Adventures in the Chinese Economy: 16 Years from the Inside

Sven Agten

Adventures in the Chinese Economy: 16 Years from the Inside

palgrave
macmillan

Sven Agten
Shanghai, China

ISBN 978-981-16-1166-7 ISBN 978-981-16-1167-4 (eBook)
https://doi.org/10.1007/978-981-16-1167-4

Cover credit: Marina Lohrbach_shutterstock.com

This Palgrave Macmillan imprint is published by the registered company Springer Nature Singapore Pte Ltd.
The registered company address is: 152 Beach Road, #21-01/04 Gateway East, Singapore 189721, Singapore

为我永远都挚爱–韩雪

Introduction

On March 16, 2004, I was at Brussels Airport, waiting for my flight to Beijing. A few weeks earlier, I had been researching job vacancies in China on the internet. The sheer energy with which the country drew me toward it, had never let go of me after a tourist trip to China in 2002. Even then I knew that I would return. And this return was now before me. With all the growth and internationalization in China, there was an acute shortage of English teachers there. My job search eventually took me to a university in Yichun City, Heilongjiang Province, a mostly rural region far from China's big metropolitan conurbations. Yichun itself, one of China's northernmost cities, had a million inhabitants at that time, but there was virtually no information about it available. My *Lonely Planet* guide spoke of a city where pigs roamed the streets. I wanted to see that for myself, and I contacted the university. Two days later, I received a call from Mr. Bai, dean of the English faculty of Yichun University. He spoke fluent English and told me after a 30-minute phone call that my level of English would be sufficient for the job. The monthly salary was €250—not much by Western-European or American standards, but at least one and a half times the salary of the average Yichuner. Mr. Bai also mentioned that there were other foreigners living in the city. Two others in all, to be specific: a 72-year-old Canadian resident in China for 25 years, who was working at the university as an English teacher at the time, and a 40-year-old Italian who owned a private school where English was taught.

Although I did not have an official contract, only an e-mail with a job offer, I decided to take the risk and plunge into the adventure. Three weeks after the phone call, I landed in Beijing. From there, I traveled to Yichun, 1400 kilometers to the northwest, in a comfortable railway sleeping compartment. The 20-hour journey took me through a breathtaking landscape, in which progress was measured by the thickness of the ice on the train windows. Although warm by comparison to average winter temperatures in the region of -22°F (-30°C), it was at that time only 5°F (-15°C) outside. A tall blond man, I must have looked like a visitor from another planet to the other passengers, who eyed my skinny jeans skeptically, and I realized that my clothes would not provide adequate protection against the freezing cold. By the end of the train ride, I had received twenty invitations to eat, and especially to drink. Those who had a camera took photos of me. Even if my fellow travelers did not speak English, that did not stop them from trying to interact with me in any way possible.

In Yichun, no pigs ran through the streets. The city was quite modern, with a number of shopping malls and many new buildings. In the suburbs, one could still see isolated wooden houses, which would soon be demolished and replaced by new blocks of flats. The meager information that I had previously gathered was nowhere near reality.

China has been my second home for sixteen years now. The saying "You will not change China, China changes you" certainly applies to me. I have lived what might be called the "Chinese Dream." I taught at Yichun University and at a private school in Beijing, worked for a Belgian interior design and renovation company there. Subsequently, in 2008, I moved to Qian'an, a city of 600,000 people, about 200 kilometers from Beijing, where I set up and built a Sino-Belgian joint venture cement company with multi-million dollar investment. As general manager, I oversaw the entire development of the joint venture and construction in 2008 of its plant, which was subsequently sold in 2013. In the meantime, I also married a young Chinese woman, with whom I have two children. In 2011, we moved back to the capital. As air pollution had become extreme there, we decided to return to Belgium, where I obtained an MBA in Business Administration at a European Business School. After my graduation, we moved back to China—the country just will not let you go!—and this time we settled in Shanghai, where I had been working for a Germanmultinational. As its Asia Pacific president, I was responsible both for overseeing the Chinese market, where they have eleven sales offices and for relations with our partners and dealers in Australia, Japan, Korea, India, South-East Asia, and Singapore.

I have thus held a number of leadership positions, lived in many places in China, and speak fluent Chinese. Of course, my Chinese wife has many local friends, who help me to get in direct contact with Chinese from all walks of life. That is often crucial in understanding the country as everything that happens in modern China is directly related to the political, economic, cultural, and social aspects of this very complex, ever-changing country. The nuances in the daily Chinese tangle are not always apparent to many people in the West. Moreover, foreigners who settle in cosmopolitan megacities like Beijing, Shanghai, or Guangzhou often miss out on what daily life is actually like for the vast majority of Chinese, or what makes Chinese citizens tick.

From my experience in Yichun, I have learned to survive Siberian temperatures and get along on the smallest possible budget, as millions of other people in China do. I also learned how important flexibility and adaptability are in Chinese culture. In Beijing, I got to know the pros and cons of the Chinese education system. I also began to understand why hundreds of thousands of Chinese go abroad each year to continue their studies there. I soon had my first experiences with the multifaceted lifestyle of China's fast-growing middle class—on my first visit to one of the 1500 Pizza Huts found all over China, I had to stand in line for almost an hour. When the Chinese began to travel overseas on a huge scale, shopping centers began to produce Chinese-language advertising for exotic travel destinations. Shopping malls abroad hire Chinese-speaking staff. Personal experience of China's food scandals changed my family's eating habits—we now strongly favor imported European and American food. We also said goodbye to Beijing owing to the intolerable levels of air pollution there. Air pollution and food scandals are two issues lamented, not only by us, but also on Chinese social media—criticism of the government in these respects has long since become reality. The Chinese government can no longer afford to ignore the environmental problems, and China has been the world's largest investor in renewable energy for several years. Green energy and social stability go hand in hand in China, with good results over the last years.

My experience in implementing the joint venture in Qian'an highlighted another problem in China: the constant shortage of skilled workers and the associated constant increase in wages. As a result, technology is now core to China's development. China's economic development over the past forty years has created an abundance of jobs. However, the constantly improving living and working conditions and the now abrogated one-child policy quickly led to a shortage of workers. Meanwhile, higher salaries have become the norm. Chinese companies and the government are facing the challenge of quickly accelerating labor shortages and the transition to a modern economy, and they are therefore focusing in an unparalleled manner on innovation and technology. China not only has almost 900 million internet users, it is also the largest digital marketplace in the world. Companies such as Alibaba are among the largest e-commerce companies in the world, while Tencent is globally recognized as a leader in digital innovation. The West's leadership role in research and development (R&D) is slowly but surely being overtaken by China. Most patent applications now come from China, and numerous well-known Western companies have now opened R&D centers in the Chinese metropolises. Apps like WeChat have become indispensable in our daily lives: a platform in which you not only can talk, but can pay utility bills and make purchases. No one uses cash anymore. Social media are now in a sense more influential than the state-controlled media, and the Chinese tech giants rule large chunks of the economy, business and daily life. Hence the pushback on Big tech and more governmental control in general. Artificial Intelligence and blockchain are also becoming key in China's technological advancement.

Chinese consumers are comparing the prices of products on Amazon and Chinese websites, and have the ability to buy products where it suits them best. While price used to be the most important criterion, quality comes first. All this also leads to more individualism. The days when the Communist Party controlled every aspect of Chinese life are long gone. Especially in the big cities, a large, individualized feeling of freedom has spread. Everything is possible and everything should be. Young people from rural areas find jobs in cities that have virtually nothing to do with their parents' origins. China's big cities are becoming more and more international, and they frequently host major international events, competitions, and exhibitions. I have also experienced first-hand how life in smaller cities like Yichun and Qian'an differs from international life in Shanghai and Beijing. There is often talk of a "new moral crisis" in China. Money is a Chinese god, and selfish behavior is becoming the norm more than the exception, something that very often annoys me personally. In overcrowded Chinese society, babies are prepared for a competitive future from their infancy. In the glittering jungle of the streets, the social Darwinist "survival of the fittest" is more and more the rule. Corruption has long been the norm, leading to social problems and food crises. My experience in Qian'an also revealed that pollution is partly due to the corrupt behavior of some civil servants. Chinese municipalities used to have a lot of free space, which they often shamelessly exploited. This was something that confronted me almost daily in Qian'an. Accordingly, President Xi Jinping's relentless anti-corruption campaign law which strengthened his position, but also enforces more the law is also supported by the general public. Rule of Law is gaining importance.

China has become the second-largest economy in the world the main driver of global economic growth. At the same time, the country is rebalancing its economy. It is moving away from the traditional drivers like export and investment, and moving toward ever-increasing consumerism and innovation. It's the "new normal." The international influence of the country is nonetheless increasing, and it's clear that China seeks to play a more important role internationally. The "Chinese Dream" is even playing an increasingly important role on the international stage. China is more assertive than ever on the global stage, changing geopolitical balances and creating new international institutions. The new Silk Road, also known as the Belt and Road Initiative, is a huge infrastructure project that will affect the economic development of all of Eurasia. During my business trips to Japan, Australia, Vietnam, and the Philippines, I have noticed again and again that China's influence is increasing at the expense of the West. However, it's equally important to understand that China's rise will be very different than that of Western empires of the past.

Because of China's rise and the continuous rule of the Communist Party, the West is getting increasingly nervous. The U.S.–China trade war is as much about trade as it is about technology. It's no wonder dat Huawei is being targeted as it's the number 1 patent developer in the world, and as such a technological competitor. The end game however is to stop the rise of China. Among others afraid of the blurry lines between the private sector and the State in China and more Chinese regional and global influence, especially the United States wants to contain China and keep it out of its market and sphere of influence. This is from American perspective also ideologically driven as there is a feeling of 'good' versus 'bad' where often rational arguments are put aside, and every argument to discredit China, will be utilized. As long as the rise of China continues, and as long as the United States feels threatened in its global leadership, the world will enter unchartered territory for which no roadmap exists. For companies, these geopolitical issues are becoming major headaches.

Irrespective of you're a student, a businessman, a teacher, or a politician, or just interested in world affairs, it's important to understand the impact that China's increasing influence in the world will have on us. China is much more than what appears in Western media and there is much more to it, than what is usually being reported. The country's rapid economic growth, rich history, geographic and linguistic complexity, and associated misunderstandings make China hard for outsiders to interpret. Even Chinese colleagues and friends often find it difficult to find their way around their own ever-changing land. Offering personal perspectives and insights, coupled with facts, data, and reporting on events that are often not discussed in the West, this book seeks both to provide orientation and to show how challenging, enriching, and exciting—in short, fun—China can be.

Contents

CHAPTER 1

"Made in China" No Longer Means Cheap

Mao Zedong, chairman of the Communist Party of China (CCP) and founder of the People's Republic of China (PRC) died on September 9, 1976, aged 84. He was succeeded first by Hua Guofeng, his chosen successor, and then, after an internal power struggle, by Deng Xiaoping, who gradually introduced the economic reforms known as the Reform-and-Opening-Up Policy.[1] China henceforth adopted economic liberalism, politically managed by the CCP. Under Deng, the country's communist planned economy was slowly replaced by a mixed economy—so-called socialism with Chinese characteristics.

But Deng's "opening-up" alsomeant opening to the capitalist world, to which China had effectively been closed since the establishment of the PRC in October 1949. Not only had the communist planned economy failed to create economic prosperity, but it also couldn't even feed the country's growing population. Every sector was underdeveloped. Industrial production barely existed. The gains China has made since Deng's reforms are one of history's great economic achievements. In 2010, the economy grew 10 percent annually, a rate twice as high as between 1960 and 1978.[2] Forty years earlier, China was an agricultural society with barely any industrial activity; today, it has evolved into the world's second-largest economy, which, despite its recent economic slowdown, is slowly and steadily advancing toward the number one position. No one who has been in China can have failed to notice its dynamism and

S. Agten, *Adventures in the Chinese Economy: 16 Years from the Inside*,
https://doi.org/10.1007/978-981-16-1167-4_1

the speed of development. The air feels electric, and the sky seems the limit. Modern China's social, cultural, and political developments cannot be understood without reference to its economic development over the past four decades.

From Agrarian Society to Industrialized Nation

In 1978, land, labor and materials were cheap in China, and taxes were low. Special economic zones (SEZs) where trade could take place without supervision by the central government were established in the country's southeast coast to stimulate foreign investment. China began experimenting on a small scale with different economic models and industrialized at a tremendous speed. Attracted by the prospects of cheap production and new opportunities, Western companies started investing on a previously unimaginable scale. They built production facilities and started producing a vast range of products for export. Already by 1981, Coca-Cola had built its first production facilities in China[3]; thousands of international companies soon followed. Despite China's slowing economy and trade, in 2019, foreign direct investment in China rose to a record $137 billion.[4]

Before 1978, there had been barely any foreign investment in China, but particularly after the country joined the World Trade Organization (WTO) in 2001, foreign companies raced to relocate their production there. It was a real gold rush, with multinationals grasping at all the opportunities available. It was also a momentous shift in globalization.[5] In 1995, the value of China's imports and exports of goods totaled $280.9 billion or 3 percent of global trade. By 2018, its total trade in goods had jumped to $4.6 trillion or 12.4 percent of global trade.[6]

At the same time, local companies began producing inferior products, which were sold at rock-bottom prices. After all, they had neither the technological means nor the experience to compete with foreign companies.Producing high-quality goods faced other obstacles as well. In the 1980s, China's education system was still underdeveloped, which meant finding skilled workers was a big problem. Furthermore, few Chinese could afford such expensive products—they often struggled to provide for their basic needs. Poverty was rampant. My wife's 55-year-old aunt remembers vividly her first visit to a restaurant, a luxury few enjoyed. In those circumstances, companies didn't feel the need to produce superior goods. It was much easier to produce low-quality products and serve 1.3 billion consumers who lacked nearly everything. Whatever they couldn't innovate themselves, they copied. Cheap production was the only competitive advantage Chinese companies had, and it quickly became their core business. Quality was not important; only quantity mattered. China became the world's factory, and the world benefited from the mass production of cheap goods. Toys, textiles, pens, and many other products were produced at razor-thin margins, which in turn led to fierce competition among local companies. Even today, China can call itself the world's factory, now producing a vaster range of products. The country builds half of the planet's ships, TVs, smart phones, and digital cameras, not to mention 60 percent of all its shoes and toys, and at least 80 percent of all its air conditioners.[7] The list is endless. China is the world's largest exporter, followed by the United States and the European Union. The country has more than two thousand ports, including 130 international harbors. One-third of global shipping activity links to China. Already by 2005, Shanghai was the world's largest cargo port.[8]

The massive influx of investment by foreign companies seeking cheap labor and new opportunities led to mushrooming job creation, and peasants flocked in great numbers to the cities in search of work and a better life. Especially in the 1980s, China's population increased proportionately, and there was massive urbanization. In 1982, only 20 percent of the Chinese population lived in urban areas—twenty years later, that figure had almost doubled.[9]

Especially in the southeastern coastal areas where most foreign companies established themselves, China's cities grew exponentially. This has laid the foundation for economic growth in nearly every sector, particularly real estate and construction. The country's urbanization wave resulted in an enormous increase in the production of cement, steel, iron, and other building materials. China produces almost 60 percent of all the world's cement, and four of the planet's ten largest steel manufacturers are Chinese.[10]

I myself have seen the gigantic plants producing steel and iron day and night in China. But even these have not sufficed to meet the enormous demand, causing China to import huge amounts of raw materials. Globally, China consumes half of the world's cement, concrete, steel, copper, and aluminum.[11]

The gross domestic product (GDP) of resource-rich countries such as Australia and Brazil depends at least in part on the China's real estate industry. This enormous economic development made many rich overnight. In 2014, China had created 4 million US-Dollar millionaires, only trailing the UnitedStates.[12] In 2020 (and due to a mini-boom because of Covid-19), there were 878 billionaires in China, compared with 788 in the United States.[13] Beijing is the billionaire capital of the world.[14] And as of 2018, four of the ten wealthiest Chinese billionaires have made their fortunes in real estate.[15]

Chinese GDP per capitadoubled between 2010 and 2018.[16] In 1981, 88 percent of China's population still lived on less than US$1.90 per day—the official poverty line. In 2020, China announced that absolute poverty had been eradicated.[17] China has rescued 700 million peasants from poverty since 1978, according to the National Bureau of Statistics.[18] These developments are the main reason why poverty has been reduced so markedly worldwide over the past thirty years, and why the United Nations' Millennium Development Goal to halve the number of people living in poverty was achieved by 2000.[19] At the same time, however, there is still a lot of room for improvement. Despite the creation of a huge middle class, when spreading the numbers across 1.3 billion people, China's disposable income per capita[20] is only around one-tenth of their American counterparts.[21]

But the Chinese Dream, with the promise of striking it rich, is still very much alive. Several years ago in Beijing, I met a young woman working long days running a food stall along a busy street. When a fancy BMW stopped in front of her stall, she told me it was her dream to buy such a car—all she needed to do was work harder. However, the Chinese Dream created its own problems. China had no experience with a capitalist system, and legislation wasn't prepared for the country's new course. This relatively lawless environment allowed many to profit enormously. Scofflaws were rife, and corruption thrived, since officials also wanted their share of the newly created wealth. Local officials responsible for achieving certain economic objectives for their city or region raced to hand out land and attract new companies. In this "Wild East," almost anything was possible with enough money. Workers toiling in factories and sweatshops for low wages had few rights, and the ruthless economic progress also had disastrous environmental consequences.

Migration and Urbanization

As economic growth continues, and China's transformation from a largely rural to a more urban society is incomplete, migration continues to play a role in the country's dynamics. Every year, between ten and fifteen million people still move from the countryside to the cities.[22] At the end of 2019, 848 million people, or 61 percent of the Chinese population lived in cities.[23] By 2025, China will have 221 cities of at least a million people[24] (by comparison, the United States has eleven).[25] Cities offer better jobs and often better living conditions, making them hugely attractive to the rural population in the poorer provinces, and they become a true melting pot of citizens from the four corners of the country. During a holiday on Hainan Island—known as the Chinese Hawaii—I was surprised to learn that many local taxi drivers actually came from northern China. Most of the young waitresses in Beijing and Shanghai hail from remote Western provinces; others do work as shop employees, cleaners, and construction workers. And like poor immigrants in Western countries, these workers often wire money back to their parents who are still working the family farms.

Especially in thebig cities, rapid urbanization has caused real estate prices to skyrocket, as much as tripling between 2005 and 2009. In 2020, the average price of a Shanghai apartment was between $7600 and $9000 per square meter.[26] Beijing prices are similar. This drives most people to buy smaller apartments with a living space of one hundred square meters or less. However, by earning an average monthly salary of $1447 in Shanghai, many young people and young couples have difficulty purchasing a new home.[27] Around 90 percent of Chinese first-time home buyers are supported by their families.[28] But that also enriched the millions of Chinese who had previously purchased apartments. For my part, I missed this opportunity. In 2006, I had an opportunity to buy the apartment I was renting in Beijing for US$180,000. Today, it is worth at least six times that.

City planning has paid a price for this breakneck urbanization. Quantity trumped quality, and many Chinese cities—especially the smaller ones—look alike. When constructing a residential building, workers follow the general rule of adding one floor per week. Because the available land had to be used in the best way possible, buildings are packed together, and even relatively new structures were quickly replaced by bigger complexes. Cities expanded to such an extent that untouched nature is hard to find, and parking is so limited that the sidewalks are packed with cars. Cyclists and pedestrians are always surrounded by vehicles, and the many traffic jams affect the quality of life in cities.

For several years, however, there have been hopeful signs. Local and municipal governments know that green spaces are an essential part of improving the quality of city life. Complete city districts are therefore being renovated and redesigned, and entirely new modern towns are being built, often tens of kilometers away from the old city centers. My trips to Osaka, Taipei, Seoul, or Hong Kong never fail to remind me how modern Chinese cities have become. Hong Kong may be famous for its skyline, but Shanghai and Beijing are much more modern. In addition to investments in water and transport infrastructure, there is a strong focus on smart cities. There are more and more green boulevards of trees and parks, where townspeople gather after work to chat or do exercises—something vital to Chinese traditional culture. In squares and open spaces, elderly and even middle-aged men and women regularly hold informal dances. Many cities have extensive metro networks, and bicycle paths are being upgraded.

Rapid urbanization also had other drawbacks. Because many smaller towns aspired to be a new Beijing, few took care of their population's real needs. When constructing new cities, local governments rarely consult residents; they have, however, become rich by selling land to wealthy property developers. It is no surprise that the annual Hurun Report of China's richest people is dominated by real estate tycoons. Household names such as Wanda, Greenland, and Vanke generate tens of billions of dollars annually.[29]

The building boom and related property speculation has also ledto bubbles. Many new apartments were empty. Numerous ghost towns, built to house thousands of people, lied completely deserted. However, despite the fact that China has most of the top ten most expensive cities in the world for residential real estate,[30] the situation may not be as dramatic as it seems. Since the purchase of private property was not allowed in the Maoist era, Chinese citizens hold home ownership in high regard. China has one of the highest percentages of home owners in the world, with 90 percent of families owning their own homes, most of them even paid for without mortgages.[31] Parents also try to support their children in buying homes. To enable their newlywed son to buy a house in Beijing, friends of mine sold their apartment and moved to a smaller house in a less attractive location. My in-laws tell me they would have done the same. In many areas, there is still a strong tradition that only young men who own homes can get married.

Labor Shortages and the One-Child Policy

This ongoing migration has, however, passed its peak. After nearly four decades of urbanization and swift economic growth, the past few years have seen a turnaround, one with far-reaching global consequences. It was long accepted that China would continue to benefit from cheap labor, low production costs, and a competitive advantage over other countries, but this situation is changing rapidly. The once seemingly endless source of poor rural workers who moved to the cities looking for work is drying up. In many cases, the depopulated countryside now only accommodates the elderly and the sick. In some rural towns, up to 30 percent of the population, especially the young, have moved to the big cities.[32] In 2013, when I visited old friends in Yichun, Heilongjiang, where my China story started, they told me that now only older people still live there. Youngsters moved to the bigger cities. And local restaurant owners insist that it's increasingly difficult to find employees.

This has much to do with China'sfamous family planning, or One-Child Policy, which limits most families to only one child. Its implementation in 1979 had been politically motivated, with fears of overcrowding and the possibility of food shortages. Families were discouraged—usually with monetary fine—from having more than one child. But contrary to its portrayal in Western media, the policy was not always as strictly enforced, and in the 1990s, enforcement became significantly looser. There were many exceptions, especially in rural areas. If the couple's first child was a daughter, families were authorized to have a second child. Members of China's fifty-five ethnic minority groups were exempt from the One-Child Policy,[33] as were mixed couples like my wife and I. Nevertheless—as is so often the case in China—implementation varied from region to region, being stricter in more populated areas. But the regulations had their desired effect. Whereas a Chinese woman in 1980 had, on average, 2.6 children, by 2009 this figure had dropped to 1.6 in 2019, the lowest ever.[34] As a direct consequence, China is now facing a decreasing workforce and an aging population.

The International Monetary Fund has calculated that in the near future, China is likely to face a deficit of 100 million workers. The United Nations assumes that by 2050 the working-age population will decrease by 225 million people compared to 2011[35] (equivalent to the population of Brazil[36]). To cope with this situation, the government has begun further relaxing the One-Child Policy. Already by 2007, couples who were both only children were allowed to have two children themselves.[37] Since 2015 everyone is.[38] However, most of my Chinese friends have little desire for a second child. In China, raising a child as well as possible is far from cheap. Parents prefer to spend their money on the proper upbringing of one child, rather than dividing their resources.

These developments also significantly impact foreign companies. Whereas in the past they set up shops in China because labor costs constituted only a small part of total production costs, the situation has now changed dramatically. For many companies, rising wages are an ever-growing concern. Western companies operating in China indicate that they face more challenges related to human resources than to unfair competition. These surveys also indicate for years that next to controlling rising labor costs, recruiting and retaining talented employees is one of their greatest concerns. Chinese employees realize their value and will quickly request salary raises. In 2009, when I worked in Qian'an, in Heibei Province, the general manager of a huge steel company that employed close to eight thousand people told me he had a permanent shortage of two thousand workers. A new production line lay empty because there were not enough production workers. Of course, steel is not the most attractive sector, and pollution concerns force many companies to operate far from city centers. This means workers need to be recruited in poorer Chinese regions. But even given the sector's higher wages, companies still faced difficulties in recruitment. One manager told me he didn't invest much in training, because it only increased the likelihood that his staff would seek other and better job opportunities. And despite paying higher wages every year, he still wasn't able to find sufficient workers.

Because of this ongoing battlefor talent within and between both domestic and foreign companies, there is a huge staff turnover. An annual employee turnover rate of only 10 percent is now regarded as a great success. Furthermore, foreign companies have gradually lost their attractiveness to Chinese workers. In 2004, more than two-thirds of graduates preferred a Western multinational as a first employer. By 2011, this had already dropped to 25 percent. For Chinese students, companies like Huawei or Alibaba are often the most popular choice.[39] In the past, employees preferred big foreign companies because of the high wages they paid, opportunities to work abroad, and a chance to learn Western best practices. Over time, however, Chinese state-owned enterprises and multinationals are increasingly in need of talent. Years of economic growth have made them profitable, which in turn generated a surplus of cash. Now they can offer the same or higher wages as Western companies. Generally speaking, Chinese companies also promote their employees faster than their Western counterparts, and, unlike most foreign multinationals, there is no glass ceiling. And despite claims in Western media that Chinese women being discouraged from pursuing professional careers, it's my experience that very often the opposite is true: Chinese women have great career opportunities in Chinese companies. In fact, China's female employment rate has become one the highest in the world, and women contribute more to GDP in China than in any other region in the world.[40]

The role and influence of women inChinese society should not be underestimated. Chinese women are also just as ambitious as men. From personal experience, I know that Chinese women's job performance is not in any way inferior to that of their male colleagues, and in an economy that increasingly depends on the service sector, women have started to earn higher salaries than men, most of whom are working in factories. In all economic sectors, women are top-level executives. On the 2016 Fortune 50 list of the world's most powerful women, a record number of fourteen were Chinese.[41] Finally, patriotic feelings also play an important role for some employees. For many, working for Chinese companies that are expanding and investing abroad is now regarded as a personal contribution to the global growth and prestige of China.

New Working Conditions

Companies unable to provide good working conditions will inevitably lose the race for skilled employees. Sweatshops are more and more a relic of the past. Companies can pay good salaries but still lose workers on a daily basis. Poor working conditions are the reason for high turnover, not low pay. To remain competitive in the labor market, Chinese companies need to offer not only higher wages, but also better and safer working conditions. Gone are the days when companies could impose long hours and a standard seven-day work week on their employees. Chinese workers have their pick of jobs.

Mega factories are increasingly being organized as small towns equipped with all the necessary facilities. In Chongqing, for instance, a metropolis of nearly 25 million people in Western China, the Taiwanese company Quanta manufactures computers for HP and watches for Apple. The site, called Quanta Chongqing Manufacturing City, boasts TV rooms, karaoke bars, a huge cafeteria, a gym, and a cinema, all free for staff. Workers sleep in modern ten-story dormitories.[42] If Quanta didn't offer these facilities, it would lose staff.

Media and independent interest groups such as China Labor Watch increasingly focus on better working conditions. Employees are also much more aware of their rights. Companies that violate labor laws face public criticism—especially foreign companies. The most famous example is Foxconn, the Taiwanese manufacturer of Apple's iPhones and iPads, which in China employs an astonishing 1.3 million people.[43] In 2010, the company came under public scrutiny because it systematically violated labor laws by forcing its workers to work ten or more hours daily without overtime. No fewer than ten company employees committed suicide because of psychological pressure. The public outcry and campaigning caused Foxconn to act, and it improved working conditions and increase salaries by 70 percent.[44]

In China'spoorer provinces, where industrialization started later, some companies continue to violate labor laws despite penalties. China is undeniably a safer place to work than it was a decade ago, but still in 2019, about 30,000 Chinese workers died in work-related accidents.[45] Especially for the nearly three hundred million unskilled migrant workers in Chinese cities, everyday life continues to be tough.[46]

Working conditions inthe construction sector especially need improvement. Although salaries are higher there than for other low-skilled labor, workers toil long hours and spend little on themselves so as to send money to distant families they see only during Chinese New Year. And in the past, some company owners failed to pay salaries on time, or even fled the area without paying at all. According to the *China Labor Bulletin*, an NGO that advocates for worker rights, in 2018, there were more than 1700 strikes and workers' protests directly related to violations of fundamental labor rights.[47] In the past, Chinese workers had little awareness of their rights; today, they staunchly defend them, especially before the Chinese New Year, when many of these problems occur. Anxious to receive their salaries and bonuses before they travel often thousands of miles to see their families, they may occupy factories or construction sites demanding wages and harassing management.

In any case, the trend toward better working conditions extending to less-developed provinces is only a matter of time. The fewer workers are available, the more quickly conditions improve and wages rise. Companies that invest now in better working conditions will benefit later. Conversely, companies that do not offer an adequate work environment will gradually lose their workforces. The Chinese government is also making efforts to better protect workers. As China seeks to transform itself into a service economy and to move away from polluting industrial sectors, the country also needs a population that can spend more money on goods and services. Higher wages fit into this picture.

But higher wages create major problems for companies, leading to more expensive production processes and transportation, higher energy prices, higher rents, and so on. It's a myth that starting a business in China is cheap. The Boston Consulting Group calculated that in 2000, Chinese manufacturing labor costs averaged only 46 cents per hour—53 times lower than the $25 per hour average in the United States. Since then, Chinese manufacturing labor costs have been rising by 15.6 percent annually on average.[48]

Incertain labor-intensive sectors, production costs in the United States are only 4 percent higher than in China.[49] Entrepreneurs complain bitterly about wages rising too quickly, telling me that their competitive advantage has deteriorated significantly.

Entrepreneurs also complain about the increased burden of taxes in China, but the value of the Chinese renminbi (RMB), or yuan, is partly to blame for rising costs. In 2018, almost 20 percent of all China's exports go to the United States.[50] Whereas in 2005, a dollar was worth 8 RMB, this had fallen to 6.5 RMB by 2020. Exporting from China to the United States in particular thus became much more expensive.

Modernize or Leave

Companies confronted with constantly rising wages and correspondingly expensive production processes, as well as a high worker turnover, declining economic growth, and more expensive exports have to choose between a strong commitment to modernization and innovation or exiting the market. It is inevitable that investment in improved productivity and efficiency will increase significantly. Relying on cheap labor and extreme cost-cutting to make products of barely acceptable quality no longer works. Nowadays, in an environment of rising costs and stricter regulations, it's much more important to produce high-quality products, which leads companies to focus on new technologies and automation.

China has fully embraceda policy of smart factories and cities, part of its "Made in China 2025" plan, which sets goals to increase domestically produced content in the automotive, aerospace, IT, pharmaceutical, semiconductor, medical devices, machinery, and robotics industries to 40 percent by 2020 and 70 percent by 2025.[51] Consumer demand for higher quality goods has also required companies to walk this path. Because of this, China is for a consecutive seven years the biggest market in the world for industrial robots. In 2018, one in three robots worldwide was sold in China. Although the Chinese industrial sector employs only 140 robots for every ten thousand workers[52]—half of the United States[53]—the use of robots will certainly increase in the coming years.

Majorforeign robot producers realize that China has become the biggest market for their products and are now building production facilities in China. The switch to advanced automation occurred first in the automotive industry, which feels the effects of rising labor costs like no other sector. Automation is also extensive in the logistics sector. In 2018, Cainiao, a Chinese logistics firm majority-owned by Alibaba, opened an almost fully automated warehouse staffed by over seven hundred robots.[54] In fact, China's surge in the employment of robots might lead to structural unemployment for some workers. A 2018 report published by China Development Research Foundation and Sequoia Capital China, a venture capital firm, shows that several companies in export manufacturing industries have reduced their labor pool by 30–40 percent over the past three years, a trend that will be accelerated by the push to upgrade the technological base and the implementation of artificial intelligence.[55] Some local and municipal governments are even considering various kinds of "robot taxes" to make up for the loss of human taxpayers.[56]

Consequently, the best Chinese companies are now as capital-intensive as their Western counterparts. China is transforming itself from a manufacturing giant to an industrialized nation. In the past, many Chinese companies were sweatshops with poor working conditions, but today they can boast state-of-the-art production facilities. Since 2003, one of our clients has had a factory near Guangzhou in southern China. It was an old, worn-out site, where workers had to manually operate machines in temperatures of as much as 95°F, but because of rising wages and outdated technology, the owner decided to build a new factory. The contrast with the previous factory is enormous: this is a modern building with state-of-the-art equipment, a ventilation system that ensures a comfortable temperature, and a modern management system—in short, it has it all. I have seen German plants in much worse shape. And the most important factor is that the owner now needs only half the number of workers he needed before. Moreover, he can now produce better-quality products to respond to the increased demand from within China.

Meanwhile, countriesin Southeast Asia are increasingly attracting investment from foreign companies that had previously opted for China. According to the American Chamber of Commerce in China, nearly one in three U.S. industrial companies had moved or considered moving their production to cheaper countries.[57] Vietnam has become especially attractive. Year by year, the country attracts more and more foreign companies. Nike already produces more goods in Vietnam than in China,[58] and a Korean manager working for Samsung told me that his company had already invested billions of dollars in Vietnam.

Whether these companies made the right choice by relocating remains to beseen. Labor costs are already on the rise in Vietnam, which has also increased the minimum wage.[59] Simply speaking, it's not easy to replace China.

Because of huge investments in infrastructure, China has an excellent transportation and communications network. In terms of depth and the volume they can handle, Chinese ports are among the world's best. Investment in education has also produced excellent results. Moreover, there is no other country that has such a dense and well-developed industrial network. The reality is that companies need to take a holistic view of costs and operating conditions, beyond labor arbitrage, to optimize location strategy. Western companies should not expect the same scale and manufacturing ecosystem advantages that they may realize in China.[60]

Manufacturing will clearly continue to play an all-important role in China's future, notwithstanding such gloomy scenarios. The domestic market has grown exponentially because of the growing middle class and its ever-increasing consumption. "Made in China" products are increasingly sold in China itself, and production close to its market has a great advantage. The traditional industrial model where products were produced in huge quantities and shipped thousands of kilometers to overseas markets is changing rapidly. The future belongs to smaller, high-tech production facilities focused on the local market that can respond rapidly to the new needs of the local middle class. Catering to niche markets and a commitment to the production of high-quality products will become much more important, and here also, China has made tremendous strides.

Notes

1. *The Irish Times*. 2008. Mao's successor, 'Wise Leader' Hua Guofeng, dies in Beijing aged 87. www.irishtimes.com/news/mao-s-successor-wise-leader-hua-guofeng-dies-in-beijing-aged-87-1.932930%3fmode=amp. Accessed March 4, 2018.
2. *The Guardian*. 2012. China GDP: How it has changed since 1980. www.theguardian.com/news/datablog/2012/mar/23/china-gdp-since-1980. Accessed May 16, 2018.
3. *Fortune*. 2014. Opening happiness: An oral history of Coca-Cola in China. https://fortune.com/2014/09/11/opening-happiness-an-oral-history-of-coca-cola-in-china. Accessed April 7, 2020.
4. Reuters. 2020. China 2019 FDI up 5.8%, outbound investment slumps. https://www.reuters.com/article/us-china-economy-fdi-idUSKBN1ZK05I. Accessed December 29, 2020.
5. *The Wall Street Journal*. 2017. The impact of China joining the WTO. www.wsj.com/amp/articles/the-impact-of-china-joining-the-wto-1495504981. Accessed March 18, 2018.
6. Chinapower. 2020. Is China the world's top trader? www.chinapower.csis.org/trade-partner/#toc-0. Accessed December 20, 2020.
7. *Chinadaily*. 2015. Top 10 products China manufactures most in the world. www.chinadaily.com.cn/business/2015-09/16/content_21886983.htm. Accessed February 20, 2019.
8. The Maritime Executive. 2006. Shanghai now world's largest cargo port. www.maritime-executive.com/article/2006-01-12shanghai-now-worlds-largest-cargo-por. Accessed November 3, 2018.
9. The World Bank. 2020. Urban population (% of total population) China. https://data.worldbank.org/indicator/SP.URB.TOTL.IN.ZS?locations=CN. Accessed November 19, 2020.
10. *Forbes*. 2018. China produces more cement than the rest of the world combined. www.forbes.com/sites/niallmccarthy/2018/07/06/china-produces-more-cement-than-the-rest-of-the-world-combined-infographic. Accessed March 19, 2019.
11. Visual Capitalist. 2018. China's staggering demand for commodities. www.visualcapitalist.com/chinas-staggering-demand-commodities. Accessed May 12, 2019.
12. *Newsweek*. 2015. China adds 1 million new millionaires in 2014. www.newsweek.com/china-adds-one-million-new-millionaires-2014-343175%3famp=1. Accessed December 1, 2017.

13. CNBC. 2020. China's billionaires see biggest gains ever, adding more than $1.5 trillion to their fortunes. https://www.cnbc.com/2020/10/20/chinas-billionaires-see-biggest-gains-ever-fueled-by-ipos.html#:~:text=China%20minted%20257%20billionaires%20over%20the%20past%20year%20—%20averaging%20five,as%20measured%20by%20Wealth-X.
14. Hurun. 2019. Loong Palace—Hurun Global Rich List 2019. www.hurun.net/EN/Article/Details?num=24DD41EE3B19. Accessed October 20, 2020.
15. CNBC. 2018. Here are the 10 wealthiest people in China—A country leading the way for self-made billionaires. www.cnbc.com/2018/02/20/self-made-billionaires-chinas-10-richest-billionaires.html. Accessed August 9, 2019.
16. Trading Economics. 2020. China GDP 1960–2019 data. www.tradingeconomics.com/china/gdp. Accessed November 2 2020.
17. CNN. 2020. Why China's Communist Party isn't celebrating a major poverty milestone. www.cnn.com/cnn/2020/11/27/asia/china-xi-jinping-poverty-alleviation-intl-hnk/index.html. Accessed December 8, 2020.
18. *Shanghai Daily*. 2015. 70 million out of poverty by 2020. www.shanghaidaily.com/nation/70-million-out-of-poverty-by-2020/shdaily.shtml. Accessed June 3, 2018.
19. United Nations Development Programme China. 2015. China, the millennium development goals, and the post-2015 development agenda. www.undp.org/content/dam/china/docs/Publications/UNDP-CH_discussionpaper-MDGPost2015.pdf. Accessed March 20, 2018.
20. National Bureau of Statistics of China. 2020. Household's income and consumption expenditure in 2019. www.stats.gov.cn/english/PressRelease/202001/t20200119_1723719.html. Accessed January 6, 2021.
21. Statista. 2021. Per capita disposable personal income in the United States from 2000 to 2019. www.statista.com/statistics/710215/us-disposable-income-per-capita/#:~:text=Per%20capita%2C%20Americans%20had%2045%2C579,dollars%20in%20the%20same%20year. Accessed January 6, 2021.
22. *The Financial Times*. 2015. China migration: at the turning point. www.ft.com/content/767495a0-e99b-11e4-b863-00144feab7de. Accessed October 9, 2019.
23. Xinhuanet. 2020.China's urbanization rate hits 60.6 pct. https://www.xinhuanet.com/english/2020-01/19/c_138718450.htm. Accessed September 7, 2020.
24. *The Guardian*. 2017. More than 100 Chinese cities now above 1 million people. theguardian.com/cities/2017/mar/20/china-100-cities-populations-bigger-liverpool. Accessed November 3, 2020.

25. Culturemap Austin. 2020. Austin officially pops onto list of cities with 1 million residents. www.austin.culturemap.com/news/city-life/08-04-20-austin-pops-onto-list-of-us-cities-with-population-of-at-least-1-million/ Accessed December 1, 2020.
26. *Forbes*. 2020. Shanghai real estate market hit hard by coronavirus outbreak, with new home transactions plummeting 56%. www.forbes.com/sites/amydobson/2020/03/10/shanghai-developers-see-56-drop-and-more-sobering-statistics-as-first-numbers-roll-in/amp/. Accessed December 3, 2020.
27. *Chinadaily*. 2019. Shanghai pays highest monthly wages in China. www.chinadaily.com.cn/a/201904/10/WS5cad86f7a3104842260b565c.html. Accessed November 29, 2019.
28. *Forbes*. 2019. China now has an answer to its housing crisis—It's called rent. www.forbes.com/sites/wadeshepard/2019/10/29/china-now-has-an-answer-to-its-housing-crisisits-called-rent/#4da3b3761a60. Accessed December 2, 2020.
29. Statista. 2019. Revenue of China Vanke Co., Ltd. from 2010 to 2019. www.statista.com/statistics/258061/revenue-of-china-vanke. Accessed December 2, 2019.
30. *Forbes*. 2016. How people in China can afford their outrageously expensive homes. https://www.forbes.com/sites/wadeshepard/2016/03/30/how-people-in-china-afford-their-outrageously-expensive-homes/#142151f0a3ce. Accessed March 29, 2018.
31. *Forbes*. 2016. How people in China can afford their outrageously expensive homes. https://www.forbes.com/sites/wadeshepard/2016/03/30/how-people-in-china-afford-their-outrageously-expensive-homes/#142151f0a3ce. Accessed March 29, 2018.
32. *Wall Street Journal*. 2015. As China's workforce dwindles, the world scramble for alternatives. www.wsj.com/articles/as-chinas-workforce-dwindles-the-world-scrambles-for-alternatives-1448293942. Accessed January 6, 2019.
33. Investopedia. 2020. Understanding China's former one-child policy. www.investopedia.com/articles/investing/120114/understanding-chinas-one-child-policy.asp. Accessed December 28, 2020.
34. BBC. 2020. Chinese birth rate falls to lowest in seven decades. www.bbc.co.uk/news/world-asia-china-46558562. Accessed December 5, 2012. Macrotrends. 2020. China fertility rate 1950–2020. www.macrotrends.net/countries/CHN/china/fertility-rate. Accessed December 5, 2012.
35. World Economic Forum. 2016. China's working-age population will fall 23% by 2050. www.weforum.org/agenda/2016/07/china-working-ageing-population. Accessed November 20, 2018.
36. Worldometer. 2020. Brazil Population 1950–2020. www.worldometers.info/world-population/brazil-population. Accessed November 22, 2018.

37. BBC. 2013. China reforms: One-child policy to be relaxed www.bbc.com/news/world-asia-china-24957303. Accessed November 2, 2018.
38. BBC. 2018. China birth rate: Mothers, your country needs you! www.bbc.com/news/world-asia-china-46558562. Accessed March 4, 2019.
39. *South China Morning Post*. 2017. China's graduates long for a job at Alibaba and Huawei. www.scmp.com/tech/china-tech/article/2098293/chinas-graduates-long-job-alibaba-and-huawei. Accessed February 20, 2019.
40. World Economc Forum. 2018. Women in China contribute more to GDP than in the US. Viewing them as "leftover" is problematic. www.weforum.org/agenda/2018/04/women-in-china-contribute-more-to-gdp-than-in-the-us-viewing-them-as-leftover-is-problematic. Accessed April 5, 2019.
41. *Forbes*. 2016. The world's 100 most powerful women list. www.forbes.com/power-women/list/ Accessed November 3, 2017.
42. Quanta Computer. 2020. https://www.quantawork.com/h-col-111.html. Accessed December 10, 2020.
43. Business Insider. 2018. Inside "iPhone City," the massive Chinese factory town where half of the world's iPhones are produced. https://www.businessinsider.com/apple-iphone-factory-foxconn-china-photos-tour-2018-5. Accessed December 2, 2020.
44. BBC. Foxconn gives workers second pay rise. 2010. www.bbc.com/news/10252344. Accessed December 5, 2018.
45. China Labour Bulletin. 2020. Work safety, https://clb.org.hk/content/work-safety. Accessed December 4, 2020.
46. *South China Morning Post*. 2019. China's army of migrant workers is becoming older and less mobile, new government data shows. www.scmp.com/economy/china-economy/article/3008285/chinas-army-migrant-workers-becoming-older-and-less-mobile. Accessed December 1, 2020.
47. China Labour Bulletin. 2019. State Labour Relations in China 2018. https://clb.org.hk/content/state-labour-relations-china-2018. State Labour Relations China.
48. Boston Consulting Group. 2018. China's next leap in manufacturing. www.bcg.com/publications/2018/china-next-leap-in-manufacturing.aspx. Accessed May 4, 2019.
49. Boston Consulting Group. 2018. How shifting costs are altering the math of global manufacturing. www.bcg.com/publications/2018/how-shifting-costs-are-altering-math-global-manufacturing.aspx. Accessed May 8, 2019.
50. Chinapower. 2020. Is China the world's top trader? www.chinapower.csis.org/trade-partner/#toc-0. Accessed December 20, 2020.

51. China Briefing. 2018. What is Made in China and why is the world so nervous? www.china-briefing.com/news/made-in-china-2025-explained/ Accessed December 11, 2020.
52. The robot report. 2019. China robotics outlook: A state of the industry 2019. https://www.therobotreport.com/china-robotics-outlook-state-industry-2019/. Accessed December 28, 2020.
53. International Federation of Robotics. 2019. US robot density now more than double that of China. https://ifr.org/news/us-robot-density-now-more-than-double-that-of-china-ifr-says. Accessed December 28, 2020.
54. CNBC. 2018. Alibaba cainiao is China's biggest robot warehouse for singles day. https://www.cnbc.com/2018/10/30/alibaba-cainiao-chinas-biggest-robot-warehouse-for-singles-day.html. Accessed October 2, 2020.
55. *The Financial Times*. 2018. China's AI push raises fears over widespread job cuts. ft.com/content/1e2db400-ac2d-11e8-94bd-cba20d67390c. Accessed November 2, 2020.
56. Inkstone. 2019. China's young workers ditch factories for deliveries. www.inkstonenews.com/society/chinese-factories-struggle-find-staff-young-migrant-workers-switch-delivery-jobs/article/3000958. Accessed Ocotber 2, 2020.
57. *The Epoch Times*. 2018. The global manufacturing industry is moving out of China. www.theepochtimes.com/the-global-manufacturing-industry-is-moving-out-of-china_2694398.html. Accessed March 4, 2020.
58. The end of cheap China. 2012. Shaun Rein.
59. Vietnam Briefing. 2019. Vietnam to increase minimum wage from January 2020. https://www.vietnam-briefing.com/news/vietnam-increase-minimum-wage-january-2020.html/ Accessed March 3, 2020.
60. Chief Executive. 2020. www.chiefexecutive.net/is-it-time-to-look-for-manufacturing-locations-beyond-china/amp. Is it time to look for manufacturing locations beyond China?

CHAPTER 2

Pragmatic China

Each Chinese New Year, our family travels to Tai'an in the eastern province of Shandong to spend the holidays with my in-laws. Between one of the many family lunches and dinners, we were strolling around the town, my wife had once called home. As we passed the local park, watching children playing and elderly people doing exercises, an old building caught my attention. Recently renovated, it is now a museum, and I asked my mother-in-law what it had been in the past. She replied that it had been a prison. She then casually recounted how when she was a schoolgirl, she and her classmates had sometimes been summoned to this now peaceful spot to attend public executions. At first, I thought my Chinese had failed me, especially since no one else in the family seemed surprised. But my mother-in-law reaffirmed that in the old days, the square used to be the scene of public executions, and that locals were often "invited" to attend these horrific events.

But what was utterly normal in the 1960s would be unthinkable today. Starting forty years ago, Chinese citizens have experienced tremendous changes. No other country has undergone such a fundamental and profound transformation in such a short time. When I ask elderly business associates or friends about their youth, the same stories often surface. Most of them have endured poverty, much government interference, and almost no individual freedom. From the proclamation of the People's Republic in 1949 to the 1980s, life in China was anything but easy. It's

S. Agten, *Adventures in the Chinese Economy: 16 Years from the Inside*,
https://doi.org/10.1007/978-981-16-1167-4_2

hard to imagine the living conditions of those days, especially compared to those in the Western world, where most people enjoyed material comfort and a high degree of political freedom. In the China of those days, the state was omnipresent and the government was fully in control over political, economic, cultural, and social life. But times have changed. Almost everything once considered dangerous and a potential threat to the state has now become normal. Although my mother-in-law recounted experiences with public executions in a matter-of-fact manner, these profound and intense events have left mental scars on many. The history of the Wang family is just one example of how twentieth-century political events have impacted the lives and minds of the Chinese citizens.

The Wang Family

Grandmother Wang, my wife's grandmother, was born in 1933, when China was not yet a communist country, but a nationalist republic. Throughout her lifetime, social revolutions were common, and she was always trying to adapt to new circumstances. Being part of a rich landowning family, her childhood was peaceful—for a time. The Wangs had rolling estates where servants and numerous tenants cultivated the land. She vividly remembers the kennel of thirty-two hunting dogs. But when Japan invaded China in 1937 and World War II broke out in Asia, dark clouds began rolling in.[1] The Wang family estates were confiscated by the Japanese army. Already, China had been embroiled in a civil war that began in 1927 but stopped during the occupation, but after World War II ended in 1945, China's conflict began again in earnest.[2] The year 1949 saw the defeat of the nationalists and the victory of the communists, and the communist People's Republic of China was proclaimed under the leadership of Mao Zedong. The new government put land redistribution among farmers high on the political agenda, so the Wang family's lands were confiscated again, this time by the regime. Wealthy landowners were declared "enemies of the Chinese people and the communist revolution."

The land was divided among the farmers and tenants who worked it. Every minute it seemed, yet another centuries-old, well-off family was wiped out. The Wang's lives turned upside down. Although the possession of private property had become a crime, the Wangs were able to keep the family home, along with a small piece of land. But that wasn't enough to live on. Grandmother Wang's father started teaching at a local high school—he was educated, which was still exceptional at that time.

She herself found a job as a civil servant in the local government. In 1951, she married an army officer who was a World War II veteran. He was seriously injured from a bullet wound, but managed to continue his army career after the war.

In 1955, the couple decided to move to the city because living conditions were better there. Since inefficient state-owned enterprises were responsible for the production of everything, everything was lacking. People used coupons to purchase rice, oil, and sugar. Meat was barely available; when it was, people had to line up for hours to get it. As late as the 1980s, rationing was common, while poverty and hunger were rampant. From 1958 to 1960, the calamitous political movement known as the Great Leap Forward established agricultural communes. The Chinese government also encouraged the personal production of steel, which was done in small ovens throughout the countryside. This left crucial agricultural work badly coordinated and often neglected.[3] Widespread famine was the result. Grandmother Wang told me there wasn't a tree with leaves to be found for miles; hungry people had stripped them bare. Estimates claim that between ten and forty-five million people died during that period. When I asked her if people knew about these staggering numbers, Grandmother Wang replied they knew only too well about these high death rates, since nobody had enough food to eat.

Despite the arduous living conditions, the couple managed to bring up three daughters and two sons. My mother-in-law, born in 1959, was the youngest daughter. She has no memory of severe food shortages, but she does remember that there was barely enough to go around. To this day, she speaks of the wooden crate filled with apples in the living room; her parents had affixed a rusty padlock to keep the children out. My father-in-law, born in 1960, remembers his older brother and sister violently arguing over a small piece of meat they had to share, one that had come from an illegally poached rabbit.

Unbelievably, times were about to get worse. My in-laws and others their age were especially marked by the so-called Cultural Revolution, a violent period of social unrest and lawlessness that targeted foreign, traditional, educational, or artistic ideals, and lasted from 1966 to 1976. To curry favor with the masses, Mao mobilized a teenage paramilitary organization called the Red Guards and ordered them to attack—psychologically and physically—the country's most educated and internationally minded citizens.[4] This revolution started as an internal struggle that sought to strengthen Mao Zedong's political power and evolved into a decade of horror that has left permanent scars on the nation.

For example, because most high schools and universities were forced to close temporarily, the 1970s generation received little schooling. My mother-in-law was lucky enough to receive some kind of education, and from age seven to seventeen, was enrolled in a school. But her oldest sister, born in 1954, received very little schooling. Cultural Revolution-era education focused on teaching practical skills for doing the heavy work in fields or factories. Nothing else was important. Both my in-laws learned to read and write in school, but nothing more. The few teachers left were instructed to limit themselves to the basics and saw little reason to go any further. Teachers, as part of the "elite," were targets; they had to be wary of students who might tell authorities they lacked ideological spirit. My mother-in-law's regular homework was writing meaningless and vicious verbal attacks on the intellectual elite. She remembers seeing teachers being paraded through the city streets with cowbells around their necks, loudly proclaiming that they hadn't done good work.

After her school career, my mother-in-law—as was required in those days—was sent to the countryside for three years to help the local farming population in their ideological development. In 1978, she met her husband, there for the same reason. He stayed one year, and afterward added two more years of compulsory military service. Chinese authorities had established a minimum age of marriage eligibility, twenty-five for men and twenty-three for women, so they had to wait six years. Even then, my father-in-law was one year too young to get married, so he falsified his birth certificate. That same year, my mother-in-law gave birth to a daughter, my future wife. The One-Child Policy had come into effect in 1980, so they stopped at one.

Changing Course

Meanwhile, China started to implement a new economic policy that included more opening up to the outside world. Like millions of others, my in-laws fully benefited from this change of course. After his mandatory military service, my father-in-law started his career in a bank, while my mother-in-law worked as a bookkeeper for one of the many state-owned enterprises. Like everybody else, they rented a state-owned apartment, since having private property was not yet allowed. But the economic transformation began to bear fruit. Although salaries remained low, urban citizens gradually felt an upswing in living standards, not to mention an ever-increasing supply of goods and more personal freedom. Universities and high schools were being upgraded again and education was brought back to standard. Restaurants, which barely existed in the 1960s and 1970s, began appearing. The first time my in-laws visited a restaurant was in 1987, when they were almost thirty years old. That same year I, at age eight, boarded my first airplane, en route to a family holiday in Greece. Anybody who has visited China during the past twenty years and enjoyed the diverse range of restaurants may find it hard to imagine that this was nonexistent not long ago. The typical lavish, alcohol-fueled banquets so intrinsic to Chinese business life only started appearing after the year 2000.

For its part, the Chinese government began exercising less and less social control. Citizens could decide for themselves how they spent their free time, what kind of work they did, and how they lived their lives. My wife's family enjoyed their first family holiday in 1993 in the coastal city of Qingdao, in Shandong Province, which was for many an unprecedented luxury. Seven years later, in 2000, my in-laws bought the apartment where they still live today. The ban on owning property had been lifted a few years earlier, although many still lacked the means to purchase a home. In 2001, their daughter began college at the prestigious Beijing Film Academy and, seeking better job prospects, stayed in the capital after graduation. Meanwhile, while her father still works at the bank, her mother is enjoying a very early retirement—not uncommon in China, especially when retiring from government jobs—and runs a small shop that sells duck necks, a delicacy for many. And after they came to Europe for our 2009 wedding in Belgium, they returned for a holiday—something they had most likely never imagined possible.

My wife and her grandmother grew up in vastly different worlds. To bridge these generational chasms and participate in the rapidly changing society, Chinese citizens must have enormous flexibility and mental resilience. In 1978, Deng Xiaoping introduced the policy of liberal reforms and openness, saying, "It doesn't matter whether the cat is black or white, as long as it catches mice.[5]" This kind of pragmatism is still present in contemporary China and in the thinking of its people. The citizen has learned that some things are just temporary and that change is always possible. The country's recent history is a vivid illustration. For example, owning private property is now part of China's official policy, but it is a 180-degree turn in communist ideology. Legally, it was not until 1982 that the door opened for reforms and this new vision was actually entrenched in the constitution. This includes specific mention of the private sector being complementary to the state-run economy.[6] However, it took until 2004, before a new constitutional amendment stipulated that private property and private companies enjoy legal protection.[7] Considering that China started sailing down this more open and liberal course in 1978, that means that for more than a quarter of a century, these policies did not have a constitutional basis. In practice, citizens could open a private company or purchase an apartment but would not enjoy 100 percent legal protection. They had to trust that pragmatism would carry the day, not ideology.

The government encouraged private companies and strengthened private ownership regulations, realizing this was an engine for the economy. In 1978, for example, there were only 110,000 people who were not employed in state-owned enterprises and cooperatives. Private companies were illegal.[8] In 2018 however, the Chinese Administration for Industry and Commerce estimated China had about thirty million private companies, and seventy million self-employed households.[9] Adapting the constitution was therefore a mere formalization of an existing situation, driven by changing market conditions. The same applies to buying a private home, although this situation is more complex. Although citizens have enjoyed four decades of private ownership, even today their land comes with seventy-year government leases. Chinese homeowners do not dwell on this. Everyone realizes that ideology is flexible and adaptable to market requirements.

Diversity and Complexity

Chinese citizens also need to possess the virtues of pragmatism and flexibility because of China's enormous complexity and diversity. There are vast regional differences in legislation, and rules are often open to interpretation. Regulations are subject to change and can be downright contradictory, either because the conditions under which they were established have already changed or because an existing situation was never formalized in the legislation. Moreover, local authorities can determine how rules are interpreted.

Take an example from my own life. Our two children were both born in China. Because I am Belgian, they both have Belgian passports. They do not possess Chinese passports because Chinese law does not support the concept of dual nationality. However, Chinese law *does* stipulate that if one parent is a Chinese citizen, the child automatically obtains Chinese citizenship. In other words, although the law says both children are Chinese citizens, they cannot get Chinese passports. But because they *are* Chinese citizens, they can't get a Chinese visa in their Belgian passports, which is required for non-Chinese nationals to enter or reside in China. To complicate matters further, different regions and authorities interpret these regulations in their own ways. In the cosmopolitan cities where authorities are more familiar with such cases, there are practical procedures in place. Officials in smaller cities have less experience with children of international marriage and don't always have solutions. As a result, my children's Belgian nationality—or better, their non-Chinese nationality—took a full three years to establish.

But as always in China, pragmatic interim solutions exist. My children were granted one-time exit and reentry visas to travel abroad. Bureaucratic reasons prevented us from starting a procedure in Beijing which would have quickly and resolutely solved the nationality issue. Instead, the procedure had to be completed in Tai'an. This led to fierce discussions between my family and the authorities, during which my mother-in-law repeatedly showed that her respect for Chinese officials was not what it once was. Fortunately, we found a way out. The Chinese embassy in Brussels provided us with an official document stating that our children had never obtained Chinese citizenship. But to receive this document, the whole family needed to go to Belgium.

This issue had been dragging on for almost three years and, calculating travel expenditure alone, cost us nearly $10,000. (The sleepless nights, annoyances, and endless discussions with authorities were free of charge.) But had we been in Beijing, we could have resolved everything in a week and spent no more than $50.

Governments are often pragmatic in implementing legislation. For example, prostitution is officially banned, yet it is still relatively easy to find.[10] Migrant workers on huge construction projects live in temporary urban housing for months before they return home. Authorities would rather they seek some (relatively) harmless fun than indulge in excessive drinking or worse. Companies can easily negotiate with local authorities regarding regulations or certain benefits. I often needed to convene with Chinese officials to negotiate certain projects, and it always struck me how reasonable and approachable they were. Practical solutions always outweighed ideology or strict enforcement of the law. The Western world sees Chinese companies or government as untrustworthy, but in my experience, this is not often the case. In China, just as in the rest of the world, reasonable, fair people will be treated reasonably and fairly. The vast majority of Chinese companies want to develop honest, long-term, mutually beneficial partnerships with foreign organizations.

For Westerners accustomed to following rules, China's vast amount of regulations is mystifying. It can seem as if they have entered a world almost completely at odds with their own. But as mentioned, rules are flexible and subject to interpretation, and strict enforcement is not a priority. Especially for the wealthy, the country can be a playground. Once I asked a friend why Chinese citizens have so little trouble breaking the rules. Joking, he replied that rules in China are never really broken, just bent as far as possible. When I asked him why, he quoted a well-known proverb: "As long as enough people break the rules, no one is punished for it." I think this fairly accurately describes the prevailing attitude to authority. After all, it's not easy for the government to make a population of 1.3 billion obey all existing laws and regulations.

Even with the rules on birth control, interpretation is flexible. Since my wife is Chinese, the doctors were not allowed to tell us our children's gender, because many Chinese parents having a girl have traditionally opted for abortion. But for us, there were hints. Maybe it's because I am a foreigner, but at a checkup a few months before the birth of our son in 2009, the doctor told us laughing that the baby "had something special between his legs." Three years later, another doctor told us that the baby my wife was carrying was "not like the father." We prepared for—and had—a girl. The doctors had not violated the rules, but they had "told" us our children's gender.

The traffic, too, is an example of Chinese flexibility. I found that rigorous attention to traffic regulations won't do any good in this neo-Darwinian environment. Strangely enough, however, road rage is rare. Even when someone is clearly breaking the traffic rules, Chinese drivers and cyclists tend to wait patiently. Also, most motorists drive much more slowly than those in the Western world. They know that other road users often don't follow the rules and need to stay on guard. China is the world's biggest car market, and cars rule the streets; cyclists and pedestrians have to take care. Yet this situation is improving, especially with stricter police controls and enforcement. These days police often stop offenders, some of whom acquiesce and some of whom argue. Shanghai, with its 2.5 million vehicles creeping along the streets, enforced its first ban on honking horns in 2007, albeit to little effect.[11] Since 2018, as the government started to battle noise pollution more vigorously, acoustic cameras that film honking cars are being installed to catch offenders.[12] And the situation improved drastically, because cars rarely honk anymore. After receiving several fines, I needed to adapt my driving style as well.

I must admit I have had my fair share of penalties, but I've also been lucky. When I was living in Beijing, four other drivers and I were pulled over because we all broke the same traffic regulation: turning left at a T-junction where vehicles were allowed only to turn right. The road sign indicating this fact was barely visible behind a tree, which made it clear why the police officer had chosen that spot to catch offenders. I was the last of the five cars to be pulled over. There was a sixth driver behind me, but he just kept driving, well aware that the police officer was on his own and could not pursue him. The first four drivers got out of their cars, all complaining that the road sign was obstructed and that they refused to pay the fine. Tempers were running hot, but I decided to observe, rather than join them. Without a trace of emotion, the stoic officer wrote ticket after ticket, much like a referee who throws a flag on the play and ignores the inevitable protests. As the four drivers drove off, still cursing, I took a different approach, explaining politely that I didn't see the sign. My attitude must have helped, because I got away with only a reprimand.

Flexible interpretation of new legislation is a problem, especially since old habits die hard. One of those habits is smoking. China is not only the world's largest cigarette manufacturer, the country also consumes one-third of all cigarettes and is home to largest group of smokers on the planet. There are no fewer than 300 million smokers, while another 700 million others—among which 180 million children—are regularly exposed to second-hand smoke.[13] Estimates claim that more than one million people die every year from the effects of nicotine. The most important cause is lung cancer, with 800,000 newly diagnosed patients annually.[14] Public pressure, air pollution, and increasing health care expenditures have led the Chinese government to push through tougher anti-smoking legislation. Smoking in public buildings has been banned since 2014, but implementation is weak. Tobacco is a huge source of revenue for the Chinese government. The tobacco industry in China contributes between 7 and 11 percent of its annual tax revenues, which makes the tobacco lobby very powerful.[15]

In big cities like Beijing and Shanghai, the legislation has had an impact, and people generally follow the regulations, but in smaller cities, people have kept on smoking in public buildings. There is also a cultural aspect to this. It was common to see Chinese politicians in photographs or on TV with cigarettes between their fingers, and smoking remains a traditional symbol of power. In business, the time-honored habit of handing out expensive cigarettes as gifts still persists, especially in the smaller towns. Although the central government asks local officials to lead by example, until a few years ago, it was still normal to step into public officials' offices and find them immersed in smoke. I learned that cigarettes were indispensable in contacts with local government officials or businesspeople.

Those who should set an example are often the first to violate the smoking ban. Although smoking in medical facilities has been prohibited, plenty of small-town hospitals have older-generation doctors still smoking in their offices or in the halls. In 2015, 35 percent of people still had witnessed smoking inside hospitals.[16]

Flexibility in Business

That the business world shows some flexibility in interpreting the rules shouldn't surprise anybody. The first Chinese private enterprises were established in the 1980s, in a world and market unfamiliar with a capitalist system. There were no rules in place for it, nor any examples to learn from. Everything was new. The only way to successfully develop a new business was to be pragmatic and creative in utilizing the limited resources available. This approach has left its mark. As markets keep evolving, and because statistics or reliable information are difficult to come by, companies must keep a finger on the social pulse and respond quickly to new trends. Chinese enterprises launch new products quickly. There may at first be issues of quality or user-friendliness, but by upgrading first-generation products quickly, companies can improve quality. This happens in a fraction of the time that Western companies need to achieve the same results. In China, speed and flexibility are vital to keep companies afloat in the ever-changing market.

Western companies cannot even imagine how intense and fiercely competitive the Chinese market is. Chinese entrepreneurs have learned the hard way what it means to be successful. No matter what industry you're operating in, there are already dozens or hundreds—sometimes thousands—of competitors. Chinese entrepreneurs are masters at doing business and skilled veterans of many battles. Some of them have successfully built real business empires from scratch in very difficult circumstances. They fought many battles with competitors, many of which were state-owned enterprises. To their disadvantage, their own customers often associate their products with lower quality, assuming that Chinese goods are less reliable than those of their Western competitors, which is increasingly no longer true. In the rapidly evolving Chinese business landscape, companies need to reinvent their businesses again and again while navigating the bureaucracy, uncertainty, and market trends. When meeting Chinese CEOs and businessmen, it always strikes me that while they attach great importance to formalities and status, they can also be down to earth and approachable. They are hands-on and feel the need to be close to the market.

The vast majority of the elder generation of Chinese entrepreneurs I know personally grew up enduring tremendous hardships and poverty. They all remember what it means to be desperately poor and to face daily struggles to bring food to the family table. Especially in Qian'an, which experienced staggering economic development, stories from the past were striking. Some owners of steel and cement companies were working in the fields or on state-owned production lines less than fifteen years ago. During meetings, I always try to inquire about my business partner's personal history, and I hear similar stories. The owner of a large steel company told me that until twenty years ago, he had used to be a truck driver and worked sixteen hours a day, seven days a week, earning barely enough to support his family. Like almost everyone else in the country, he lived in a simple house he couldn't afford to heat. It was luck and a lot of guts that led him to start his own business.

A senior government official told me he was the eldest son of a family with six children. Two of his brothers died—one from malnutrition—but he was lucky enough to be selected by the Communist Party of China at a young age, which enabled him to pursue a career in state administration. That amounted to winning the jackpot, since it opened the gates to all sorts of financial gains. In Tai'an, I heard similar stories. Even in Beijing and Shanghai, people vividly remember their impoverished youths. A good friend in Beijing made her fortune in real estate. She was born in the early 1960s and told me that for her sixth birthday, her parents had somehow managed to find a birthday cake. However, she was only allowed to look at it. After the Party, the cake needed to be returned to the bakery display window. Nowadays under normal circumstances, she takes family holidays in Thailand twice a year. She doesn't eat cake anymore, however; she needs to keep fit.

Clearly, Chinese entrepreneurs are not people that give in easily or avoid challenges. One by one, they managed to climb their way out of poverty. They are living the Chinese Dream and believe they are at the forefront of the resurrection of the Chinese nation. They want to show the world what China is capable of. Many are passionate about their work and anxious to scale even higher peaks with their companies. It's true that most lack proper education and have few analytical skills; but then again, analysis wasn't always possible anyway. After all, Chinese companies have grown up a market in which accurate data or information were hardly available, and where fast-growing sectors prized flexibility and adaptability over traditional skills. Even today, I receive reports that are incomplete or already invalid by the time they land on my desk. When I was analyzing the cement market in Hebei Province, I originally based my information on official reports and data. However, I realized it was much more useful to talk to people in the field to get a better market overview. Sometimes I just counted the new cement plants under construction while I was driving through the countryside. There were no official figures about that.

Chinese businesspeople often lack the qualities that foreign companies value so highly, which means their abilities are misjudged and grossly underestimated. This can be a big mistake. In a country that changes so often and so quickly, in society—and certainly in business—pragmatism and flexibility have become second nature. In China, this is a huge asset. Companies facing economic hardship can react quickly. One of the top managers of a large Chinese automotive supply company told me that during the 2009 financial crisis, they reduced production, temporarily laid off workers, and terminated suppliers' contracts quickly without any significant problems. He added proudly that many of his European competitors were amazed at such a high degree of flexibility. It gave his firm a huge competitive advantage. And during the Covid-19 crisis, Ziva, a global manufacturer of fitness equipment, changed his B2B model into B2C within forty days, including new website and sales channels. The British owner living in Shanghai and a friend of mine claimed this speed of execution could only be possible in China.

Chinese companies are fighting daily battles in a highly volatile and rapidly evolving market. There were no standard formulas for success; everything has had to be learned from scratch. Many managers do not follow existing patterns or rules, because they need to constantly reinvent themselves and their products. Western companies spend a lot to master being lean and agile, but these characteristics are simply part of the Chinese DNA.

Notes

1. Britannica. 2020. Second Sino-Japanese War.www.britannica.com/event/Second-Sino-Japanese-War. Accessed February 16, 2018.
2. History Channel. 2019. China: Timeline. www.history.com/.amp/topics/china/china-timeline. Accessed February 16, 2018.
3. Britannica. 2020. Great leap forward. www.britannica.com/event/Great-Leap-Forward. Accessed February 23, 2018.
4. *The Guardian*. 2016. The Cultural Revolution: all you need to know about China's political convulsion. theguardian.com/world/2016/may/11/the-cultural-revolution-50-years-on-all-you-need-to-know-about-chinas-political-convulsion. Accessed February 4, 2019.
5. *The Guardian*. 2008. The great pragmatist: Deng Xiaoping. www.theguardian.com/business/2008/dec/18/globaleconomy-economics. Accessed July 1, 2018.
6. Cato Institute. 2003. Ownership with Chinese characteristics: private property right and land reform in the PRC. http://www.cato.org/publications/congressional-testimony/ownership-chinese-characteristics-private-property-rights-land-reform-prc. Accessed April 28, 2018.
7. World Socialist Web Site. 2004. Chinese regime amends constitution to protect private ownership. www.wsws.org/en/articles/2004/04/npc-a02.html. Accessed May 4, 2018.
8. The development of private businesses in China: 1978–2004. Guibin Zhang & Zhong Qin. www.apebhconference.files.wordpress.com/2009/09/zhang-qin-20081.pdf. Accessed June 21, 2018.
9. CGTN. 2018. Historic changes in China's economic structure in past 40 years. https://news.cgtn.com/news/3d3d674d77677a4d31457a6333566d54/share_p.html. Accessed April 15, 2019.
10. South China Morning Post. 2019. Inside China's sex trade: seduction, sympathy, survival, and pride in 'emotional labour'—prostitutes and their clients tell all to a Hong Kong academic. www.scmp.com/lifestyle/arts-culture/article/3032354/inside-chinas-sex-trade-seduction-sympathy-survival-and. Accessed December 1, 2020.
11. *Shanghai Daily*. 2016. Number of cars on city's streets increases to 2.5 M. https://archive.shine.cn/metro/public-services/Number-of-cars-on-citys-streets-increases-to-25m/shdaily.shtml. Accessed October 3, 2019.

12. Business Insider. 2018. Chinese cities wanting peace and quiet are using acoustic cameras to catch honking drivers. www.businessinsider.de/china-using-acoustic-cameras-to-catch-car-honking-2018-4?r=US&IR=T. Accessed March 23, 2019.
13. World Health Organization. 2020. Smoking in China. https://www.who.int/china/health-topics/tobacco. Accessed December 1, 2020.
14. Supchina. 2019. China's cigarette smoking epidemic. https://signal.supchina.com/chinas-cigarette-smoking-epidemic/. Accessed December 1, 2020.
15. Supchina. 2019. China's cigarette smoking epidemic. https://signal.supchina.com/chinas-cigarette-smoking-epidemic/. Accessed December 1, 2020.
16. *The Financial Times*. 2017. Smoking remains one of China's burning. www.ft.com/content/0817f89c-3fa5-11e7-82b6-896b95f30f58. Accessed April 20, 2018.

CHAPTER 3

Multifaceted China

In April 2012, we paid a short visit to a good friend of my wife's and her husband, a high-ranking official in Beijing's central government. Like so many others, Mrs. Li had made her fortune in real estate, while for a long time her husband was responsible for many of the infrastructure projects China carried out. After dinner, we discussed government policies and the problems of implementation. The husband explained that the government had very good long-term plans and a clear vision for the future. But, he added joking, implementation isn't always easy, because nobody can predict what will happen in five minutes' time, let alone in a month, a year, or longer. This is one of the most important things to understand about China, where thinking and behavior are inextricably linked to the country's enormous complexity. This country cannot be seen as a homogeneous entity and cannot be understood if one has not grasped its internal functions.

China has a population of 1.3 billion—more than the United States and Europe combined. This leads to varied views and competing interests. The country is subject to a complex administrative division into twenty-three provinces, five autonomous regions, and four municipalities, all under the authority of the central government, which also governs two special administrative zones (Hong Kong and Macao), operating under the principle of "one country, two [political] systems." The provinces

S. Agten, *Adventures in the Chinese Economy: 16 Years from the Inside*, https://doi.org/10.1007/978-981-16-1167-4_3

and autonomous regions are further divided into prefectures, municipalities, cities, counties, and districts. And if that weren't complicated enough, there are special economic zones and other districts that operate by different rules to of the rest of China. There are more than 113 cities with more than one million inhabitants and six cities with more than ten million inhabitants and three more on the way, not to mention the thousands of smaller towns and hundreds of thousands of villages.[1]

Although not officially divided into them, Chinese cities can be grouped into broad categories. The most developed are Tier 1 cities, centers of economic activity that include Beijing, Shanghai, Shenzhen, and Guangzhou. About twenty-four cities, usually provincial capitals, can be considered Tier 2 cities, such as Jinan, Chengdu, and Fuzhou, in Shandong, Sichuan, and Fujian provinces, respectively. Tier 3 cities are less economically developed, but can be crucial for many businesses. The majority of the population lives in Tier 4, Tier 5, and Tier 6 cities. These cities and regions may lag behind economically, but many enjoy great autonomy and are catching up fast.[2]

It's a mistake to believe that Beijing's central government entirely controls all these areas. Local governments often act independently, pursuing their own goals and directions as far as possible. In implementing the central policies, they consciously make local adjustments and show a high degree of freedom. This is similar to the United States, which also considers the views and needs of its fifty states and allows every region to develop its own dynamics. China is a huge country with significant geographic, economic, social, regional, and cultural differences. It extends from Russian Siberia in the north to Afghanistan in the west and Vietnam in the south. Tropical forests, white sandy beaches, high mountains, deserts, snow-capped peaks, and extensive grasslands are all within China's borders. Of course, every Chinese citizen knows that China is enormously complicated. The different societies and sometimes opposing forces that shape China can also carry seeds of instability.

China has achieved almost unprecedented economic growth in the four decades since the 1978 opening of its economy. However, this growth was unevenly spread throughout the country. Eastern China's geographical location and numerous ports meant that development came early there, spearheaded by the many export companies that established themselves in the area. The northern provinces are dominated by heavy industry and state-owned enterprises, while southern China has primarily private companies focusing on exports. The needs of large cities with richer, more demanding citizens and complex service networks will differ from the needs of rural communities entering their first phase of industrialization.

Moving even ten miles out of the big cities, visitors find themselves in a different world, one that is diametrically unlike modern, international China. Some smaller urban areas still suffer from energy shortages, something unthinkable in the country's megacities. Time and time again, I have seen hotels suffering from electricity and water shortages. This uneven economic development not only furthers the gap between rich and poor, but also poses a potential threat to stability. China's *hukou* system, a family registration program that functions as a domestic passport, regulating population distribution and rural-to-urban migration, virtually institutionalizes inequality.[3] For fear that peasants seeking work will overwhelm urban centers, the *hukou* system ensures authorities can control migration and monitor social stability, but at the expense of citizen mobility or worse. Most of China's estimated two hundred and fifty million migrant workers can only receive social services such as education and health care in their home towns, not their place of employment.[4] Many of these migrants are like illegal immigrants in the West, doing the jobs the locals don't want, without benefits or protection. The concern is valid; without the *hukou*, a city's financial burdens would inevitably skyrocket—overcrowding of schools is just one problem. But it creates difficulties for many people. For instance, although my wife has a Tai'an *hukou*, she lives in Shanghai. She has to return regularly to her hometown to apply for official papers and endure countless administrative challenges as a consequence. Another problem is feeling displaced, even at an emotional level; after all, you're never really "home" when you're carrying proof that you actually belong somewhere else. Seeking to solve the *hukou* problem at least partially, China's government expanded the urban *hukou* to 100 million migrant workers in 2020.[5]

Inequality

Despite China being forecasted to have a $25,307 per capita GDP in 2025,[6] inequality remains a big issue. The international Gini coefficient captures income inequality around the world: a Gini of 0 would represent perfect income equality, a Gini of 1, complete inequality. China's Gini was 0.465 (the international alert line is 0.4) at the end of 2019, worse than the 1978 value of 0.3.[7] This means that income inequality in

China has grown over the past four decades. The rich are getting richer. No one can deny that China's standard of living has improved tremendously; nevertheless, while the growing middle class enjoys comparative comfort, the working class finds every day a tough fight. In Shanghai, a senior executive manager for an FMCG company can make more than the equivalent job in New York. Whereas people in China's poorer provinces will have an income which equals that of poor developing countries.[8] Shanghai residents have purchasing power on par with Switzerland.[9]

In Qian'an, income inequality has taken extreme forms. The city has a disproportionate number of cement and steel companies receiving coal shipments, sometimes in convoys of fifty trucks each loaded with a hundred tons of coal. In the winter, elderly people and children desperate for heat stand by the roadside hoping to pick up a few pieces of coal dropped by passing trucks.

Still, ostentatious wealth is everywhere. Qian'an's super-rich drive their Aston Martins and Ferraris through the city's impoverished neighborhoods. On the Luan River that bisects the city, construction companies have built artificial islands strong enough to hold villas—one of which has a private zoo. The owner of a private steelworks, now a good friend of mine, told me that he often takes a private jet with other steel barons for weekends in Europe. Each of the fellow passengers takes care of one aspect of the journey, be it hotel accommodations for everyone, restaurant visits, or shopping. The only exception is casino visits, where the sums can skyrocket—for that, everyone picks up their own tab.

On my many journeys through China, I encountered poverty in all its forms—mostly in small villages where time seemed to stand still. In 2015, 57 million households reportedly did not have a sanitary toilet of their own.[10] However, 93 percent of the rural population did have access to an improved drinking water source.[11] These figures are broadly consistent with my own observations in Qian'an, where most of our production workers come from surrounding villages. Most village homes are two-bedroom houses with a small kitchen, a dining table with four chairs, a TV, a wardrobe, and a wooden bunk. Indoor plumbing is rare, but most villages have public facilities where locals can take weekly showers. Running water is often limited, particularly in the drier north. In villages of only a few hundred, residents grow their own fruit and vegetables for personal use and sell the remainder to the city dwellers who come to the country for visits. This is often the elderly's only source of income. The main roads between villages are paved, but their internal roads are sandy walkways. Here and there, a goat runs through the streets, and horse-drawn carriages still make the rounds.

The tremendous dynamism of modern China has missed the villages, where, with their children doing menial labor in the big cities, the country's elderly inhabitants sink further and further into poverty. I once saw an elderly bed-ridden man suffering from cancer just waiting to die, because he could not afford the cost of treatment. For many, the statutory health insurance covers only part of the costs and, in cases of serious illness, does not apply. Children in remote mountain villages with no electricity still walk for hours every day to school, just as their parents did forty years ago. In this economically and socially developed country, where everything is more expensive and everyone is more demanding, the rural population has been left behind. The younger generation looks for work and a better life in the cities—and most of the time, they find both. The contrast between the countryside and the vibrant metropolises could not be greater. The government is therefore promoting further urbanization to lift more people out of poverty, seeing this as the only way to ensure social stability. If the larger proportion of the poor remain poor while a small number keep getting richer, social unrest or even revolution is looming.

Ethnic Diversity

Often unobserved in the West, China also has a great ethnic diversity. The country has fifty-six ethnic groups, many of whom speak their own language and maintain their own distinct cultures.[12] Of these groups, Tibetans and Uyghurs—the latter from Xinjiang, in northwestern China—are the best known abroad; they often launch protests against what they see as government oppression, garnering vast international news coverage. When I traveled through Tibet in 2006, I sensed the unique atmosphere. On a nocturnal stroll through the streets of Lhasa, an older man grabbed me and started speaking, looking hard into my eyes. Even through his Tibetan dialect, his meaning was clear. When he released my arm, he gave me a medallion embossed with a Tibetan flag. He said that Tibet was once an independent country, something the Chinese authorities have never accepted.

Although the majority of the population speak Mandarin, there are countless regional dialects and languages, the best known being

Cantonese. This diversity means communication can be difficult, particularly between northerners and southerners. When my wife and I traveled through southern China a few years ago, we reached the stunning mountainous region of Guangxi, which borders Vietnam. But my wife struggled to make herself understood. A restaurant owner in the village actually asked her if she was Chinese. After studying in Canada, a good friend moved to Toronto, which has the world's largest Chinatown. He came from one of the northern provinces, but many of his Toronto neighbors were Cantonese speakers from Guangzhou, and he found communication impossible. Many Chinese restaurants in the United States and Europe are run by southern Chinese immigrants who have retained their own dialect and accent. I am fluent in Mandarin, but when I tried to speak to a restaurant owner in Belgium, the conversation ended after a few words. The same applies to my colleagues in Shanghai speaking Shanghainese—I have no idea what they are talking about.

Apart from the language differences, there are regional customs and habits. At the beginning of meetings, I ask colleagues where in China they're from. This is not only small talk; it gives me hints about what habits to expect. These regional differences are especially reflected in China's food culture; each village has their own traditional dishes. An old proverb says that it is possible to try a new dish every day in China for the rest of your life. In the Western world, people like to meet for coffee and a chat. In China, restaurants—and copious amounts of alcohol—are crucial for developing and maintaining contacts with business partners. The northern Chinese are used to lavish meals, while the southern provinces have smaller portions and less to drink. Beijingers who visit business contacts or friends in Shanghai always complain about the small meals, while Shanghaiers gripe about being overfed.

In fact, when my wife and I weighed the pros and cons of moving to Beijing versus Shanghai, for my wife, one major drawback was that the food in Shanghai was not as good. Guangzhou residents are so proud of their food that they hold meetings in teahouses or restaurants. The diversity of Guangdong province's cuisine has inspired its own saying throughout China: they eat anything that swims except submarines, anything that flies besides airplanes, and anything with four legs besides tables and chairs. When our employees travel to other cities and regions on business trips, they always bring local specialties back to Shanghai.

For my part, I have had plenty of experience with Chinese-style eating and drinking—at the expense of my waistline. Attending Chinese banquets, an essential part of everyday business life, never ends well—especially in the north. Food is incidental, and hosts prioritize the constant and efficient consumption of alcohol, with predictable results. Chinese table neighbors love to test foreigners' drinking resistance and, not surprisingly, things disintegrate rapidly. One time, I was the only foreigner sitting at a small table in Inner Mongolia, a province of China that borders Mongolia. Residents of Inner Mongolia are notorious drinkers, believing that alcohol consumption can help one defy the cold in the vast steppes. They promised me an unforgettable night. That may be true, but unfortunately, I cannot remember any of it. However, such evenings promote strong bonds and play a big part in success for any endeavor in China.

Religious Diversity

China's broad diversity also extends to religion. China has an official and fairly consistent antagonistic policy to religion. One notable exception was the crackdown on the Falun Gong in 1999.[13] Amid China's economic boom and rapid modernization, the emergence of a spiritual vacuum has led to a growing number of religious believers. The Chinese constitution guarantees freedom of any "normal" religion, which, of course, is open to interpretation. The government officially recognizes five religions: Buddhism, Catholicism, Daoism, Islam, and Protestantism, all of which have millions of followers. There also are a variety of small local religions. In total, China has more than 5500 religious organizations and 140,000 places of worship.[14] It's estimated that there are up to 350 million religious believers in China, which is almost four times more than all the members of the Communist Party combined.[15] In western China, especially in Xinjiang, there are large numbers of Muslims; in fact, the area feels more like the Middle East than China. Buddhism is deeply rooted throughout the country, and Buddhist temples are often major tourist attractions. But above all, Christianity enjoys great popularity, partly because it's seen as trendy. Every Sunday, more people gather in the churches of China than in all the churches in Europe. Christmas is not an official holiday, but young people have started to celebrate this "modern" holiday, if not always in a religious way.

In 2005, I went to a Chinese church for the first and last time. A Canadian colleague in Yichun was a devout, almost militant Christian. Her mission in China was not only to spread the doctrine of Christianity, but also to win some souls for the "good cause"—a task she performed with zeal. She was also trying to save my soul, but was not ultimately successful. She regularly attended mass in one of the city's two churches and, because I wanted to experience how a church in China is designed, I ventured inside. The white, American-style church seemed normal enough, but what transpired was like a bad Hollywood movie. A Chinese priest in white robes, flanked by a gospel choir dressed in purple, performed ecstatically, and after a few minutes, the worshippers began to sing and even dance along. Many—including my Canadian colleague—seemed to have fallen into trances, as if they were communicating directly with Jesus; others spoke loudly, their emotions running wild. To this day, I am not sure if this was a Christian group or an extreme sect, but the experience seemed less like an authentic Chinese church and more like American Christians in the Bible Belt. I managed to remain fully conscious, though astonished by the spectacle around me.

The majority of Chinese believe in some form of religion. My Chinese friends all believe in "something," including widespread nature religions. In my role as general manager of the Qian'an Cement Factory, I heard that employees believed that a female spirit haunted the surrounding fields. Several workers reported having heard a female voice during their night shifts and seeing a shadowy figure. In the past, villagers buried their dead, and many workers feared that the construction of the cement factory might have accidentally released some ghosts. One day, the factory workers decided to burn down a doghouse—the closest thing to a real house—to offer the spirit a new resting place. Apparently this was the right approach, because from then on, no one mentioned the female spirit.

Superstition remains strong in China. In the luxury block of Beijing flats, we shared with other Westerners and Chinese, there were no fourth, thirteenth, fourteenth, or twenty-fourth floors. The number four (and derivatives) is considered a cursed number, much the way some people in the West feel about thirteen. Feng shui, the philosophical system that promotes harmony with the environment, instructs followers to demolish new buildings if they do not conform to the harmonious system. And those who commune with spirits can earn a good living; I know a successful businesswoman who never makes decisions until she has consulted her fortune-teller. Most of the time, the modern Chinese belief in "something" serves a pragmatic purpose—whether in love, in games, or in business, where anything that helps make money is allowed, be it one of the five recognized religions or something more exotically mystical. Shopkeepers place small Buddha figures on store counters all over China to ensure that business goes smoothly. And as in the Western world, opportunity counts for something. My father-in-law, a sober, nonreligious man, still went to the temple after my son's birth to pray for his grandson's good health. Even within the Communist Party of China (CCP), religiosity is not an absolute taboo. Although the CCP is officially atheist, many of its members profess belief in some religion.[16] Some pragmatic local governments in China still actively support churches as a new social fabric to replace outdated CCP dogma.

Although China's constitution allows religious belief, many religious organizations nevertheless increasingly face more scrutiny or sometimes a certain level of persecution. In recent years, there were campaigns to remove crosses from churches, demolitions of churches, while some Christian priests were harassed or even imprisoned. Because of the region's ethnic and religious links to neighboring countries such as Kazakhstan, Kyrgyzstan, Tajikistan, and Afghanistan, crackdowns in Xinjiang have been particularly harsh. In 2018, UN experts estimated that upwards of three million people there had been detained or sent to reeducation camps. Beijing denies claims of human rights abuses in the region, calling these camps vocational training centers aimed at countering extremism.[17]

Stability Through Integration

But China's diversity goes beyond language, food, and religion and extends to hundreds of other details. This is not surprising in a country and society that is in constant flux, and where social, economic, and cultural trends are rapidly changing. In addition, the large migration flows into the cities increase the complexity. Culinary customs, consumer behavior, lifestyles, traditions, and other habits vary from region to region, from city to city. Shanghai is China's most international urban center and more people speak English there than anywhere else in China. It is also one of the world's most dynamic cities. Beijing has more traditional culture and history. Guangzhou is a culinary adventure. Shenzhen is the digital innovation capital, while daily life in Chengdu, the capital of the southwestern province of Sichuan, is still slower than in other major cities. In smaller cities like Tai'an or Qian'an, people still wake up at dawn, and some go to sleep at sunset.

As in the West, some people prefer the stability of their small area as opposed to the frenetic pace of the megacities. A friend from Sichuan says he hopes his daughter will marry someone from the same region, so that at least they share a cultural background. Despite the country's enormous size, there is only one time zone, Beijing standard time, which can cause problems. In Xinjiang, in China's far northwest, the locals often use a time zone of their own, and I have found that Beijing time is not always used in regional public transport.

All this means that it is impossible to speak of a Chinese culture or mentality. Nor is there a common recipe for what works and what doesn't. Many Westerners have trouble believing this, but in fact my Chinese colleagues do not always know what to expect from their fellow citizens, and people everywhere generalize about those from other regions of China. After fifteen years of living in this country, this is the most important lesson I have learned is that China has so many facets that it is virtually impossible to fully understand it.

Precisely because of this complexity, the Chinese government is trying to further integrate the country—paying special attention to the economy. Authorities realized early on that a modern economy depends on a well-developed motorway and rail network as well as a reliable power supply and functioning telecommunication systems. In 1978, the country began to build new infrastructure to connect and supply the various cities and industrial areas with sufficient water and electricity. China also facilitated communication by laying new telephone lines and later by setting up internet servers. In 1957, the first bridge was built over China's longest river, the Yangtze; today, there are a hundred and sixty-two of them.[18] The country has more than two hundred and thirty international and regional airports, with hundreds more planned[19]; nine major airlines; 34 cities with metro services covering more than 3000 miles; 3 million miles of road network and a very modern highway network; more than 80,000 miles of railways[20]; and the world's largest broadband network, with more internet users than the United States and Europe combined.[21] In October 2019, three of China's largest mobile-phone carriers launched 5G services, making it the world's largest 5G network.[22] All this has enabled the Chinese to live and travel more comfortably than ever before.

Until a decade ago, traveling in China was a complex venture. Even one-way train tickets were hard to get; return tickets were virtually impossible. On holidays, trains were so crowded that the only way some passengers could board was by climbing through the windows; sometimes family members would come to say a long goodbye and then be trapped on board for the rest of the journey. Air travel was possible, but expensive. There were highways but no interlinked motorway network, and most Chinese couldn't afford cars anyway. I remember in 2005, when I was an English teacher in Beijing, a student invited me to visit him in his hometown of Luoyang in Henan Province on May Day, one of China's two "Golden Week," holidays (the other is October 1, China's national day). These week-long vacations gave citizens a chance to travel the often considerable distances to their hometowns, which could take two or three days by train. Luoyang is one of China's ancient dynastic capitals and is steeped in historical attractions, most notably the famous fifth-century Shaolin Temple, home of the Shaolin monks and the birthplace of kung fu. This invitation (common between students and teachers) was a great opportunity for me to indulge in my love of history and to get a sense of daily life in Luoyang, and I gratefully accepted.

We set off on the five-hundred-mile, fourteen-hour journey. The holiday crush meant we couldn't get sleepers, and managed seats only for the first four hours. For the rest of the trip we had to stand in a crowded train. The stench of sweat and food was overpowering, and it was impossible to get to the restrooms. I almost fainted. We reached our destination completely exhausted. It was an unforgettable experience, one I hope I never repeat!

No one traveling by train today can imagine such conditions. In 2020, China's high-speed rail network covered a total of 24,000 miles—about two-thirds of the world's total—and it will expand to 45,000 miles by 2035.[23] By comparison, Spain's network covers 1900 miles, while Japan, the industry's former leader, has 1600 miles of track.[24] 550 Chinese cities are now connected through this network.[25]

Creating the world's largest high-speed rail network has been a quantum leap for Chinese mobility. Every day, over four million people race through China's countryside at speeds of 186 miles per hour.[26] Two decades ago, traveling the 1430 miles between Beijing in the north and Guangzhou in the south took fifty hours. On today's high-speed trains, it takes ten. My uncomfortable fourteen-hour journey from Beijing to Luoyang would today take under four hours, and could be done in a comfortable seat in a punctual manner, with no luggage limitations and snacks available for purchase.

Unsurprisingly, China's high-speed rail network has propelled the country's social and economic integration forward. My wife used to travel to her family in Tai'an twice a year, always dreading the travel stress, but she now goes at least five or six times annually and enjoys it. Beijing travel agencies now offer day trips to see the terracotta soldiers in Xian, a city 715 miles away. Our managers attend the quarterly symposium in Shanghai and always prefer the comfort of the comparably priced train over a plane. High-speed train terminals are as slick and gleaming as the airports, and this applies to all infrastructure components used by the masses: in China, you have to think big in every sense of the word.

Notes

1. Visual Capitalist. 2020. Meet China's 113 cities with more than one million people. www.visualcapitalist.com/chinas-113-cities-one-million-people-population/. Accessed December 1, 2020.
2. *China Briefing*. 2010. China's second tier cities? The third and fourth tiers are catching up. https://www.china-briefing.com/news/chinas-second-tier-cities-the-third-and-fourth-tiers-are-catching-up/. Accessed May 5, 2018.
3. ThoughtCo. 2019. China's Hukou system. https://www.thoughtco.com/chinas-hukou-system-1434424. Accessed March 5, 2020.
4. *New Horizons*. China's hukou system explained—what is "hukou" and how it works https://nhglobalpartners.com/the-chinese-hukou-system-explained/. Accessed December 29, 2020.
5. *The Diplomat*. 2017. China is speeding up hukou reform, but that won't be enough to solve the migrant worker problem. https://thediplomat.com/2017/02/chinas-hukou-reforms-and-the-urbanization-challenge/. Accessed June 4, 2020.
6. Bloomberg. 2020. China to leapfrog 56 nations during quarter-century income surge. www.bloomberg.com/news/articles/2020-11-17/china-to-leapfrog-56-nations-during-quarter-century-income-surge. Accessed December 30, 2020.
7. CEIC. China Gini Coefficient. www.ceicdata.com/en/china/resident-income-distribution/gini-coefficient. Accessed December 20, 2020.
8. Bloomberg. 2018. China's got a $46,000 wealth gap problem. https://www.bloomberg.com/news/articles/2018-05-20/china-s-wealth-gap-teslas-for-the-rich-footpaths-for-the-poor?utm_source=news_chinaskinny_com&utm_medium=email&utm_content=The+Weekly+China+Skinny&utm_campaign=20210112_m161581909_20210113+-+1&utm_term=Gansu+province+share+income+per+capita+similar+to+Guatemala.

9. China Skinny. 2018. Lower tier cities in China—Considerations before jumping in. www.chinaskinny.com/blog/marketing-china-lower-tier-cities/?utm_source=news_chinaskinny_com&utm_medium=email&utm_content=The+Weekly+China+Skinny&utm_campaign=20210112_m161581909_20210113+-+1&utm_term=Shanghai+residents+have+purchasing+power+parity+on+par+with+Switzerland. Accessed January 3, 2021.
10. ScienceDirect. June 15, 2018. *Journal of Environmental Management*. Toilet Revolution in China. www.sciencedirect.com/science/article/pii/S030147971730912X. Accessed May 10, 2019.
11. ChinaWaterRisk. 2018. 8 key challenges in rural water security. www.chinawaterrisk.org/resources/analysis-reviews/8-key-challenges-in-rural-water-security/. Accessed April 20, 2020.
12. Asia Society. 2020. Ethnic minorities in China. https://asiasociety.org/ethnic-minorities-china. Accessed December 20, 2010.
13. *The Globe and Mail*. 2020 Religion is under assault in China. But Canada may not have the moral high ground it needs to defend it. www.theglobeandmail.com/opinion/article-religion-is-under-assault-in-china-but-canada-may-not-have-the-moral/. Accessed December 23, 2020.
14. Xinhuanet. 2018. China focus: China pledges to protect freedom of religious belief. www.xinhuanet.com/english/2018-04/03/c_137084970.htm. Accessed February 3, 2019.
15. Council on Foreign Relations. Religion in China. www.cfr.org/backgrounder/religion-china. Accessed December 2, 2020.
16. *The Straits Times*. 2017. Having Chinese Communist Party membership is like having 'a diploma', 'opens doors'. www.straitstimes.com/asia/east-asia/having-chinese-communist-party-membership-is-like-having-a-diploma-and-opens-doors. Accessed October 23, 2020.
17. Council on Foreign Relations. Religion in China. www.cfr.org/backgrounder/religion-china. Accessed December 2, 2020.
18. *Chinadaily*. 2016. A history of bridges over the Yangtze River. www.chinadaily.com.cn/china/2016-10/21/content_27132070.htm. Accessed January 23, 2018.
19. CNN. 2019. Beijing is building hundreds of new airports as millions of Chinese take to the skies. https://edition.cnn.com/travel/article/china-new-airports/index.html. Accessed February 4, 2020.
20. HSBC. 2019. China's infrastructure builds fundation for growth. www.gbm.hsbc.com/insights/global-research/china-infrastructure-builds-foundation-for-growth. Accessed December 20, 2020.
21. www.stats.gov.cn/english/statisticaldata/yearlydata.
22. HSBC. 2019. China's infrastructure builds fundation for growth. www.gbm.hsbc.com/insights/global-research/china-infrastructure-builds-foundation-for-growth. Accessed December 20, 2020.

23. Bloomberg. 2020. China doesn't need 125,000 miles of track. www.bloomberg.com/opinion/articles/2020-08-17/china-doesn-t-need-another-125-000-miles-of-high-speed-rail. Accessed December 11, 2020.
24. Smartcitiesdive. 2017. The five best high-speed rail networks in the world. https://www.smartcitiesdive.com/ex/sustainablecitiescollective/five-best-high-speed-rail-networks-world/164916/.
25. TravelChinaGuide. 2020. China high speed train (bullet train). www.travelchinaguide.com/china-trains/high-speed/. Accessed December 29, 2020.
26. *Railjournal*. 2018. Ten years, 27,000 km: China celebrates a decade of high-speed. www.railjournal.com/passenger/high-speed/ten-years-27000km-china-celebrates-a-decade-of-high-speed. Accessed April 6, 2020.

CHAPTER 4

The Unwritten Contract

The complexity of China may seem unfathomable to newcomers. But the Chinese grew up with this complexity—they virtually imbibed ways of handling it with their mothers' milk. Moreover, China's complexity is not always obvious. No one was more surprised than the Chinese when federal government coalition negotiations in my homeland, Belgium, lasted an astonishing 541 days in 2010.[1] How on earth, the Chinese wondered, could a country function for so long *without a government*? If China went even a single day without one, it would collapse into instability—a state of affairs called *luan*, which literally means "messy"—and the result would be chaos!

As a Chinese proverb has it, a lake may seem calm despite many currents beneath the surface. This is an excellent analogy for China. At first glance, Chinese society may appear balanced, but geographic and economic realities create hidden currents. Open conflict in Chinese society would have unpredictable and undesirable consequences, which requires the government to perform a difficult balancing act.

Between 1850 and 1949, China experienced feudal society, civil wars, foreign occupation, warlord governments, and Western imperialism, which—not surprisingly—led to political and social instability. The Maoist Cultural Revolution between 1966 and 1976 was a global pinnacle of instability and bloodshed. These events also left deep wounds in Chinese society. My in-laws remember all too clearly the disintegration of society

S. Agten, *Adventures in the Chinese Economy: 16 Years from the Inside*,
https://doi.org/10.1007/978-981-16-1167-4_4

and the widespread reign of *luan*. The idea behind the Cultural Revolution was that although the bourgeoisie had been overthrown, it was still trying to use the old ideas, culture, customs, and habits to exploit the masses. Gangs of students and Red Guards set out to destroy the so-called Four Olds. In the process, they abused, tortured, and killed thousands of Chinese, even attacking people wearing "bourgeois clothes" on the street. As a result, the Cultural Revolution crippled the economy, ruined millions of lives, and thrust China into ten years of turmoil, bloodshed, hunger, and stagnation.[2] The current president, Xi Jinping, has his own vivid memories of this terrible time. He worked in the countryside for six years and saw his father fall victim to the Red Guards and purged.[3]

Since then, China has undergone tremendous changes. Together, the government and citizens have created a modern country, where stability is key. This historically inspired need for security is the main reason Chinese continue to accept CCP leadership: the promise of stability is also the foundation of Chinese politics. Westerners and foreign China experts interpret this relationship as meaning that there is an unwritten contract between the Chinese and their government to the effect that the Party will maintain its legitimacy as long as the government can continue to improve citizens' living conditions and generate further economic growth. But the reality is not that simple: people see the opportunities their country offers them and are optimistic about their future. They are ready to acknowledge the benefits of CCP rule, but expect much more than just steady economic growth.

People have high expectations and trust the government's ability to create a healthy and safe environment for its citizens. This of course was highlighted very clearly during the COVID-19 crisis when China was one of the very few countries in the world which was able to contain the virus very quickly. That by itself boosted the legitimacy of the Party in China.

In addition, the Chinese want to live their own lives and expect the state to protect—to a certain extent—their privacy. Many in the West believe that the Chinese people have no opportunity to express their opinions, that they are constantly monitored, and that they are compelled simply to keep quiet, but this is oversimplification. Every year, millions of Chinese travel abroad as tourists or on business. Most citizens can get a passport within a few days. In a truly repressive state like North Korea, this would not be possible.

The Chinese people of course know that censorship exists, but this kind of monitoring does not usually affect most of their daily lives, although of course political activists and artists might have a different experience. The government does not allow its authority to be undermined—but otherwise it allows every citizen to live his or her life as he or she pleases, as long as it does not jeopardize overall stability or escalate from public criticism into a mass movement. The media are state-controlled and the internet is always monitored, but there is room for personal expression. Despite undeniable stricter control social media feature numerous daily comments that are not necessarily government-friendly. In conversations with friends or family, I rarely hear any requests for greater political freedom or even democracy based on the Western model. Some discuss the U.S. elections—which, incidentally, I watched live on the internet with my colleagues in 2016 and 2020—or Western-style freedom of speech, but they usually say that such models would not work in China. And contrary to what Western media claim, this has little to do with brainwashing. Many of my friends have studied abroad, and have been exposed to western societies and its liberal values. But even they don't necessarily think this will work in China.

Rather, the fact that China has so many people leads to countless opinions and differences. Everyone wants to go their own way, but many feel this poses a potential threat to the nation's development and the population's prosperity. The same applies to the death penalty debate. What the West considers a terminally divisive issue, most Chinese see as an effective way to ensure the country's stability. In 2013, controversy erupted when a businessman was executed for widespread fraud. However, the debate did not address the death penalty itself, but rather the related process—in particular, the fact that family members were not informed prior to the execution.[4] The idea of sacrificing liberty for stability is supported by much of China's population. Like the West, China was horrified by the World Trade Center attacks in 2001, the Paris events of November 13, 2015, and the Brussels bombing of March 22, 2016, and, as a country, has sacrificed some freedom for the sake of greater security. It is also striking that the Chinese government uses the words "stability" and "harmonious coexistence" in its communications; these have become national ideals.

The Consensus

But widespread stability requires consensus. The Chinese government does not necessarily simply make decisions and then enforce them; in fact, the decision-making process is much more subtle. Given the economic, social, and cultural diversity of the country consulting, communicating, and understanding local needs and interests are of the utmost importance. Theoretically, all power is in the hands of the central government, the CCP bureau, and the Party leader, but the reality is more involved. Just as the American president must consider the varied interests of the states, Beijing is not always the absolute center of power—nor are all its regulations rigorously and consistently implemented by local governments. In fact, there is an accepted scope to apply central policy locally. The great domestic differences allow for individual interpretations of the rules. As a result, some laws are implemented only partially, or not at all.

The old Chinese proverb "The sky is high and the emperor far away" is still valid today. Once while traveling in Gansu in 2006, a poorer and less populated province, I met a woman with five children. Surprised, I asked her if then still in place One-Child Policy did not apply to her. She explained that while the policy existed, the local government had barely enforced it. "Beijing is far away," she added with a shrug. My wife's uncle—the archetypal sober Chinese man—once estimated that China's actual population was probably 20 percent higher than the given number of 1.3 billion. After a glass too much, this estimate goes up to 30 percent. Some economically motivated local governments imposed retroactive fines for policy violators, but many regional authorities with scarcely populated regions refuse to participate. They focus on local, not national interests. The central government often negotiates directly if it wants policies implemented.

And this goes beyond family planning. The massive scale of environmental pollution creates problems too big for Beijing. The government must cooperate with local authorities to find solutions. China is a one-party state and not a Western-style democracy, but imagining this state issuing dictatorial decisions that follow the Party line, whatever the cost, is not necessarily the case. There are different currents vying for power within the CCP. For example, the current president, Xi Jinping, whose father was vice prime minister in the 1960s, is one of the so-called princelings, children of elite senior officials are often the children of former leaders,[5] comparable to the Bush and Kennedy clans in the United States.

As in the Western democracies, many in the CCP's political families compete for power. This often does not make any headlines as of course as Chinese media obviously won't report this, but a well-known consequence of these power relations is the idea of collective leadership. Authorities see close cooperation as essential both for the survival of the Party and for China's socioeconomic development. Since there are conservative and more liberal factions within the CCP, and as both have large bases, every decision must be deliberated, because internal disagreements could have a lasting impact on society.[6] Since Xi's inauguration, however, the situation has changed quite a lot and with it the idea of collective leadership.[7] President Xi Jinping has not only emerged as one of the strongest leaders China has ever known, and as the rules changed in 2018 which would let Xi Jinping remain in power for a third or fourth term, he can now in theory also remain president for life.[8] As such there might be a long-term shift in the old model of governance.

The Chinese government is also lobbied by many different groups. Of the millions of entrepreneurs whose ventures make up the private sector of the Chinese economy, 20–25 percent are Party members.[9] Regardless of the CCP's stated political ideology, capitalists thus play an important role. In addition, the CCP is constantly modernizing through the use of social media or other technological advancements. Xi went to a pub with the former British Prime Minister David Cameron,[10] took a selfie with the star footballer Sergio Agüero during a visit to Manchester City football club,[11] and has ridden a tractor with an American farmer on an official visit to the United States[12]: all this is part of the Party's new modern outlook. In addition, the CCP does not want to lose popularity among the population, though not always for the right reasons. At the end of 2019, there were 19 million applicants wishing to join the CCP but only one of every eight applicants was allowed to join the party.[13] The CCP chooses its members, not vice versa, and selects only the most suitable ones.

From what Party members tell me, many felt that joining would bring them career opportunities and—in the past—quick financial success. Their commitment to communist ideology varies, depending on how much it intersects with their own interests or the interests of their department, city, or region. In many ways, they are the opposite of the storied communist apparatchiks who blindly obey rules. Most mayors run their cities like business managers. A friend whose Beijing-based consulting firm often works with foreign and Chinese clients told me that when he was once assigned to perform due diligence on a Chinese company, he realized that its actual profit was well below the tax office's official report. The opposite is much more common. When he asked the manager about it, he was told that administrative officials had systematically artificially increased the annual result. A better economic performance overall would advance their career.

But corruption—and especially the associated environmental and food crises—has been a stain on both the CCP and the country. The CCP knows that it depends on public goodwill, which makes raising citizens' quality of life and combating corruption essential to its survival. Chinese hold local authorities responsible for the country's many environmental and food safety issues, and the central government generally still enjoys a good reputation. In the end, however, the population expects the central government to provide solutions.

Food Scandals

Although much improvement has been made now, in the last decade, a number of food scandals have exposed the poor quality of the domestic food supply. Examples include contaminated milk powder, frozen meat that has been in storage for decades, rat meat disguised as pork, fake alcoholic beverages, fake gelatin, and poisonous mushrooms.[14] For those outside China, the psychological effects of these scandals are difficult to comprehend. Among the greatest problems faced by Chinese people, food scandals were a constant source of outrage. They used to be a nightmare also for my wife and me.

Like everything else in China, food safety is a complex issue stemming from multiple causes. For a start, only 12.66 percent of China's land is arable, and 1.3 billion people have to be fed.[15]

There is tremendous pressure within China to use its scarce farmland effectively, which encourages a liberal use of pesticides and other chemicals. Ever-expanding cities claim farmland and convert agricultural areas into industrial zones, leading to soil pollution. A 2014 government report showed that one-fifth of China's agricultural land was contaminated by heavy metals such as cadmium and nickel.[16]

All this causes the already limited agricultural area to keep shrinking. But farmers are part of the problem too. More than 260 million rural households grow fruit and vegetables, using whatever means necessary to produce abundant harvests.[17] Again and again, I see poorer farmers putting essentially organic vegetables on their own tables while selling chemically treated crops in the cities. But most Chinese people still cannot afford to buy expensive food, and chemically treated produce is cheaper and more readily available.

Food safety in China has often fallen victim to corruption, the profit motive, and inefficient regulation, with civil servants embroiled in corruption scandals and large companies resorting to illegal practices to maximize their profits. Local governments should audit these companies, but they feel pressure from Beijing to ensure regional economic growth, in addition to securing their jobs and protecting social stability. Since consumers have no confidence in the domestic market, they prefer food of foreign origin. Food scandals cause widespread anxiety. Some consumers limit themselves to a few select shops, and a friend even leased a piece of land in Beijing to grow food for personal use. For him, this is the only way to ensure absolute security. In my first year in China, after an upset stomach, I learned that vegetables should be washed not only with water, but with a special detergent. Chinese consumers also follow food safety issues on the internet. By now they are among the world's most experienced consumers when it comes to ingredients and quality.

Foreign companies don't hesitate to use the food scandals to their advantage: imported products are clearly marked with the country of origin, and when Western companies produce food in China, they claim (loudly) to avoid using Chinese ingredients. Foreign products are still expensive but used to be sold at peak prices in Chinese supermarkets. The milk powder scandal of 2008, in which tainted milk killed at least six infants and sickened 300,000 others,[18] led to a shortage of milk powder in some Dutch, Australian, and English supermarkets as Chinese consumers scouted the globe for safe milk powder.[19]

Companies involved in food scandals cannot shake the stigma easily. Bad news spreads like lightning, and CEOs end up in jail. Sanlu, the largest producer of dairy products in China, went bankrupt after the baby milk powder scandal.[20] Shuanghui, one of the nation's largest food manufacturers, saw its stock value plunge after word got out that the company injected artificial hormones into meat.[21] The government closed all its distribution channels within one working day, fearing that large department stores like Tesco and Carrefour might sell contaminated meat.

Then, in July 2014, an undercover television report showed that Chinese supplier Husi—part of the U.S. OSI Group—was selling spoiled meat to American fast-food chains such as McDonald's and Kentucky

Fried Chicken (KFC) in China.[22] Already weary of China's food scandals, Chinese consumers were shocked to find that even Western restaurants were unsafe. Fearful customers began to shun temporarily U.S. fast-food restaurants. The consequences for McDonald's—now with more than 3300 restaurants in China[23]—were dramatic: within months, sales dropped 15 percent.[24] Yum! Brands saw a 30 percent decline in sales at its Pizza Hut and KFC outlets in China.[25] This was a cause for concern: after all, Yum China is the company's largest market with 5000 KFCs—more than in the United States—and 1500 Pizza Huts, which account for more than half of global sales and 35 percent of worldwide revenue.[26]

Opportunities

Despite these problems, the Chinese middle class's demand for more food diversity provides big opportunities and has enormous global consequences. The Chinese diet is becoming increasingly Western, with more consumption of meat and grains. Domestic production of grains, vegetables, and meat is increasing by 3 percent annually. China's imports of foreign agricultural products have also grown exponentially over the past decade. Since the beginning of 2018, China has been the world's largest food importer.[27] The appetites of the Chinese middle class are changing the way the world grows and sells food in every way imaginable.[28]

For many Western companies, the Chinese market is of vital importance. In 2020, Starbucks had 4400 stores in 150 Chinese cities[29] with 800 in Shanghai alone[30]—including the world's largest Starbucks, opened in 2017. On average, the company opens a new China Starbucks every day, a rate that shows no signs of slowing.[31] Increasingly integrated into the global food market to meet domestic demand, as of 2016 Chinese companies' foreign direct investment in agriculture totaled $26 billion, with investment in 100 countries.[32] In 2017, China was the second-largest export destination for U.S. agricultural products, spending $23.8 billion on them.[33] U.S. farmers' sales of soybeans to China that year amounted to $12.25 billion.[34] In that year more than half of the U.S. soybeans exports, went to China. And given the history of scandals combined with growing incomes, the demand for organic produce was perhaps inevitable. In 2018, Chinese consumers spent close to $10 billion on organic products, making China the world's third-largest market for them.[35] The market is expected to grow to $13 billion by 2025.[36]

Oddly, considering that China has barely enough agricultural land to feed its own people, the country is also exporting more food. In 2014 already China was responsible for 90 percent of the vitamin (C) consumed by Americans, 78 percent of the tilapia, 70 percent of the apple juice, 50 percent of the cod, 43 percent of the processed mushrooms and 23 percent of the garlic.[37] More than half of the world's commercial caviar farms are in China,[38] and Chinese caviar is to be found in Michelin star restaurants all over the world.[39] Unlike companies that produce for the domestic market, exporting companies follow stringent foreign food safety regulations. The prices of foreign food are higher than in China, and that covers the greater cost of producing safer food. Clearly, as long as it is profitable, Chinese companies are indeed capable of producing "clean" foods.

Just like their western counterparts Chinese companies also understood that food-industry problems also offered great opportunities, and that a firm commitment to quality can offer a long-term competitive advantage over foreign companies, as well as restoring consumer confidence. Chinese companies such as Yili Group and China Mengniu Dairy Company have been pioneers in what has become the world's largest dairy market. Since the 2008 milk powder scandal, both companies have produced high-quality dairy products, building new production lines, and forming partnerships with foreign dairy producers to acquire technical know-how.[40]

In 2014, the Inner Mongolia Yili Industrial Group invested more than $180 million in a dairy plant in New Zealand, and later also built one in the United States. All the milk powder produced in the New Zealand plant, at that time the company's first overseas facility, was intended for the Chinese market.[41] And in 2017 Feihe International started to build a $225 million baby formula plant of which 85 percent of its output will be bound for the Chinese market.[42]

To meet long-term food demand as well as ensure better quality agriculture, China has started modernizing. To improve not just quality but also productivity, small-scale farming was replaced by U.S.-style industrial production. In 2007, 80 percent of China's pork was produced by small farmers; by 2017, just under a third was.[43] The acquisition in 2013 of the largest U.S. pork producer, Smithfield Foods, by the Hong Kong-based WH Group was part of this trend.[44] China has also become the world's largest market for agricultural machinery[45] which of course attracted the likes of U.S. industry giant Deere & Company.[46]

As is often the case, China's government long misjudged the scale of the problem and neglected to pass new food regulation legislation until 2015.[47] Xi Jinping's anti-corruption campaign has also forced many officials to reconsider illegally supporting local businesses. But despite stricter controls and a significant decrease in scandals, the Chinese population is still suspicious of the domestic food industry. Regaining this trust still will take years.

Pollution

In addition to the food scandals, an enormous side effect of rapid economic growth has been rampant environmental pollution. But this is nothing new. The first director of China's National Environmental Protection Agency, Qu Geping, noted in a 1991 book, *Environmental Management in China* that the ecological situation in the country was deteriorating.[48]

Since then, the situation has gotten worse. According to a 2012 official government report, 40 percent of Chinese watercourses are heavily polluted, and in a fifth of water sources, "water quality is so toxic that it is dangerous to even come into contact with it." Not surprisingly, the problem is partly related to the ten thousand petrochemical factories along the Yangtze River and the other four thousand along the Yellow River.[49]

Air pollution problems still exist in over half the country but are most serious in the north, because coal is used for industrial purposes and coal stoves remain the primary source of heating.[50] The peak of the problem was in 2013, not surprisingly the year our family moved out of Beijing. In Beijing that year, 189 days fell into the "polluted" or "heavily polluted" category.[51] According to the World Health Organization, in 2015 only 22 of the 122 Chinese cities met the criteria of healthy air quality. And although the situation has improved a lot—decisive action reduced particle pollution in 74 key Chinese cities by an average of 33 percent between 2013 and 2017—still about 1.25 million Chinese people still die early each year as a result of air pollution.[52]

The long-term effects of air pollution on public health are difficult to assess, since in terms of sheer numbers, this phenomenon is unique. Never in human history have so many been exposed to so much for so long. One study estimated that in 2010, about 1.2 million premature babies died from pollution problems.[53] Because the number suffering from lung cancer has quintupled in the past thirty years, while the number of smokers has remained roughly the same, scientists predict that by 2060, the effects of air pollution will be even worse.[54] And a team of international scientists, including those from top Chinese universities, published a report stating that pollution in northern Chinese provinces could shorten the life expectancy of its five hundred million people by 5.5 years.[55]

Foreigners new to Beijing and unaccustomed to such levels of air pollution suffered myriad problems, from inflamed eyes and allergies to migraines, chest infections, and severe coughs, accompanied in extreme cases by vomiting. As I experienced myself, spending a day out in Beijing in 2013 often meant feeling sticky with dirt and taking evening showers to wash off the filth. But physical problems were just one aspect; severe pollution took a psychological toll as well. Being confronted with bleak gray skies and filthy air for days on end had a direct influence on minds and spirits. On clear days, when the previous night's wind or rain has left the sky blue, Beijing came to life. People opened windows and took kids to parks or other outdoor activities, while social media overflew with pictures of happy people against the rare backdrop of blue sky.

Because the quality of everyday life in Beijing had declined too much to live a healthy life, many foreigners—as mentioned including my own family—have fled the city. The figures of the Beijing Exit-Entry Administration Bureau are significant: in 2014, more than 20 percent fewer foreigners had a Beijing work permit than in 2010.[56] Although more and more foreigners were attracted to China's continued economic growth and corresponding opportunities, they avoided Beijing. As Chinese workers increasingly choose not to visit Beijing, too, companies have trouble finding suitable personnel on the ground. *Forbes* estimated the economic costs of pollution at 10 percent of Chinese GDP.[57]

Especially for families with children like us, pollution still factors into planning daily activities. Like many others, my wife and I have smartphones apps that monitor the level of air pollution. Updated hourly and giving air quality readings all over China, these apps have become indispensable tools. When the pollution reaches a certain level, we keep the kids indoors or go to malls or museums. The schools are also adapting to pollution conditions. Signs on school doors indicate the daily values, which in turn determine indoor or outdoor activities. Wealthier families send their children to private schools fully equipped with air filtration systems, and many people install air and water purifiers in their homes.

Specialty companies such as IQ Air and Blueair have experienced unprecedented sales as many of my friends bought several air purifiers for their homes.

Social Protest

For a long time, China's government dismissed such concerns because it feared that admitting the problem would cause social unrest. To angry citizens, the pollution however was visible (and sometimes tangible), but without precise data and official communication, for long no one knew the extent of the problem. Instead, people started to voice their frustrations on social media and demanded more transparency. Large Chinese microblogging websites like Weibo grew into platforms for bloggers who railed against the poor air quality. "Our standards are not high; we just want pure water, clean air, and safe food," a radio journalist said.[58] From its part the U.S. Embassy in Beijing—always ready to stir things up—began to disseminate air pollution readings. By January 2011 however, which was a period of unusually poor air quality, the public had become outraged at their government's false reporting, and their complaints were finally too loud to ignore. Recognizing that only more transparency would regain public confidence, the government was forced to admit the problem. China's premier, Wen Jiabao, demanded that the government supply reliable information on air quality. Increasing dissatisfaction carries the seeds of social instability, which made creating pollution solutions a priority for Beijing. In 2013, the government estimated that between thirty thousand and fifty thousand so-called mass incidents against environmental problems were taking place every year.[59] The actual number is probably much higher. This means that the country's environmental issues were the number one cause of social unrest. In China, social stability and a clean environment went and still go hand in hand.

The depth of public concern revealed itself in February 2015, when Chai Jing, a well-known Chinese investigative journalist, released her self-funded documentary *Under the Dome*, which was viewed in a two-week period by two hundred million people, or about a third of Chinese internet users at that time. Initially released uncensored, *Under the Dome* openly criticized government agencies and highlighted the most visible side effect of China's unchecked economic growth. The film soon disappeared.[60]

Coal is the main contributor to China's air pollution. More production also means demands for more energy, and coal is an abundant resource. Until 2001, the global use of coal was declining, but China's economic growth has reversed this trend. Between 2001 and 2013, Chinese coal consumption tripled.[61] New policies and slower economic growth slowed consumption in 2014, 2015, and 2016, but then increased again slightly in 2017 and 2018. Despite China having invested heavily in green and renewable energy, the country still relies on coal for 50 percent of its electricity production. As of 2018, China was burning over 3.9 billion tons of coal annually, which is still more coal than the rest of the world combined.[62]

The large number of cars also contribute to air pollution. Until the 1990s, China was a country of bicycles; today there are 170 million cars and another 130 million other motorized vehicles on China's roads, with more to come.[63] The reason is partly due to air pollution itself. The worse the smog, the more cars are sold, because everyone wants to avoid spending too much time outdoors.

Cities with polluting industries have conflicting interests. While citizens criticize local industrial pollution and its negative impact on their quality of life, they realize these companies drive local economies. Closing these industries can shatter smaller cities and provinces, leaving massive unemployment and social instability. Officials from smaller cities often balk at enforcing environmental legislation or penalizing violators; their palms are greased and locals get jobs.

The lack of food safety and the extreme environmental impact leave its traces. At the same time Chinese citizens are eating more calorie-rich food, with all the obvious effects. End 2020 an official report found that over half of adults in China were overweight, which is a significant increase compared to 2002 when only 29 percent of adults were overweight.[64] As a result more and more Chinese increasingly value a healthy lifestyle.

Memberships in the thousands of fitness studios, joggers in city parks, and sports club openings are increasing apace. In 2019, more than 1800 marathons were organized in China.[65] The rising popularity of outdoor activities explains the success of chains such as Decathlon, which in 2017 had 214 Chinese stores, more than in other countries outside of France, its home market.[66] Shops that sell fresh fruit juices are mushrooming all over the country. Our family finds that the pollution problem forces us to pay more attention to healthy food and a healthier lifestyle. COVID-19 has of course accelerated this trend even more, but in fact in China it was the air pollution and food scandals that galvanized the people into pursuing a healthier lifestyle.

Green Revolution

To tackle these problems while remaining mostly independent of foreign energy imports, China started a war on pollution. At the same time it's successful Green Revolution has put the country at the center of a global energy transition, fueled by technology and the falling costs of renewable energy. The impressive numbers could serve as an example worldwide. China has long been investing some $100 billion annually on average in renewable energy, leading the pack year after year in the context of a global decreasing trend.[67] In 2018, it invested $91.2 billion in renewables, which is double the amount of the United States, and one-third more than European countries.[68] By the end of 2019, China had an installed capacity of 695 gigawatts (GW) of renewable energy according to official data from the International Renewable Energy Agency. In comparison, the United States had installed 245 GW and Europe 536 GW.[69] In addition, China has ambitious goals as it aims to produce 50 percent of its energy from non-fossil fuels by 2030.[70] In 2018, the combined proportion of natural gas, hydropower, nuclear energy, and wind power accounted for 22.1 percent of China's energy mix.[71]

China is now also the world's largest producer, exporter, and installer of solar panels, wind turbines, batteries, and electric vehicles.[72] The country's thriving green industry was in 2019 responsible for 4.1 million jobs. This accounts for 39 percent of the world's total jobs in the sector.[73]

The explosion of this green industry and the large single market for renewable energy and technology have led to a sharp fall in green technology prices, which benefits the entire world. In terms of green sector patent development, China is leading the way, with well over 150,000 renewable energy patents as of 2016. That represents 29 percent of the global total, and one-third more than the second-place United States.[74] China is on its way to becoming a renewable energy superpower.

Chinese citizens feel government measures most keenly in car ownership restrictions. To counteract pollution and traffic, a growing number of cities have limited the number of registered cars and the corresponding license plates.[75] This has made license plates invaluable, also for us. Both my spouse and I still have a car with Beijing license plates. Although we now live in Shanghai, it seemed advisable to keep both license plates.

Buying a car in Beijing or Shanghai is easy, but getting the license plate is far more difficult, with waiting lists up to several years.

To clean up its cities, the Chinese government also encourages the purchase of electric cars. China is already the world's largest producer and consumer of electric vehicles. In 2019, 1.2 million electric and plug-in hybrid cars were sold,[76] far more than any other market, and that doesn't include the more than 20 million new e-scooters that hit the Chinese roads every year.[77] Started in 2019, new legislation required that 10 percent of all new cars be electrically powered,[78] and by 2025 China wants new energy vehicles to make up at least a fifth of the country's auto sales.[79] In Shenzhen, 100 percent of the buses and taxis are already electric.[80]

Plenty of my friends drive electric cars now. It's no wonder that in 2019, the U.S. technology giant Tesla opened a huge factory in China, its first outside the United States.[81] And because in Shanghai it's also much easier to get a license plate when buying an electrical car, at the end of 2020 we decided to buy an NIO—one of these emerging Chinese premium electrical car brands which are by no means much cheaper than western cars. In this way we didn't have to wait years to get the license plate.

Meanwhile, China is also taking other drastic measures to clean up its act. Starting in 2018, the government of Jiangsu Province, a highly industrialized area on China's east coast, ordered a thousand chemical plants that used older technology or were located next to the Yangtze River to close by the year 2021.[82] The central government has also taken new measures to give NGOs and citizens more power to fight pollution. Since the end of 2017, it has been easier to file lawsuits against companies and government agencies that pollute the environment or are negligent, and 55 percent of the 89,000 lawsuits filed in China between January and November 2018 were related to the environment.[83] Thousands of citizens in Wuhan, the capital of Hubei Province, took to the streets in 2019 over a planned waste incineration plant that would bring dangerous levels of pollution to their town.[84]

China is also much greener—literally—than it was ten or fifteen years ago. In 2018, the government assigned sixty thousand soldiers to plant at least 84,000 square kilometers of trees, roughly equivalent to an area the size of Ireland.[85] Because of China's greening campaign, the country's forest coverage increased from 12.7 percent in 1976 to almost 23 percent in 2018.[86]

This range of drastic measures is taking effect. People feel that the air quality, although still not always good, is improving rapidly, and that China will slowly and steadily get its environmental problems under control. A clear sign was that in 2019 Beijing was on track to drop out of the list of the world's top 200 most-polluted cities.[87]

Nationalism as a Unifying Factor

All these problems give Chinese citizens a multifaceted relationship with their own country. They are its biggest critics, and know exactly where the trouble spots are. At the same time, they are fiercely patriotic and proud of what China has achieved in the past four decades. They are well aware of their glorious history, accomplishments, and inventions, subjects focused on in Chinese education. One of the world's oldest civilizations, China's culture in many ways surpassed that of the West. While Europeans in the Middle Ages were enduring witch burnings and plague, China had more advanced medicine and well-developed, hygienic cities. From 1500 till around 1870, China's advanced economy made it one of the world's richest countries,[88] leading it—perhaps inevitably—to see itself as the center of the world, surrounded by barbarian nations. As with empires throughout history, internal problems and civil wars led the country into a steep decline. Subsequent Western invasions, Western enclaves on Chinese territories such as Hong Kong and Macao, and humiliating, Western-imposed treaties were a deep, lasting scar on Chinese national pride.

Although Chinese citizens are generally open to foreigners and curious about current Western trends, they have not forgotten their country's past subjugation and humiliation at international hands. These experiences are engraved in the collective memory. The idea that China should learn from abroad but should never fall into the Western sphere of influence is present everywhere. Between its own traditions and Western methods, China has always sought a third, even unique way to modernize. Foreign media often speaks of China as the personification of emerging countries, but the Chinese would not agree: to them, the developments of the past four decades have been in line with its exalted past as the physical and innovation center of the world. Remember that China birthed four inventions that changed the course of history: paper, gunpowder, the compass, and moveable type—four centuries ahead of Gutenberg.[89] To Chinese, the past few hundred years are the exception, not the rule. Even the Chinese name for China, Zhongguo, or "Middle Kingdom" indicates the Chinese regard for their own country. Also significant is that China's enormous size, rich history, and long periods of isolation can result in a binary division of the world—China and everyone else. When Chinese friends traveled abroad for the first time, they told me that they had never seen so many *laowai*, or foreigners, before. The idea that they were foreigners when they left China had not occurred to them. According to the 2010 census, which for the first time included foreign residents, China had a foreign population of only one million. Estimates that included the many non-registered non-Chinese nationals might double that figure.[90] This is less than 0.0001 percent of the population, making foreigners a rarity.

Over the last 150 years, several strong personalities have tried to revive China's glorious past, but in the end, it was Deng Xiaoping who found the winning formula. He saw the 1997 Hong Kong's return to China as one of his greatest achievements, as if a past mistake had been corrected and a visible wound of Western colonialism had been healed. However, no one should assume that the average person is anti-Western; in fact, Westerners are still treated preferentially. But visitors should pay due respect to Chinese achievements and history. Chinese citizens are known for their modesty, their generosity, and their sense of humor, but can react strongly to perceived insults to their country. This could include comments about government or society that we in the West see as casual conversation; most Chinese see their country as Westerners see their family—insiders can criticize all they want, but outsiders should proceed with caution!

As an employee of a Western company in China, your daily routine can feel like walking on eggshells. This was illustrated in 2013 when Apple was accused of not providing replacement iPhones for major repairs. The state-controlled flagship newspaper *People's Daily* launched a two-week media campaign denouncing Apple as "one of those Western companies that exploit Chinese citizens," which resulted in a public apology from its CEO, Tim Cook.[91]

At the same time, many Chinese citizens find this anti-West outrage misguided when compared with domestic company performance. After all, the homegrown articles often take more liberties with local legislation, commit many more violations, and abuse consumer confidence to a greater extent.

Regained Self-Confidence

Now that China has regained its national self-esteem, citizens are happy to acknowledge their government's achievements. This awakens national pride. And although, as mentioned before, China's development is unique, every world power has taken similar steps. Just as the 1964 and 1988 Olympic Games in Tokyo and Seoul, respectively, signaled that Japan and Korea had found their way onto the world stage, the 2008 Olympics in Beijing and Expo 2010 Shanghai sent the same message. China was now a power player.

During these and other high-profile events, the government actively promotes a positive image. Polluting factories are shut down to keep air pollution at an absolute minimum. When Beijing hosted the Asia-Pacific Economic Conference (APEC) in November 2014, the government took half of all cars off the roads, temporarily closed factories, and gave workers special leave. Throughout the conference, the sky's radiant color gave rise to the term "APEC blue."[92] In fact, when Beijing residents saw a few days of blue sky, their first thought invariably would be to wonder what international dignitary was visiting (flags posted downtown would reveal the answer). For the September 2016 G20 meeting in Hangzhou, all polluting factories in the surrounding provinces were closed for a month. For four weeks, over a large part of China including Shanghai, there was a bright blue sky.[93]

Great numbers of citizens support international events. When Beijing was picked to host the Olympic Games, many felt real euphoria. The city almost broke out into a kind of spontaneous folk festival. The Chinese citizen knows his country has a—rightly or wrongly—bad image abroad and wants to show the city at its best. For the Beijing Olympics—which cost the Chinese government more than $40 billion[94]—no fewer than 2.2 million volunteers applied for the 500,000 spots.[95] The Shanghai Expo inspired the same countrywide pride. The population turns out in droves to support all events that put China in an internationally positive light.

National euphoria also surrounds China's Nobel Prize recipients. Tu Youyou was awarded the Nobel Prize in Physiology or Medicine in 2015 for her malaria research, the first Chinese woman to receive it and the first Chinese scientist to earn her prize on the basis of scientific work in China. Astoundingly, as one commentator put it, "much of her work happened in China during the darkest periods of the Cultural Revolution."[96] Similar adulation surrounded Mo Yan, who received the 2012 Nobel Prize in

Literature.[97] But in China, even the Nobel Prize can be controversial. The best-known Chinese Nobel Peace Prize laureate, Liu Xiaobo, was under house arrest until his death in 2017 from liver cancer,[98] and the Dalai Lama, who won in 1989, is still persona non grata in China.

Nationalist feelings manifest themselves in other areas as well. The September 2015 Tiananmen Square parade in Beijing, which officially commemorated the seventieth anniversary of the victory over Japan in World War II but was in fact a clear indication of China's growing military might, had countless viewers on television. Like all war veterans, my wife's grandfather received a medal, which earned him a full day of his family's absolute pride. Events of World War II, not to mention the lack of a Japanese apology, has caused a latent anti-Japanese sentiment, just as exists in South Korea and Taiwan. Now and then, the Chinese government stirs up these feelings for its own political purposes, and nationalist flare-ups can incite protests and even violence and against other countries. A dispute over the Diaoyu Islands, claimed by both China and Japan, caused outraged Chinese to hold demonstrations, burn Japanese flags, and damage Japanese-owned property and restaurants. I witnessed demonstrations at the Japanese Embassy in Beijing,[99] while my wife could not get gas for her Honda at most gas stations. Others have seen their Japanese cars completely destroyed by angry fellow citizens. When in 2017, a row broke out between South Korea and China over the installation of the American THAAD missile system as a protection measure against North Korean missiles. China objected concerned the missile shield's radars could be used to spy on China instead.[100] As a result, Chinese customers boycotted Korean companies, especially the big retailer Lotte, while local Chinese authorities increased their safety and sanitation inspections of the company.[101] In China, geopolitics and business go hand in hand.

The 2019–20 U.S.–China trade war and Hong Kong protests also incited growing nationalism and more local support for government. It's wrong and even dangerous for Western media and observers to assume that China and its citizens will choose a different pathway than the one they are on; if anything, the U.S.–China trade war strengthens Chinese citizens' resolve to back the current growth trajectory. Many of my friends say that given China's rapid growth and competition with the United States, an economic conflict was inevitable.

One of my more cosmopolitan friends always claims she was born in the wrong country, because she considers herself Western and not really

Asian. She's not interested in patriotic demonstrations, is critical of official media coverage, and encourages me to move my family back to Belgium whenever there's a new food or corruption scandal. Unlike me, she wasn't even interested in the Beijing Olympics. But she was so embarrassed by all the "Chinglish" (a combination of Chinese and English) attached to the official Olympic signage that she wrote the Beijing Municipal Government Ombudsman's Office to complain. Despite her constant criticism of China, she acutely felt that sloppy English would be an international embarrassment and harmful to the country's image.

Foreign media have observed that many Chinese emigrate, or at least invest their wealth abroad, because of dissatisfaction with their government. After all, Chinese have been the top foreign buyers of U.S. residential property for six years straight.[102] But that's not the complete picture: in fact, not all Chinese citizens who have the opportunity to go abroad actually leave. Far from it. China used to be the world leader in illicit capital outflows,[103] but capital flight was mainly caused by wealthy Chinese seeking to secure their assets, while they themselves remained in China. The transfer of money is simply a way to spread risk between different investments and countries. Most of those who do emigrate do so because they want to raise their children in an environment of clean air and safe food, and to give them Western educations.

Notes

1. *The Telegraph*. Belgium to have new government after world record 541 days. www.telegraph.co.uk/news/worldnews/europe/belgium/8936857/Belgium-to-have-new-government-after-world-record-541-days.html. Accessed October 9, 2018.
2. CNN. 2016. How the Cultural Revolution changed China forever. https://edition.cnn.com/2016/05/12/asia/china-cultural-revolution-dikotter/index.html. Accessed April 13, 2018.
3. *Business Insider*. 2019. The life of Xi Jinping, China's authoritarian leader who is fighting Trump in the trade war, and presides over the mass oppression of the Uighur Muslim minority. www.businessinsider.com/xi-jinping-who-is-china-president-2018-2?r=DE&IR=T. Accessed May 2, 2020.
4. *South China Morning Post*. 2013. Revealed: Truth behind tragic secret execution of businessman Zeng Chengjie. www.scmp.com/news/china/article/1292842/questions-asked-over-execution-hunan-businessman-zeng-chengjie. Accessed December 4, 2020.

5. BBC. 2018. Profile: China's President Xi Jinping. https://www.bbc.com/news/world-asia-pacific-11551399. Accessed January 10, 2019.
6. CNN. 2012. 'One Party, two coalitions'—China's factional politics. https://edition.cnn.com/2012/10/23/world/asia/china-political-factions-primer/index.html. Accessed February 4, 2019.
7. *Nikkei*. 2017. Xi Jinping and the end of collective leadership. https://asia.nikkei.com/Politics/Xi-Jinping-and-the-end-of-collective-leadership. Accessed March 2, 2019.
8. BBC. 2018. China's Xi allowed to remain "president for life" as term limits removed. www.bbc.com/news/world-asia-china-43361276. Accessed December 5, 2020.
9. London School of Economics Business Review. 2018. The paradox of communist entrepreneurs in China. https://blogs.lse.ac.uk/businessreview/2018/11/06/the-paradox-of-communist-entrepreneurs-in-china/. Accessed April 6, 2020.
10. *The Guardian*. 2016. Chinese firm buys pub where David Cameron and Xi Jinping enjoyed a pint. https://www.theguardian.com/uk-news/2016/dec/06/chinese-firm-pub-david-cameron-xi-jinping-pint-plough-cadsden. Accessed December 29, 2020.
11. BBC. 2015. Selfie of the year? Sergio Aguero, the PM, and Chinese President Xi Jinping. https://www.bbc.com/news/newsbeat-34620535. Accessed May 5, 2019.
12. CNN. 2016. Chinese Xi Jinping keeps Iowa close to his heart. https://edition.cnn.com/2016/12/07/asia/china-iowa-xi-jinping-branstad-trump/index.html. Accessed November 19, 2019.
13. *Nikkei*. 2020. Communist Party Secrecy hampers China's trust building efforts. https://asia.nikkei.com/Spotlight/Comment/Communist-Party-secrecy-hampers-China-s-trust-building-efforts. Accessed November 4, 2020.
14. *Der Spiegel*. 2012. The hidden price of food from China. www.spiegel.de/international/world/europe-worries-about-health-hazards-of-cheap-food-from-china-a-861406.html. Accessed February 3, 2018.
15. Trading Economics. 2020. China—arable land (% of land area). www.tradingeconomics.com/china/arable-land-percent-of-land-area-wb-data.html. Accessed October 10, 2020.
16. *The Wall Street Journal*. 2014. China details vast extent of soil pollution. www.wsj.com/articles/SB10001424052702304626304579507040557046288. Accessed September 3, 2019.
17. *Bloomberg*. 2017. Farming the world: China's epic race to avoid a face crisis. www.bloomberg.com/graphics/2017-feeding-china/. Accessed February 21, 2019.

18. *China Briefing*. 2015. China releases harshest food safety law in history. www.china-briefing.com/news/china-releases-harshest-food-safety-law-in-history/. Accessed November 4, 2020.
19. What's on Weibo. 2015. We want milk! Australian baby formula sold out due to Chinese demand. www.whatsonweibo.com/we-want-milk-australian-baby-formula-sold-out-due-to-chinese-demand. Accessed March 20, 2019.
20. CNN. 2008. Milk scandal-tainted Sanlu files for bankruptcy. http://edition.cnn.com/2008/BUSINESS/12/25/sanlu.bankruptcy/. Accessed December 2, 2020.
21. CNN. 2013. Maggots, bacteria allegedly plagued China's number one meat brand. https://edition.cnn.com/2013/05/31/business/china-food-tainted-shuanghui-maggots/index.html. Accessed November 23, 2019.
22. BBC. 2014. Bad taste lingers over China's latest food scandal. www.bbc.com/news/blogs-china-blog-28450308. Accessed December 3, 2020.
23. *The Guardian*. 2020. Mcdonald's shuts 300 restaurants in China as coronavirus spreads. www.theguardian.com/world/2020/jan/29/mcdonalds-shuts-300-restaurants-in-china-as-coronavirus-spreads. Accessed December 13, 2020.
24. *Forbes*. 2014. McDonald's faces sales in Asia after China food scandal. www.forbes.com/sites/greatspeculations/2014/09/11/mcdonalds-faces-declining-sales-in-asia-after-china-food-scandal/#6326cb516de1. Accessed December 3, 2019.
25. *South China Morning Post*. 2014. KFC owner admits China rotten food scandal causing "significant" damage to sales. www.scmp.com/news/china/article/1563324/kfc-owner-admits-china-rotten-food-scandal-causing-significant-damage.
26. *Business Insider*. 2019. KFC is by far the most popular fast-food chain in China and it's nothing like the U.S. brand—here's what it's like. www.businessinsider.de/most-popular-fast-food-chain-in-china-kfc-photos-2018-4?r=US&IR=T. Accessed February 20, 2020.
27. The Heritage Foundation. 2018. Agricultural trade with China: what's at stake for American farmers, ranchers. And families. https://www.heritage.org/agriculture/report/agricultural-trade-china-whats-stake-american-farmers-ranchers-and-families. Accessed October 3, 2019.
28. *Bloomberg*. 2017. Farming the world: China's epic race to avoid a face crisis. www.bloomberg.com/graphics/2017-feeding-china/. Accessed February 21, 2019.
29. Starbucks. 2020. About. www.starbucks.com.cn/en/about/. Accessed December 19, 2020.

30. Retailnews Asia. 2020. Starbucks China opens first coffee outlet made of containers. https://www.retailnews.asia/starbucks-china-opens-first-coffee-outlet-made-of-containers/. Accessed December 3, 2020.
31. Starbucks. 2020. About. www.starbucks.com.cn/en/about/. Accessed December 19, 2020.
32. Asia Sentinel. 2019. The driving forces behind China's agri-food FDI. https://www.asiasentinel.com/p/driving-forces-china-agri-food-fdi. Accessed December 3, 2020.
33. Minnesota Department of Agriculture. 2018 China: Top market for U.S. AG exports. www.mda.state.mn.us/sites/default/files/inline-files/profilechina.pdf. Accessed April 5, 2019.
34. *Chinadaily*. 2019. U.S. soybeans may lose China's market. www.chinadaily.com.cn/a/201906/26/WS5d12a5baa3103dbf1432a34e.html. Accessed Marc 4, 2020.
35. Daxue Consulting. 2020. The organic food market in China. https://daxueconsulting.com/organic-food-in-china/. Accessed December 1, 2020.
36. GlobeNewswire. 2019. China organic food market, 2024. https://www.globenewswire.com/news-release/2019/11/04/1940427/0/en/China-Organic-Food-Market-2024.html. Accessed December 20, 2020.
37. Alliance for American manufacturing. 2014. The U.S. imports a lot of food from China—and you might be surprised what's on the list. www.americanmanufacturing.org/blog/the-u-s-imports-a-lot-of-food-from-china-and-you-might-be-surprised-whats-on-the-list/. Accessed December 29, 2020.
38. *South China Morning Post*. 2019. Chinese caviar: the Singapore pair farming "black gold" in Yunnan—and trying to change perceptions. www.scmp.com/lifestyle/food-drink/article/3018198/chinese-caviar-singapore-pair-farming-black-gold-yunnan-and. Accessed December 5, 2020.
39. *South China Morning Post*. 2019. How China came to satisfy the world's appetite for caviar. www.scmp.com/news/china/society/article/3041777/how-china-came-satisfy-worlds-appetite-caviar. Accessed December 5, 2020.
40. *New Zealand Herald*. 2014. China business: Chinas champions of the dairy boom. www.nzherald.co.nz/business/china-business-chinas-champions-of-the-dairy-boom/246CKBMX56UXTE27HUFM6CBVW4/. Accessed April 5, 2018.
41. *Chinadaily*. 2014. Yili opens first major overseas factory in New Zealand. www.chinadaily.com.cn/business/2014-11/25/content_18974143.htm. Accessed May 20, 2018.

42. CBC. 2017. A winning formula? China invests in Canadian dairy to help feed its baby boom. www.cbc.ca/news/politics/feihe-plant-kingston-con struction-1.4228501. Accessed October 21, 2020.
43. *South China Morning Post*. 2017. China's "backyard" pig farmers squeezed as sectors scales up. www.scmp.com/news/china/policies-politics/article/2098877/chinas-backyard-pig-farmers-squeezed-sector-scales. Accessed May 5, 2019.
44. *Forbes*. 2020. The Chinese billionaire whose company owns troubled pork processor Smithfield Foods. https://www.forbes.com/sites/jennif erwang/2020/04/16/the-chinese-billionaire-whose-company-owns-tro ubled-pork-processor-smithfield-foods/.
45. GlobeNewswire. 2019. China agriculture equipment market volume forecast report. www.globenewswire.com/news-release/2019/02/19/1733997/0/en/China-Agriculture-Equipment-Market-Volume-For ecast-Report-2019.html. Accessed February 2, 2020.
46. *Chinadaily*. 2012. Farming machinery maker Deere to reap rich harvest. www.chinadaily.com.cn/business/2012-11/03/content_1587 1664.htm. Accessed April 4, 2018.
47. Brookings. 2016. What China's new food safety law might mean for consumers and businesses. www.brookings.edu/blog/up-front/2016/05/13/what-chinas-new-food-safety-law-might-mean-for-consumers-and-businesses. Accessed May 4, 2019.
48. Council on Foreign Relations. 2013. China: dirty air, dirtier water? https://www.cfr.org/blog/china-dirty-air-dirtier-water. Accessed April 21, 2019.
49. *The Diplomat*. 2013. Forget air pollution. China has a water problem. http://thediplomat.com/2013/01/forget-air-pollution-chinas-has-a-water-problem. Accessed June 19, 2019.
50. *The New York Times*. 2018. In China's coal country, a ban brings blue skies and cold homes www.nytimes.com/2018/02/10/world/asia/china-coal-smog-pollution.html. Accessed April 21, 2019.
51. *The Beijinger*. 2014. Fewer than half of Beijings 2013 days were "blue sky days." www.thebeijinger.com/blog/2014/01/04/fewer-half-beijings-2013-days-were-blue-sky-days. Accessed December 20, 2020.
52. *The Guardian*. 2020. Pollutionwatch: air pollution in China falling, study showswww.theguardian.com/environment/2020/sep/10/pollut ionwatch-air-pollution-in-china-falling-study-shows. Accessed December 6, 2020.
53. *South China Morning Post*. 2018. Air pollution is killing 1 million people and costing Chinese economy 267 billion yuan a year, research from CUHK shows. www.scmp.com/news/china/science/article/2166542/air-pollution-killing-1-million-people-and-costing-chinese. Accessed September 3, 2019.

54. National Center for Biotechnology Information. 2018. Epidemiology of lung cancer in China. www.ncbi.nlm.nih.gov/pmc/articles/PMC6312841. Accessed December 19, 2020.
55. *Financial Times*. 2017. China smog cuts 5.5 years from average life expectancy. www.ft.com/content/eed7c0be-e7ca-11e2-9aad-00144feabdc0. Accessed June 5, 2020.
56. eChinacities. 2014. An anxious Beijing to departing expats: "please stay, guests from far away." www.echinacities.com/china-media/An-Anxious-Beijing-to-Departing-Expats-Please-Stay-Guests-from-Far-Away
57. *South China Morning Post*. Air pollution is killing 1 million people and costing Chinese economy 267 billion yuan a year, research from CUHK shows. www.scmp.com/news/china/science/article/2166542/air-pollution-killing-1-million-people-and-costing-chinese. Accessed September 3, 2019.
58. *The Guardian*. 2015. Beijing's smog is increasingly toxic for China's politicians.www.theguardian.com/environment/2015/jan/20/beijings-smog-increasingly-toxic-chinas-politicians. Accessed June 4, 2019.
59. *Bloomberg*. 2013. Chinese anger over pollution becomes main cause of social unrest. www.bloomberg.com/news/articles/2013-03-06/pollution-passes-land-grievances-as-main-spark-of-china-protests. Accessed May 11, 2019.
60. BBC. 2015. Under the dome: the smog film taking China by storm. www.bbc.com/news/blogs-china-blog-31689232. Accessed August 5, 2018.
61. Chinese climate policy. 2020. Guide to Chinese climate policy. https://chineseclimatepolicy.energypolicy.columbia.edu/en/coal-3. Accessed December 28, 2020.
62. Chinese climate policy. 2020. Guide to Chinese climate policy. https://chineseclimatepolicy.energypolicy.columbia.edu/en/coal-3. Accessed December 28, 2020.
63. *South China Morning Post*. 2017. China now has over 300 million vehicles... that's almost America's total population. www.scmp.com/news/china/economy/article/2088876/chinas-more-300-million-vehicles-drive-pollution-congestion. Accessed December 2, 2020.
64. BBC. 2020. Over half of Chinese adults overweight, study finds. www-bbc-com.cdn.ampproject.org/c/s/www.bbc.com/news/amp/world-asia-china-55428530. Accessed January 6, 2021.
65. Xinhua. 2020. Seven million Chinese runners participate marathons in 2019: CAA. http://www.china.org.cn/sports/2020-05/01/content_75998626.htm. Accessed December 29, 2020.

66. *Chinadaily*. 2017. China home to most Decathlon stores outside France. https://www.chinadaily.com.cn/business/2017-02/18/content_28251519.htm. Accessed November 4, 2019.
67. Renewable Energy World. 2019. Driven by China, global investment in clean energy falls. www.renewableenergyworld.com/2019/07/11/driven-by-china-global-investment-in-clean-energy-falls/#gref. Accessed November 3, 2020.
68. United Nations Environment Programme. 2019. Renewable energy investment in 2018 hit USD 288.9 billion, far exceeding fossil fuel investment. www.unenvironment.org/news-and-stories/press-release/renewable-energy-investment-2018-hit-usd-2889-billion-far-exceeding. Accessed April 4, 2020.
69. International Renewable Energy Agency. 2020. Renewable energy capacity statistics 2020. https://irena.org/-/media/Files/IRENA/Agency/Publication/2020/Mar/IRENA_RE_Capacity_Statistics_2020.pdf. Accessed December 29, 2020.
70. Brookings. 2018. Utility of renewable energy in China's low-carbon transition. https://www.brookings.edu/2018/05/18/utility-of-renewable-energy-in-chinas-low-carbon-transition/. Accessed December 5, 2020.
71. Xinhuanet. 2019. Coal shrinks in China's energy mix. www.xinhuanet.com/english/2019-02/28/c_137857755.htm. Accessed March 5, 2020.
72. *Forbes*. 2019. China is set to become the world's renewable energy superpower, according to new report. https://www.forbes.com/sites/dominicdudley/2019/01/11/china-renewable-energy-superpower/?sh=63ccdbe1745a. Accessed February 3, 2020.
73. Climate scorecard. 2019. China leads green jobs in energy sector. www.climatescorecard.org/2020/09/china-leads-green-jobs-in-renewable-energy-sector/. Accessed December 5, 2020.
74. *Forbes*. 2019. China is set to become the world's renewable energy superpower, according to new report. https://www.forbes.com/sites/dominicdudley/2019/01/11/china-renewable-energy-superpower/?sh=63ccdbe1745a. Accessed February 3, 2020.
75. *Automotive news*. 2014. China's car sales up 13 percent as buyers rush to beat ownership limits. www.autonews.com/article/20140509/GLOBAL03/140509801/chinas-car-sales-up-13-as-buyers-rush-to-beat-ownership-limits. Accessed December 19, 2020.
76. CNN. 2020. China's car sales fell 8 percent in 2019 and the slump is entering its third year. https://edition.cnn.com/2020/01/13/business/china-car-sales/index.html. Accessed December 4, 2020.

77. *Wired*. 2019. The problem with China's electric scooter revolution? It is too quiet. https://www.wired.co.uk/article/why-electric-motor-scooters-are-leading-electric-vehicle-revolution-in-asia. Accessed December 23, 2020.
78. *Bloomberg*. 2018. China is about to shake up the world of electric cars. www.bloomberg.com/news/articles/2018-11-14/china-is-about-to-shake-up-the-world-of-electric-cars-quicktake. Accessed December 3, 2019.
79. CNN. 2020. China's car sales fell 8 percent in 2019 and the slump is entering its third year. https://edition.cnn.com/2020/01/13/business/china-car-sales/index.html. Accessed December 4, 2020.
80. *Techcrunch*. 2019. First buses, now Shenzhen has turned its taxis electric in green push. https://techcrunch.com/2019/01/04/shenzhen-electric-taxis-push/?guccounter=1&guce_referrer=aHR0cHM6Ly93d3cuZ29vZ2xlLmJlLw&guce_referrer_sig=AQAAAFfHIx58L71bvIRiCC6j2CR0Iq-g_A9G9GbEnIA32qA0rBxq_5oxzOs1MUjNYZb04w6w9YzvG-wyhthbHrAKRkHwtUVO8Umo4FqJadZEaKAMwn7z7CkUAe4If54GHqYV3DaK7q3pWrT3G5cXkZb7QlQgssSw6De_EZ7RByV187g5. Accessed December 3, 2020.
81. Bloomberg. 2019. Elon Musk in China to break ground for first Tesla factory outside United States. www.bloomberg.com/news/articles/2019-01-07/elon-musk-in-china-to-break-ground-for-tesla-s-china-factory. Accessed December 11, 2020.
82. *Chemical & Engineering News*. 2018. China's Jiangsu province will close 1000 chemical plants. https://cen.acs.org/environment/Chinas-Jiangsu-province-close-1000/96/i37. Accessed March 2, 2019.
83. China Dialogue. 2019. China's prosecutors are litigating government agencies for being soft on pollution. https://chinadialogue.net/en/pollution/11095-china-s-prosecutors-are-litigating-government-agencies-for-being-soft-on-pollution/. Accessed March 9, 2020.
84. BBC. 2019. Wuhan protests: Incinerator plan sparks mass unrest. www.bbc.com/news/blogs-china-blog-48904350. Accessed January 9, 2020.
85. *The Independent*. 2018. China reassigns 60,000 soldiers to plant trees in bid to fight pollution. www.independent.co.uk/news/world/asia/china-tree-plant-soldiers-reassign-climate-change-global-warming-deforestation-a8208836.html. Accessed March 21, 2020.
86. *Global Times*. 2019. 70 years: China's contributions to the world. www.globaltimes.cn/content/1165930.shtml. Accessed January 5, 2021.
87. U.S. News. 2019. Beijing set to exit list of world's top 200 most-polluted cities: data. www.usnews.com/news/world/articles/2019-09-11/beijing-set-to-exit-list-of-worlds-top-200-most-polluted-cities-data. Accessed February 23, 2020.

88. Newgeography. 2015. 500 years of GDP: a tale of two countries. https://www.newgeography.com/content/005050-500-years-gdp-a-tale-two-countries. Accessed October 2, 2020.
89. China Highlights. 2019. The four great inventions of ancient China. www.chinahighlights.com/travelguide/culture/four-great-invention.htm. Accessed May 4, 2020.
90. Mercator Institute for China Studies. 2019. How immigration is shaping Chinese society. https://merics.org/en/report/how-immigration-shaping-chinese-society. Accessed September 3, 2020.
91. BBC. 2013. Apple's Tim Cook says "I'm sorry" to Chinese customers. www.bbc.com/news/business-21996134. Accessed March 13, 2018.
92. CNN. 2016. China: "Political" blue sky comes at a price. www.cnn.com/cnn/2016/12/15/asia/china-air-pollution-study/index.html. Accessed April 3, 2019.
93. *The Wall Street Journal*. 2016. China basks in "G-20 Blue" as factories ordered to shut. www.wsj.com/amp/articles/china-basks-in-g-20-blue-as-factories-ordered-to-shut-1472199891.
94. *Business Insider*. 2013. Why the Beijing Olympics were a huge mistake for China. www.businessinsider.com/the-beijing-olympics-were-a-mistake-2013-3. Accessed January 19, 2019.
95. *Chinadaily*. 2008. Record volunteers apply for Beijing Olympics. www.chinadaily.com.cn/olympics/2008-03/05/content_6509316.htm. Accessed March 14, 2018.
96. *The Atlantic*. 2015. The significance of a Nobel Prize for a Chinese scientist. www.theatlantic.com/notes/2015/10/the-significance-of-a-nobel-prize-for-a-chinese-scientist/409105. Accessed April 21, 2019.
97. *The Guardian*. 2012. Mo Yan wins Nobel Prize in literature 2012. www.theguardian.com/books/2012/oct/11/mo-yan-nobel-prize-literature. Accessed March 3, 2019.
98. *The Guardian*. 2017. Liu Xiaobo, Nobel laureate and political prisoner, dies at 61 in Chinese custody. www.theguardian.com/world/2017/jul/13/liu-xiaobo-nobel-laureate-chinese-political-prisoner-dies-61. Accessed May 5, 2019.
99. *South China Morning Post*. 2012. Protests over Diaoyu islands turn violent outside Japanese embassy. www.scmp.com/news/china/article/1037967/protests-over-diaoyu-islands-turn-violent-outside-japanese-embassy. Accessed June 18, 2019.
100. *Nikkei*. 2018. Korea Inc. mostly freed from China's missile shield wrath. https://asia.nikkei.com/Business/Business-trends/Korea-Inc.-mostly-freed-from-China-s-missile-shield-wrath. Accessed April 18, 2019.

101. Caixin. 2018. South Korea's Lotte, hit by consumer boycott, sells more China stores. www.caixinglobal.com/2018-05-12/south-koreas-lotte-hit-by-consumer-boycott-sells-more-china-stores-101248605.html. Accessed August 19, 2019.
102. CNBC. 2019. Chinese buyers expand their reach in the U.S. housing market as the middle class gets in on the act. www.cnbc.com/2019/01/08/chinese-middle-class-buying-up-american-residential-real-estate.html. Accessed April 25, 2020.
103. Huffpost. 2012. China: $4 trillion in dirty money should worry us all. www.huffpost.com/entry/china-4-trillion-in-dirty_b_2024732?guccounter=1. Accessed November 2, 2019.

CHAPTER 5

Why Chinese Students Go Abroad

My first class began a week after my arrival in Yichun at the end of March 2004. A little nervous, I stepped into the classroom, where just over twenty students were eager to meet their new teacher. After introducing myself, I asked the students to do the same, which most did—very shyly, using one or two sentences in halting, hesitant English. They were in their early twenties and had been studying English all through middle and high school, but still lacked the confidence to start even a basic conversation. Throughout the entire class, no one asked a single question.

As I was puzzling over the lack of interaction, however, four students came to my office, considerably chattier, and invited me to lunch. Their self-confidence had returned. When I asked them why they didn't have any questions during class, they replied that this would be a lack of respect for the teacher, because it would only disturb the class and the other students. I raised my eyebrows and wondered about the world in which I had landed. Clearly, I had a lot to learn about China.

Chinese society shows tremendous respect for teachers and professors. To students, a teacher's word is the gospel, and asking questions and entering into discussions are out of the question. But in Chinese culture, education has always played a central role. Almost two thousand years ago, China was one of the first countries to introduce an exam system for civil servants.[1] Instead of being born into a respected position, candidates

S. Agten, *Adventures in the Chinese Economy: 16 Years from the Inside*,
https://doi.org/10.1007/978-981-16-1167-4_5

were tested on their knowledge and needed to display specific qualities. When Europe was still in the dark Middle Ages, China had already established an advanced education system.

But upon coming to power in 1949, the CCP made drastic changes. During the Cultural Revolution, most schools and universities were closed, denying a whole generation of Chinese people an education. Since 1978, however, that same CCP has changed course, sparing no efforts to reinstate and upgrade the education system. The government realized China's only chance at a modern future was to invest in education. Especially after the 1989 Tiananmen uprising, organized by students, Beijing took a course that emphasized modernization and openness, and launched new policies that encouraged students to study abroad (hoping and expecting them to return).[2]

Government spending on education has since gone up spectacularly and now amounts since 2013 to 4 percent of the GDP. In 2018 total spending on education was $520 billion.[3]

I saw the human toll of Cultural Revolution–era education during my first visit to China in 2002, when I was strolling around a local market in Xian, the city known for its UNESCO World Heritage site of the terracotta soldiers. A seventy-year-old postcard seller heard me speaking Dutch and started talking to me in perfect German, a similar language. I was amazed. Since China had been closed off to the outside world for a long time, few citizens had even mastered English, and I asked him about his German skills. He told me he was a professor of German literature and had been studying and working at a university in Germany. In the 1950s, Chinese were allowed to study abroad, but during the 1966 Cultural Revolution, he and thousands of other professors and teachers were labeled subversive elements and potential dangers to socialist society. He was ostracized, publicly criticized, and lost his job when his Chinese university closed. By the time schools were opened again, he was too old to start over. Selling postcards was the best way he had found to provide for his family and utilize his knowledge of German.

The 1980s revival and expansion of the Chinese education system is definitely one of modern China's greatest achievements, as well as being a pillar of the country's continuous economic growth. When the People's Republic of China was founded in 1949, only 117,000 students were attending colleges or universities; by 2015, there were thirty-seven million. China now has the world's largest student population studying at 2900 colleges and universities in the country.[4] In 2020, an all-time record number of 8.7 million students graduated from Chinese universities, ten times higher than twenty years before.[5]

That the qualityof education is so high is nothing short of remarkable, given that before 1980 there was virtually nothing left of the school system. It always strikes me how well-educated most Chinese are. My many business and tourist trips have brought me to the diverse locations and introduced me to people from all strata of society. In most cases, they have impressive general knowledge. My saying I'm from Belgium leads to discussions about the EU, Brussels, chocolate, and beer. I have met plenty of other foreigners who don't even know that Belgium is in Europe. According to UNICEF data, 99.6 percent of Chinese aged between 15 and 24 are literate, which means that they know at least 1500 Chinese characters.[6] It takes years to master this number, as I myself have found. It took me three years to learn a thousand characters. The overwhelming majority of Chinese think that a good education is an essential way to achieve success, and most believe that studying hard will get you whatever you want. The idea that by studying diligently and working hard, one can achieve anything is ingrained in Chinese society.

Deprived for political reasons of their own educational opportunities, many in the older generation believe that school is the only way to secure their children's future. In fact, this idea is a collective obsession and, as in other East Asian countries, results in enormous pressure on students to compete and perform well, and showing scholastic prowess must start in childhood. Most parents expect their children to graduate from university or college, and entering a top university is the ultimate measure of success—for students, and especially for parents. When my wife's seventeen-year-old niece and her parents visited Beijing, her first stop was Peking University, which is known locally as China's Harvard and, according to British *Times Higher Education*, in 2020 ranked twenty-fourth in the world.[7]

Gaokao

The make-or-break moment formany students is the *gaokao* (high exam), the annual national university entrance examination that is China's version of the American SAT and British A-level exams. All the years of intensive training and study come down to a single day and, in citywide solidarity, life around Chinese schools falls quiet. Police patrol the surrounding streets to remind cars to drive slowly and keep noise to a minimum, construction work ceases, and nervous parents gather at the school gates to provide moral support. In schools drones hoover in the sky to catch cheaters.[8] In 2020, over ten million students took this university entrance examination.[9] The lucky ones who pass the exam (about 60 percent) have the chance to enroll at a university, but only 5 percent can enter the most prestigious schools.[10] The rest does not make it into any university at all because of low test scores.[11] They thus face bleak job prospects. To some extent, the *gaokao* determines whether students will become blue- or white-collar workers. A Chinese saying says that the *gaokao* is a stampede of "thousands of soldiers and tens of thousands of horses across a single log bridge."

The pressure to achieve the best possible score is unimaginable. Students take nine-hour tests spread over two days. Exams cover many topics, including geography, English, Chinese, mathematics, and politics, and unlike measuring potential knowledge, as does (in theory) the SAT, the *gaokao* is often a test of memorizing and reproducing. facts The exam not only determines whether students get into university, but also where they can enroll and what they can study. Applicants list their preferences, but only those with results that match the university's point totals for given subjects can pursue those majors. A friend of mine from a remote province was lucky enough to gain acceptance to China's most prestigious schools, but choosing Peking University (the best) meant majoring in anthropology. Instead, he chose Renmin University, just a few steps below, where he could study business. In Yichun, I knew many students who were not at all interested in English, but their *gaokao* score had dictated their course of study. Needless to say, their results were mostly below average.

To prepare their children for not only their *gaokao* but also their careers, parents spend a lot of time and resources on schooling. "Between 2015 and 2030, China is expected to spend 12.5% of overall consumption growth on education for those under 30," according to the McKinsey Global Institute.[12]

This kind of dedication and financial pressure explains why, even though the One-Child Policy has been repealed, many Chinese parents still opt for a single child. Few have the resources to give two children the best of everything. For poorer families, this can have far-reaching consequences. One of my Yichun students was the first from his village to pursue a university degree. Since his family lacked the financial means to pay for his studies, the whole village decided to chip in. His parents had given up their medical insurance to spend this money on their son's education. He was proud of his hometown, but I realized that the pressure must have been enormous. For him, failure was not an option.

Both Chinese consumers and businesses are culturally prone to seeing education as an investment and not an expenditure. Starting when their children are toddlers, families from the growing middle class spend astronomical amounts on education. Although school attendance for at least nine years has been compulsory since 1986, preschool—or what China calls kindergarten—education is thriving as never before. Legally, Chinese children need to start school at age six, but there are about 182,000 public and 84,000 private kindergartens operating across the country.[13]

Since parents want to prepare their children for the brutally demanding school environment, children receive extra after-school lessons starting from a young age. Parents provide a whole arsenal of ballet classes, piano lessons, or training in logical thinking and mathematics to provide their children with a competitive advantage. A report revealed that more than 60 percent of primary school pupils in China are tutored outside the classroom, with parents spending between $17,400 and $43,500 annually on extra classes.[14] The so-called tiger moms are everywhere. My two children have only minimal after-school tutoring, but a female colleague has a five-year-old son who already attends after-school classes four days a week, including others on weekends. She hopes to enroll her son in good primary and secondary schools and fears his classmates will be equally, if not better, prepared. Einstein once said that play is the highest form of research, but that certainly doesn't apply to the Chinese education system. The competition is simply too fierce.

In newly international China, English classes have become extremely popular. In 2004, a colleague at the university in Yichun invited me home to meet his family. To my great surprise, I was greeted by more than twenty children, all excited to see a real foreigner. Only then did I notice that his living room was filled with small desks and stools facing a blackboard hanging on the wall. As I was recovering from the surprise, my colleague told me he earned extra money teaching English to young children. That's why he turned his home into a classroom and invited me to be the—unwilling—special act for the day.

As in the United States, areas with quality schools boast higher value real estate. Some newly married couples choose their home because of nearby schools, while established couples may uproot and move across the city for the sake of their child's school opportunities. Some mothers give up their work to provide full-time assistance to their studying children. My wife told me that when her high school results were not too good, her parents invited her teachers for dinner and showered them with presents. This used to be a fairly common practice. As a teacher in Yichun, I noticed that many of my colleagues, while they were busy correcting exams, received a remarkable number of visitors, often parents who "wanted a word." In addition, cheating is common, especially during the *gaokao*. To counter this problem, some schools organize their exams in open parking spaces or sports fields. Parents also often bribe well-regarded schools to get their children enrolled. There are clear shortcuts to escape unsatisfactory *gaokao* results.

For their part, many schools apply Spartan methods to educate their students . Starting at ten years old, many children do homework until ten o'clock every night. Friends have a fifteen-year-old daughter who wakes up every day at six o'clock to leave for school. She then studies an hour in the library before classes begin and doesn't leave again until after nine at night, arriving home an hour later. She takes only two days off a month, because most weekends she attends special weekend classes at school. This puts tremendous pressure on the students.

Chinese parents, coaches, and teachers follow what to the West is a disturbing cultural trend. They believe offering praise and encouragement will make their children lazy and unmotivated, so they use criticism and negativity as inspiration. On a family trip to Guangzhou in 2009, we stayed in a luxurious five-star hotel. I saw a ten-year-old girl taking evening swimming lessons in the hotel pool. As her parents and coach followed her along the poolside, she kept swimming, with a face devoid of interest or emotion. It was clear she wished to be somewhere else. For his part, her coach made sure she knew that everything she did was wrong, while comparing her to all his other students who could swim faster and better than she could. When I wondered aloud if this girl was even interested in swimming, I have seen many scenes like this, making this normal behavior in Chinese education.

The high expectations, enormous pressure, andextreme competition leave behind mental scars. Most children consider their school lives their formative years, but I have the impression that for some Chinese pupils, those years have caused deep and emotional wounds. Research shows that 60 percent of Chinese university students said they were stressed-out by their studies.[15] Young people often feel unhappy during their school years, and more serious depression is also common.[16] I attended several of my wife's class reunions and I often noticed how negatively her classmates looked back on their school years. Even being away for over a decade hadn't softened the memories; most talked about their teachers with disgust or even hatred. In particular, teachers exhibiting authoritarian and dominating behavior caused deep resentment. Teachers did not tolerate different opinions or views and often humiliated the students to try and improve their performance. Such experiences failed to boost the students' self-confidence and may have had grave consequences for their subsequent careers.

The Problems of the Education System

Recently, however, the entire educational system has come under fire, mainly because students' entire value is measured by their *gaokao* score. Extracurricular activities, hobbies, other talents, or creative behavior are completely left out of the equation. In contrast to Western educational systems, which put a certain emphasis on individual development, Chinese students are evaluated solely on their ability to memorize and reproduce vast amounts of knowledge. The omniscient teacher still occupies the central position within this framework, and students have to accept—without question—everything they are told.

Analysis and interpretation are rarely needed, while creativity is as good as nonexistent. During my very first class I asked my students, "How do you do?" They answered in chorus, "Fine, thank you. And you?" The next day, I changed the pattern a bit and asked, "How are things going?" and was met by silence. One student explained that they didn't know the answer to this question—it was never in the textbook, so they never memorized it. A friend told me about her shockingly bright and deeply thoughtful middle-school student explaining how Chinese teachers teach literature, "After we read the story, the teacher tells us exactly what the author means, and we have to memorize it." "If the answer says 'he will die,' but I write down, 'he will not live,' that counts as a wrong answer."

This emphasis on memorization and passive behavior has some roots in specific characteristics of the Chinese language. The English alphabet has twenty-six letters that together form individual words. Chinese characters are more like Egyptian hieroglyphs. Originally an iconic, or picture-based language, Chinese has more than fifty thousand characters, each representing a word or specific meaning. To read a newspaper, one needs to master between two and three thousand characters.[17] This requires Chinese students studying their native tongue to memorize a huge number of characters just to read at all.

My students were regularly "robotized," listening quietly in the auditorium and accepting everything I taught without thinking or analyzing. Rarely did they have questions, and "critical" remarks were completely out of the question. Sometimes, overtired by the long school days and studying at night, students laid their heads on their desks, maybe even falling asleep. In the beginning, I considered sleeping in the classroom disrespectful to the teacher, and I resented their lack of cooperation. After a while, however, I understood that my students were simply exhausted. On the contrary, some students explained that they were so tired that they would have preferred to stay home to sleep, but attended classes out of respect.

The education system itself, with its focus on reproducing knowledge and students who barely leave the schools and university campuses because of their many hours of study, is completely at odds with the practical and social knowledge required to function in China's competitive society. There is actually a huge gap between education and professional life, and the practical knowledge students need to do well in society is often lacking. Personal development is neither promoted nor supported. Fresh graduates looking for jobs, especially those coming from smaller cities with less exposure to international companies, often lack social and soft skills. When we interview young job-seekers, we can see they have intelligence and potential, but still give nothing but pat answers. It often takes months of training to teach them some basic social skills.

These systemic disadvantages have many parents seeking alternatives. Private schools that provide a more Westernized education are in high demand, albeit significantly more expensive. A third of Chinese kindergartens are privately owned, and the number of private universities is also on the rise. In the big cities, a year of private kindergarten can easily cost up to $10,000, but twice as much for a high-quality bilingual (English-Chinese) kindergarten. These often originate abroad and attract the city's wealthiest students. These schools being limited to the big cities was the main reason for our family's relocation from Qian'an back to Beijing in 2011. This was the only possibility for our then three-year-old son to enjoy a Western-style education. International schools in China that only accept foreign passport holders, at which annual school fees of $40,000–$50,000 are not unusual, are an attractive option for wealthy Chinese. In the international school my two children attend, 70 percent of the students, all of whom live in Shanghai, are of Chinese origin, indicating that there are lots of wealthy Chinese citizens with foreign passports.

In China, schooling isa big business. Expenditure growth in China's private education also fueled by the after-school tutoring industry, making the whole sector between a $230 and $400 billion market. And this is a market which keeps growing.[18] EdTech—education technology—companies are booming and online tutoring is exploding. The global EdTech market is massive and is led by Chinese firms. Beijing has the highest concentration of EdTech companies in China at 120 firms per million people. New York, the Bay Area, and Bangalore follow closely behind.[19] According to Goldman Sachs, EdTech companies in China raised more than $1.2 billion in 2016 which is not only more than in the United States in the same year, but also more than triple the amount raised in China two years earlier.[20] Chinese companies TAL Education Group and New Oriental Education are globally on top, respectively valued at US$17.7 billion and US$11.3 billion in 2018.[21]

Founded in 2003 and headquartered in Beijing, TAL Education Group is China's leading education technology company, with centers in forty-two cities nationwide.[22]

In addition to the many private schools that offer general education, a number offer specific courses. Although the English courses of Global IELTS, the private school for which I worked in 2005, were by no means cheap, there was no problem attracting students. The school also offered e-learning classes, where students could communicate with foreigners living abroad via the internet.

Global IELTS owned campuses throughout China and was part of a listed holding company, whose other subsidiaries provided numerous complementary services. Government agencies were part of their customer base, and I spent several months teaching Ministry of Transport officials in Beijing. Every morning between seven and eight, I taught around twenty officials who regularly went abroad for business and were studying English before their workday started. However, most were students who wanted to enroll in foreign universities and had to take exams such as the TOEFL (Test of English as a Foreign Language) and IELTS (International English Language Testing System) to prove their English proficiency.

In addition to these English-language courses, Global IELTS also offered extra, more practical services. Students could get assistance in completing their official university applications or were taught how to apply for financial aid. The company provided a specific service for the more affluent parents—namely, Chinese staff who supervised students once they went overseas. Generally, the parents were more committed to an overseas education for their children than were the children themselves, and these same students could become unmotivated once the distractions of the West kicked in. Some parents paid in-country supervisors to ensure that their massive investment was protected. Chinese parental authority has a global reach.

Although my students all had a basic level of English, we had communication issues. I had one 28-year-old student who was funny, popular, and favored NBA shirts for his hefty frame. He was looking to study abroad, on what he described as a "career break." When I asked him about his previous employment, he casually replied, "I kill people." Assuming this was either a mistranslation or a misplaced joke, I asked him again. "I kill bad people," he further explained. Now we were all looking at him in amazement. A rotund, jolly young man in a baseball cap and matching sneakers who killed bad people? What on earth could this mean? After a few minutes of circular conversation, we finally understood that this student worked in a prison and was a member of an execution squad dispatched prisoners sentenced to death. I could see why he might need a change of scene.

Studying Abroad as an Alternative

Because Western schools and universities are held in high regard, students with foreign degrees enjoy a competitive advantage in the domestic and international labor markets, as well as a higher status in Chinese society. Others may go abroad to find new experiences and greater personal development, something that—as mentioned before—is absent in the Chinese education system. Most parents want their children to live in a different society or political system, and to experience different values and cultures. This is the kind of thinking that made *Harvard Girl Yiting*

Lu (Writers Publishing House, 2000), a how-to guide for raising academically successful children, by the journalist parents of a Chinese Harvard student, a national bestseller.[23]

For these, and many more reasons, the number ofChinese students in foreign schools has risen sharply over the past decade. Almost two million Chinese people go abroad for education or training. According to the Chinese Ministry of Education, over 600,000 Chinese students used to enroll in Western universities annually.[24] 370,000 of those studied during the 2018–2019 school year in the UnitedStates,[25] which is a third of the total amount of international students in the UnitedStates.[26]

Even President Xi Jinping's daughter studied at Harvard University. Other popular destinations are Australia, Great Britain, and Canada, not surprisingly, countries where English is the official language. But these numbers are changing dramatically. Amid the ongoing fallout of the COVID-19 pandemic and unrelenting political tensions between the UnitedStates and China, in 2020 F-1 student visas for Chinese nationals have declined by a staggering 99%. Given the fact that Chinese students alone paid $15 billion in tuition payments for the 2018–2019 school year, the economic impact is big.[27]

As a result, all of these European countries are becoming increasingly popular destinations. Over the past ten years, students have increasingly chosen European universities as cheaper alternatives to Anglo-Saxon schools, not to mention that the post-9/11 legislation has made studying in the United States more complicated. In particular, members of China's growing middle class now have the financial means to send their children abroad which is by no means cheap as they spend the full tuition fees. For working-class families, this financial burden is often too much to bear. Yet even they may spend huge sums of money to enroll their children in international universities, where tuition can amount to four times their annual family income. Research shows that 87 percent of Chinese parents are willing to borrow the necessary money to fund study abroad.[28]

Parents are also sending their children abroad even younger. Year after year, boarding schools abroad receive more and more requests from Chinese parents. A close American friend of mine living in Shanghai has two sons who go to a well-known boarding school in Connecticut. A third of their classmates are Chinese children. My spouse and I regularly get asked by friends—and sometimes by strangers in the street—whether we will send our children to a Belgian school once they are a bit older. In their view, it would be perfectly acceptable for us to continue to live and work in Shanghai while the children are brought up by my parents in Belgium. For them, close and regular contact with parents is clearly subordinate to a good education and the future that may entail.

Despite all their hopes of findinggood jobs, students who have studied abroad often fail to land suitable positions, whether because of the language barrier or shifting political or economic circumstances. But these days, the economic situation in China provides better job opportunities, especially to those with international experience. Furthermore, the Chinese government encourages students to return. China used to suffer from a brain drain—for example, out of the 1.06 million students who studied abroad between 1978 and 2007, only a third returned. Today, the situation is reversed. In the past years before 2020, China has welcomed back more than 1.5 million returnees, three times more than in the previous thirty years combined. According to the Ministry of Education in 2017, the number of returnees since 1978 was over 3.13 million—out of a total of 5.2 million who went overseas in the first place.[29] 2020 proved to be an exceptional year. Due to the impact of the coronavirus pandemic and tightening immigration and employment rules overseas, no less than 800,000 Chinese students who recently graduated from overseas universities, returned to China.[30]

Clearly, an exodus has changed into a round trip. However, the promise of a great job upon return is no longer the guarantee it once was. Nowadays only diplomas from prestigious universities such as Harvard or Oxford provide job security in the domestic labor market, something often still unknown, especially to lower middle-class Chinese families. China's top domestic universities have raised the bar and are graduating their own outstanding scholars.

Modern China has also a greater needfor international business people, CEOs, scientists, and other top talents. Tsinghua University has launched the Schwarzman Scholars Program, which aims to train the next generation of global leaders.[31] Their success will depend on how well they understand China's role on the global stage. Peking University has set up a similar program. This university has a long and proud tradition in the Chinese education system. Since its foundation in 1898, it has always been at the center of the country's political and social developments. It is also where the 1989 Tiananmen Square demonstrations started.[32] In 2014, as part of my MBA program, I spent a week on its campus and its great tradition and exceptionally free-thinking were both perceptible. Renmin University, with its focus on social sciences, also rates among the world's top universities, as do Fudan University and Sun Yat-sen University, which are household names to every Chinese citizen.

Labor Market Competition and Problems

Chinese students used to think that studying abroad would be a ticket to success back home in China. These days, the opposite is true. In the past, the Chinese economy was driven by low-skilled labor sectors, for which the country had no shortage of workers. Skilled workers, however, needed to look abroad for foreign degrees and suitable employment at competitive salaries. However, those who did return—known as *haigui* "sea turtles"—were prized by Chinese and Western companies in China because of their Western knowledge and experience. Today, Chinese universities and colleges produce more than enough high-quality graduates, so overseas returnees have to compete for jobs against high-level domestic competition. Human resource managers in China now classify sea turtles into subgroups: those with overseas diplomas but little relevant work experience are "bathing crabs" or "small turtles," while those with prestigious degrees combined with extensive work experience are "big turtles." Unlike ten years ago, having studied abroad does not in itself impress employers; only those who have combined overseas study with internships or work experience make the grade.[33]

Part of this is China's economics, but another aspect of it is financial reality. The students going abroad today may not necessarily be the most qualified, merely those who can afford to go. I see this when recruiting new staff. Many Chinese students went abroad to study, but didn't necessarily get into the best colleges, and thus are not the best-qualified ether.

As a result, more and more people are starting to question the real value of studying abroad. Furthermore, although the rate of graduate unemployment has remained relatively stable, there is an underemployment problem. Most graduates eventually find work, but too many end up in part-time low-paid jobs. There is a mismatch between the skills employers need and the skills graduates mostly possess. There is a great need for graduates with technical or quantitative skills, resulting in attractive employment opportunities for these.[34]

Graduates fill the highest-paid entry positions in the most attractive employment sectors such as engineering, IT, and finance. Since the Chinese economy has gone digital, areas like artificial intelligence, the "internet of things," and cloud computing engineering are among the highest paid. The government's "Made in China 2025" strategy of becoming a global high-tech leader in industries such as advanced IT and robotics has created plenty of opportunities for graduates in these fields.

An economy increasingly more dependent on high-tech innovation also needs creative thinkers. The Chinese government knows that the current education system is ill-suited to modern society and realizes that reforms in the education sector are necessary. But that's easier said than done. The government would have to loosen its grip on the education system, something it's reluctant to do, for obvious reasons.

But there is also the *gaokao*, which was established to prevent corruption in the education system and to ensure the best students are admitted to the best universities. This is why top scholars graduate from top universities, while all over China, students in mediocre universities are stuck with a major they didn't choose. Many of those universities are intrinsically the same and focus on quantity instead of quality. However, mounting criticism of the *gaokao*, the single exam that determines the future of high school students, has pushed the government to roll out changes. There are plans to allow some schools to choose their own curriculum more freely, outside of the government control, and to permit students to have more freedom to choose their university . The *gaokao* itself won't be abolished, but it will be relaxed.

China, however, has set our plans to further modernize its education. Detailed strategies to modernize Chinese education are listed in the 2018–2022 Plan and the 2035 Plan, respectively. Eight core concepts are being promoted: virtue; overall development; everyone; lifelong learning; individualized teaching; the unity of knowledge and practice; integrated development; and co-construction and sharing.[35] These values clearly reflect a western view of learning where student-centered learning replaces teacher-centered learning. As such a western standard of education seems to be the goal by 2035. However at the same time the policy will increase government control and encourage domestic innovation of education-related projects. Analysts believe that real in-depth reforms could take ten or even twenty years. Consequently, parents still prefer to send their children abroad instead of letting them undergo the ordeal of the *gaokao*.

The Cultural Revolution denied millions of Chinese a decent education. And although there is now huge awareness that education is a solid foundation for students' futures, China still struggles with the necessary reforms.

Notes

1. Britannica. 2020. Chinese civil service. https://www.britannica.com/topic/Chinese-civil-service. Accessed December 5, 2020.
2. China.org. 2006. Students to go abroad but encouraged to return. https://www.china.org.cn/english/education/194041.htm. Accessed December 5, 2020.
3. China State Council. 2019. China's govt spending on education above 4% of GDP for seven consecutive years. https://english.www.gov.cn/statecouncil/ministries/201910/17/content_WS5da82aa2c6d0bcf8c4c1549c.html#:~:text=Totaling%20nearly%203.7%20trillion%20yuan,for%204.11%20percent%20of%20GDP. Accessed November 3, 2020.
4. *Chinadaily*. 2016. China has 1 in 5 of all college students in the world. www.chinadaily.com.cn/china/2016-04/08/content_24365038.htm. Accessed August 4, 2020.
5. CNBC. 2020. As China's economy picks up, new university grads are still looking for jobs. www.cnbc.com/2020/10/30/as-chinas-economy-picks-up-new-university-grads-are-still-looking-for-jobs.html. Accessed December 3, 2020.
6. Unicef. 2017. Literacy rate of youth aged 15–25, 2000, 2010, and 2015. www.unicef.cn/en/figure-829-literacy-rate-youth-aged-15%E2%88%9224-2000-2010-and-2015. Accessed October 4, 2020.
7. Times Higher Education. 2020 World Ranking. www.timeshighereducation.com/world-university-rankings/2020/world-ranking. Accessed December 15, 2020.
8. That's. 2020. Explainer: everything you need to know about the gaokao. https://www.thatsmags.com/china/post/13965/explainer-gaokao#:~:text=Though%20varying%20from%20province%20to,(in%20most%20cases%20English).&text=If%20they%20choose%20science%2C%20they,physics%2C%20chemistry%20and%20biology%20tests. Accessed December 4, 2020.
9. CGTN. 2020. Gaokao 2020 ends with over 10 million taking apart. https://news.cgtn.com/news/2020-07-10/Gaokao-2020-ends-with-over-10-million-taking-apart-S0Ytldcvio/index.html. Accessed December 21, 2020.
10. *People's Daily Online*. 2018. China's college entrance exam: national obsession and idealistic evolution. https://en.people.cn/n3/2018/0606/c90000-9468247.html. Accessed January 5, 2020.
11. College stats. 2020. 15 facts about China's grueling college entrance exam. China's college. https://collegestats.org/2012/08/15-facts-about-chinas-grueling-college-entrance-exam. Accessed October 4, 2020.

12. ICEF. 2016. Growing Chinese middle class projected to spend heavily on education through 2030. https://monitor.icef.com/2016/04/growing-chinese-middle-class-projected-spend-heavily-education-2030. Accessed April 14, 2019.
13. *Global Times*. 2019. Chinese kindergarten enrollment hits record low in recent four years. www.globaltimes.cn/content/1140357.shtml. Accessed August 2, 2020.
14. *South China Morning Post*. 2018. Chinese parents spend up to US$43,500 a year of after-school classes for their children. www.scmp.com/news/china/society/article/2176377/chinese-parents-spend-us43500-year-after-school-classes-their.
15. *Sixth Tone*. 2020 Student's suicide note raised concerns about academic pressure, mental health. www.sixthtone.com/news/1006296/students-suicide-note-raises-concerns-about-academic-pressure%2C-mental-health. Accessed December 30, 2020.
16. British Herald. 2020. Student mental health in China in the spotlight with suicide rate jump. www.britishherald.com/student-mental-health-in-china-in-the-spotlight-with-suicide-rate-jump/. Accessed December 31, 2020.
17. BBC. 2014. Languages Chinese. www.bbc.co.uk/languages/chinese/real_chinese/mini_guides/characters/characters_howmany.shtml. Accessed February 21, 2019.
18. *South China Morning Post*. 2019. China's private tutoring industry is booming despite economic slowdown. www.scmp.com/economy/china-economy/article/3003163/education-education-education-chinas-private-tutoring. Accessed March 18, 2020.
19. *China Briefing*. 2019. How China's education modernization policy impacts foreign investors. www.china-briefing.com/news/chinas-education-modernization-policy-impact-foreign-investors/. Accessed December 30, 2020.
20. Quartz. 2017. Asians spend seven times as much as Americans on tutoring to give their kids and edge. https://qz.com/970130/asians-spend-15-of-their-family-income-on-extra-education-and-tutoring-for-kids-americans-spend-it-on-cars-and-gas. Accessed April 18, 2019.
21. *South China Morning Post*. 2019. China's private tutoring industry is booming despite economic slowdown. www.scmp.com/economy/china-economy/article/3003163/education-education-education-chinas-private-tutoring. Accessed May 18, 2020.
22. *Chinadaily*. 2018. China's TAL education buys Israeli learnin start-up Codemonkey. www.chinadaily.com.cn/a/201812/05/WS5c0765a8a310eff30328f371.html. Accessed March 4, 2019.
23. *Harvard Magazine*. 2002. Harvard Girl. https://harvardmagazine.com/2002/07/harvard-girl.html. Accessed December 3, 2019.

24. The Diplomat. 2018. Is the golden age of Chinese studying abroad at and end? https://thediplomat.com/2018/10/is-the-golden-age-of-chinese-studying-abroad-at-an-end. Accessed July 4, 2010.
25. *Fortune*. 2020. U.S. visas for Chinese students have all but dried up. https://fortune.com/2020/11/06/f1-student-visa-us-china/#:~:text=Around%20370%2C000%20Chinese%20nationals%20studied,the%20Institute%20of%20International%20Education. Accessed December 5, 2019.
26. China.org. 2019. U.S. colleges fret over fall in Chinese students. www.china.org.cn/china/2019-03/06/content_74537409.htm#.XH85ovTjLuI.linkedin. Accessed June 4, 2020.
27. *Fortune*. 2020. U.S. visas for Chinese students have all but dried up. https://fortune.com/2020/11/06/f1-student-visa-us-china/#:~:text=Around%20370%2C000%20Chinese%20nationals%20studied,the%20Institute%20of%20International%20Education. Accessed December 5, 2019.
28. BBC. 2013. Asia's parents suffering "educational fever." www.bbc.com/news/business-24537487. Accessed February 5, 2018.
29. *People's Daily Online*. 2018. China sees more overseas returnees as it continues to make progress. https://en.people.cn/n3/2018/1224/c90000-9531263.html. Accessed March 7, 2019.
30. *South China Morning Post*. 2020. China's overseas graduates return in record numbers into already crowded domestic job market. www.scmp.com/economy/china-economy/article/3102384/chinas-overseas-graduates-return-record-numbers-already. Accessed December, 2020.
31. Schwarzman Scholars. 2020 www.schwarzmanscholars.org.
32. Britannica. 2011. Peking University. https://www.britannica.com/topic/Peking-University. Accessed October 14, 2018.
33. Sixth Tone. 2017. Chinese grads return home with degrees and disillusionment. www.sixthtone.com/news/1001154/chinese-grads-return-home-with-degrees-and-disillusionment.
34. The Conversation. 2017. Inside the world's largest higher education boom. https://theconversation.com/inside-the-worlds-largest-higher-education-boom-74789. Accessed May 12, 2019.
35. China Briefing. 2019. How China's education modernization policy impacts foreign investors. www.china-briefing.com/news/chinas-education-modernization-policy-impact-foreign-investors/. Accessed December 30, 2020.

CHAPTER 6

One Billion Customers

I am at a Mercedes dealer in the suburbs of Beijing in January 2011, looking for a new company car. The six-person sales team is busy with a group of Chinese customers, and it takes some time before anyone notices me. This isn't the first time I've experienced this, but it reminds me again of China's blistering pace of change. I spent years entering shops and watching the sales staff rush to my side, helping Chinese customers only when I was finished. Westerners were perceived as much richer than Chinese. But even after only a few years, this has changed dramatically.

The growth inthe spending power of the Chinese middle class has worldwide consequences. Not only do the profits of increasing numbers of large multinationals depend on the Chinese market, but companies must also rapidly adapt to their consumers' whims. This evolution has happened at lightning speed. In the Maoist era, everyone was equally poor, but after economic reforms got underway, a small wealthy class started to emerge. In the year 2000, only four percent of urban Chinese families earned between $9000 and $34,000 annually, but 68 percent of urban Chinese customers were within this range by 2012, and research by McKinsey & Company suggests that by 2022, 75 percent will have attained it.[1] In the upper middle class—households earning between $2600 and $3900 per month—the total amount of people will rise to 350 million by 2025.[2]

S. Agten, *Adventures in the Chinese Economy: 16 Years from the Inside*, https://doi.org/10.1007/978-981-16-1167-4_6

Middle-class households typically have enough income to satisfy their primary needs—food, clothing, and shelter—with some disposable income left over for additional consumption and savings. This means that in China, an enormous, rapidly expanding group of people will be able to enjoy a more luxurious lifestyle and purchase more expensive products. And that shows in the numbers. Despite COVID-19, with just over $5 trillion in retail sales of consumer goods in 2020, it was projected that China would surpass the U.S. market and become the biggest consumer market in the world.[3]

There are, however, vast differences between theChinese middle class and its Western counterpart. For example, take the demographic structure. The 1980s generation, to which my wife, her classmates, and most of her friends belong, forms the core of the new middle class. This group has the highest incomes and enjoys spending on high-quality goods. More than 70 percent of all Chinese consumers of luxury goods are under the age of 44.[4] Most of their parents survived the Cultural Revolution and lived in poverty, using ration tickets for basic necessities—spending on restaurants, leisure activities, or luxury goods (what few existed) was not an option. Today's abundance and variety are hard for them to get used to; they often still focus on saving money for themselves and their children.

Also geographically theChinese middle class doesn't constitute a homogeneous whole. I have friends in all the cities where have I lived: Shanghai, Beijing, Tai'an, Qian'an, and Yichun. Statistically, they all belong to the middle class. But since these cities are at different stages of development, my friends have widely divergent preferences and spending patterns. Some products and services will sell better in Qian'an, while others need a more international market like Guangzhou or Shenzhen. My friends in Shanghai and Beijing are more prosperous and erudite than those in Tai'an or Yichun, and all have different motivations for spending. When a Beijinger buys a Mercedes, status is important, while a Shanghaier might purchase the same brand out of an internal need to feel sophisticated. In Qian'an, it is the nouveaux riches, not the middle class, who can afford these cars and feel a thrill signaling their wealth. In a city like Tai'an, only a limited number can afford the luxury of foreign travel, the latest smartphone, quality cosmetics, and Belgian beer or chocolate, while in Shanghai or Beijing, these are standard purchases. It used to be that most spending was done by the urban population of the bigger, more sophisticated cities. However, this situation is changing rapidly. Consumption in China's still less developed 193 third-tier cities and 696 fourth-tier cities is increasing.[5] These cities are becoming bigger, richer, and more eager to spend. In 2017, consumption spending in these smaller cities was $3.3 trillion, but is expected to reach $8.4 trillion in 2030, thus being the engine driving China's consumption market of US$11.8 trillion over the same period.[6]

Also crucial to understand is that in dynamic, rapidly growing China, the new middle class isn't always as affluent as equivalent economic strata in the West, and consequently does not share the same standards. Very often, supporting one's family while living in a comfortable home is not the ultimate goal in China. Social and financial advancement is critical, and many see middle-class status as a stepping stone. But in the meantime, most are satisfied with what they have. My friends (and their friends) all have stable jobs and time to spend on hobbies or travel; they are self-confident and optimistic about the future. Both the 1980s generation and the millennials have witnessed only economic prosperity and living conditions that improved year after year. In addition—and unlike their parents—they have never experienced a purely repressive system and can enjoy everything modern China has to offer. Students who revolted in 1989 in Tiananmen Square were seeking a greater democratic voice and public accountability for corruption, but the new generation is pacified by wealth and greater individual freedom.

Quality and Status

BesidesChinese consumers increasing their discretionary spending, they are also constantly looking for better and more exclusive products. This so-called trading up is driven by customers aspiring to improve themselves.[7] Apart from the focus on quality, social status also plays a huge role, because consumers often judge themselves and others on what they buy. In the extremely competitive society that idolizes money and power, those who can afford luxury products enjoy a higher status. When I ask colleagues why they want to buy the newest iPhone or Huawei—at the cost of a monthly wage—while their old smartphone still works perfectly well, I hear "my friends all have one." When smartphones were first introduced in China, Chinese raced to buy them, while Westerners held back. It was common to see Chinese riding buses and living off instant noodles but owning smartphones, while most Westerners dined in restaurants and took taxis, but hung on to their old flip phones.

Luxury products play an important role in the social environment. A good friend told me that she used to dream of owning an Esprit shirt—until that dream transformed into a Louis Vuitton bag, a product particularly aspired to in China. She finally settled for a Louis Vuitton copycat bag, which helped both her status and her wallet. Many Chinese feel that buying the latest iPad or Western textile brands or drinking red wine in restaurants shows they have climbed up the social ladder.

TopWestern brands which understand the Chinese consumer, are benefiting enormously from this collective mind-set. The best-known examples of brands that witnessed outstanding growth in China include Rolex, Cartier, Gucci, Louis Vuitton, Chanel, Lancôme, Dior, and Prada. Other top brands such as Apple also made huge profits in China despite the hefty price tag and declining sales in the last years. China remains Apple's most important international market with $44 billion in sales in 2019. At its peak a few years ago, Greater China accounted for 25% of Apple's global revenue.[8] Among the more than forty Apple Stores in China in 2020,[9] one in Shanghai is the busiest in the world, with 25,000 visitors a day.[10] The sales figures for various products illustrate perfectly the growth of the middle class. For instance, while French cognac and wines used to be a privilege of the rich, the middle class has now started to buy lots too.

The recent evolution in the Chinese car market also clearly shows how China's middle class has grown into a global force to be reckoned with. In the past, only companies had cars, with one or two at their disposal. Now, the big cities at least boast plenty of two-car households. In today's China, buying a car is almost the same as buying a bicycle. Despite since 2018 the market for the first time since the 1990s declining owing to weaker economic growth, the trade war with the United States, and tough new emission standards, more than twenty-five million cars were sold in China in 2019.[11] The Chinese market dwarfs the U.S. market, the second-largest, with about seventeen million sold cars in 2018.[12]

For China'sgrowing middle class, owning a car has become a symbol of progress. Even my father-in-law, who has ridden a bicycle his whole life, wants a car. Most of his friends now own cars, because they feel riding bikes has become too dangerous on the busy Chinese streets, where the car is king. And of course, a car is more comfortable than an overcrowded bus or subway. Many people feel that because countless traffic jams are inevitable anyway, it's better to be stuck in your car than on a bus. At a meeting of the German Chamber of Commerce in Shanghai, the CEO of Audi China told that me the big German car manufacturers sell one-third of their cars in China, accounting for more than half their global profits. Other Luxury vehicles manufacturers have fared equally well. In 2017, China became Maserati's biggest market.[13] For Mercedes-Benz is China since 2015 the largest market in the world.[14]

Products and Services

To satisfy China's growing middle class, the supply of new products has grown enormously in recent years. When I first lived in China, I kept bringing products back from Belgium that I knew could not be found locally. Now when visiting my home country, I bring back American and European products I find in Shanghai, knowing they are not available in Belgium. In Chinese cities, the selection of Western brands is endless. Between 2014 and 2017, 50 percent of all the shopping centers under construction worldwide were being built in China. In total there are now about 4500 shopping centers—and another 7000 are expected to open in the next seven years[15]—that boast international clothing stores such as H&M, Benetton, and Zara, sports stores such as Adidas and Nike, and fast-food chains such as McDonalds, KFC, Pizza Hut, and Burger King.

Shopping centers are also no longer primarily intended for shopping—this sector is occupied by the enormous Chinese e-commerce platforms such as Alibaba and JD.com—but are preferred locations for leisure activities and restaurant visits. City dwellers consider a visit to a shopping center a day out, maybe even entertainment for the whole family. Besides traditional shops and restaurants, there are hair salons, fitness centers, massage parlors, bowling alleys, medical centers, large indoor playgrounds, fountains, a cinema complex, and maybe even an indoor skating rink or other sports and entertainment facilities. These are modern, comfortable complexes, often measuring more than 100,000 square meters, with an entire day's activities in one location. And since the vast majority of megacities used to have relatively little green space or recreational facilities, shopping centers could fill that void.

Instead of limiting themselves to products, Chinese consumers also are spending more time and money on services and experiences, an increasingly important worldwide trend. These need not be elaborate or adventurous; some of my friends, for example, spend more time in cinemas than they do at home.

China was alreadythe world's second-biggest movie market with box office sales of $9.2 billion in 2019, but COVID-19 changed this. While North America was still struggling with the raging COVID-19 pandemic, China's effective prevention and control has benefited its film market as such became the biggest market worldwide.[16] Despite domestic films accounting for around more than 50 percent of the revenue,[17] Hollywood movies depend greatly on China and its 70,000 movie screens in 10,000 venues.[18] The 2019 movie *Avengers: Endgame* did especially well in China, where it grossed $629 million, or more than 20 percent of the movie's global earnings.[19]

There isa legal quota in China limiting the number of foreign films shown annually to thirty-four, and to circumvent this, some foreign filmmakers get their movies co-financed by Chinese producers.[20] Hollywood productions compete fiercely, and since censorship is still in force, this often entails self-censorship and catering to Beijing's preferences.

Iron Man 3, *Transformers IV*, and *X-Men: Days of Future Past* are but a few examples of Hollywood blockbusters that adapted their storylines and integrated positive Chinese elements into their scripts to win their share of this lucrative market.[21] Beijing thus not only determines the way American films are being shown to Chinese citizens, but also to the American public.

Tourism

Another sector that benefits tremendously from China's growing middle class is tourism. Traveling used to be a luxury beyond most Chinese people's reach; today, it is an integral part of their lives. The first phase saw the more affluent population begin exploring at home. As a new visitor to China in 2002, I rarely needed to wait in lines at Chinese tourist attractions. Now our family tries to avoid domestic tourism as much as possible because the sites are so overcrowded.

Foreign tourism is also on the rise. Until the 1980s, Chinese citizens had difficulties leaving their country, but today taking vacations abroad is common. Most are open to new trends and experiences, and since the administrative and financial burdens of foreign travel have decreased significantly, Chinese tourists are exploring the world in ever-increasing numbers. In 2019, almost 169 million overseas trips were made by Chinese residents, three times more as in 2010. For clarity these numbers also include over 100 million trips made to China's special administrative regions of Hong Kong and Macao as well as China's Taiwan region, for which mainland Chinese also need a visa or special permit. Domestically also a staggering 6 billion trips were being made.[22] This makes China the number one country worldwide for outbound tourism. In the past, the process of applying for a visa was complicated, in large part because of restrictions from other countries that feared Chinese travelers would disappear into the local population and never return home . Given China's rapid development, today these concerns are not as acute, and countries are eager for Chinese tourism. China's Southeast Asian neighbors were the first, but the world is increasingly tapping into the growing wanderlust of the burgeoning Chinese middle class. COVID-19 of course has changed things a lot, but under normal circumstances many of my colleagues took at least one regional vacation a year. South Korea attracted almost five million Chinese tourists annually, who made up one-third of all its foreign visitors.[23] On our family vacation to Seoul, I saw more Chinese at the tourist attractions than I did locals. South Korea's Jeju Island has been made visa-free, as has the island of Saipan in the Marianas, a U.S. commonwealth. In 2019 Thailand hosted about thirty-nine million tourists, eleven million of whom came from China.[24]

Visas for European countries are also much easier for Chinese to obtain than they once were. In the past,my wife needed to prepare a sheaf of official documents to get a Belgian visa. Now the procedure has been simplified a lot and she can easily get a five-year visa. In 2017 over twelve million Chinese visited Europe, usually as tour groups visiting three or four countries.[25] France alone received in 2019 2.4 million Chinese travelers.[26] Because the United States offered Chinese citizens a ten-year visa in 2015 to boost tourism, three years later close to three million tourists flocked to the United States.

But forChinese tourists, sightseeing is just one aspect of travel. Despite it not being the main reason for traveling, shopping is often still of the essence, especially during sales periods. The casual observer can be forgiven for thinking that for many travelers, shopping actually trumps sightseeing. Chinese tourists spend huge sums of money abroad, especially on well-known luxury products, which are cheaper abroad than in China itself, where high import taxes and premium prices are in force. Cosmetics, perfume, high-end handbags, wallets, and designer clothes are coveted items for Chinese tourists. According to United Nations World Tourism Organization (UNWTO), Chinese tourists overseas spent $277.3 billion in 2018, when only 9 percent of Chinese had passports, a number expected to increase significantly in the coming years.[27]

This constituted in 2018 21 percent of the world's total spending on tourism.[28] Moreover, Chinese travelers spend on average more per trip than tourists from any other country. The impact of Chinese tourism on the luxury goods industry is thus immeasurable. Chinese consumers were responsible for one-third of the €260 billion spent on personal luxury goods in 2018,[29] while two-thirds of those purchases are made by Chinese tourists abroad.[30]

Every Chinese knows the term *daigou*, which means "to buy on behalf" and describes purchasing in-demand goods overseas and reselling them back in China. This is big business. Customers purchasing Chanel and Gucci items from Chinese stores often paid 80 percent more than if they had bought them in Europe; unsurprisingly, four out of every ten luxury items Chinese customers bought, was on the *daigou* plan.[31]

This has changed the faceof international retail. Every year we go shopping at Designer Outlet Roermond, the biggest factory outlet in northern Europe,[32] where almost every shop employs Chinese-speaking personnel. Western luxury brands are aggressively lobbying American and European governments to further lower the visa restrictions for Chinese tourists, and many foreign stores have installed Chinese payment systems to cater more to Chinese tourists. Visa and Mastercard may be global players, but in China they occupy a limited market share. In contrast, UnionPay dominates the Chinese market and, for Chinese tourists convenience, has already been rolled out in more than 170 countries and regions.[33]

Every major European airport has Chinese tourists lining up at duty-free stores, and also to collect their VAT reimbursements on luxury goods purchased within the European Union (I am also there, collecting VAT on the luxury watches my father-in-law wants to give his friends). China's payment companies like Alipay have also been following tourists abroad. However a changing trend is underway. As prices on foreign luxury goods achieve greater parity in mainland China relative to the rest of the world, combined with better e-commerce penetration and a government crack-down on professional resellers, in the future more of those sales will take place within China.[34]

To accommodateChinese tourists Western hotel chains have developed special services. When I was in the Netherlands, the owner of a hotel near Amsterdam told me that Chinese tourists made up 80 percent of his guests. Accordingly, he was planning to integrate cultural and practical considerations. In 2011, Hilton Hotels & Resorts launched a special Huanying (welcome) program that provides specific services for their

Chinese guests. The service is now available in 39 countries and 148 properties popular among Chinese travelers. Guests can enjoy Mandarin interpretation services, in-room tea kettles, and an enhanced Chinese breakfast.[35] But the growth of Chinese tourism globally is also tangible in other ways. The Chinese company Fosun acquired Club Med and became largest stakeholder in the British travel company Thomas Cook. After the latter's bankruptcy in 2019, Fosun also acquired the Thomas Cook brand name.[36]

Shopping or traditional sightseeing are, of course, not the only reasons Chinese travel abroad. Tourists increasingly start to develop new appetites which are becoming more important than shopping. Experience-based travel is increasing trendy, and more experienced travelers start to undertake more solo or family trips instead of group travel. Local experiences matter much more than just sightseeing, while fine dining is on the rise as well.[37]

I myself have witnessed this trend growing rapidly, and the travel habits of my Chinese friends are clear proof of this. One friend's housekeeper, a retired cafeteria worker from a government organization, has taken several European tours, arranged by her former company. However, when visiting other continents, many Chinese take solo trips. Another friend ran into a number of Chinese women traveling alone through Iran.

These days, China's super-rich are also opting for more exotic destinations. For them, having the latest Gucci handbag or BMW is no longer good enough—those who can afford them want more exclusive experiences. For example, the parents of one of our daughter's classmates regularly go to the Maldives, and African safaris are becoming increasingly popular. Chinese have become the second-largest tourist contingent in Antarctica. During the 2017–2018 tourist season, more than 8000 Chinese tourists traveled to the South Pole, a twenty-day trip one of my friends undertook that cost her and her family over $10,000 per person.[38] Chinese have now become the second-largest tourist force in Antarctica.

Wine tasting in France is another new trend. In Qian'an, a steel company owner told me that he had acquired a French wine chateau, adding proudly that he brought friends over several times a year for wine-tasting events. During a banquet I was at, he also served his own French wine—flown in directly from Europe.

Medical tourism is also on the rise. Friends of my wife travel to South Korea for plastic surgery, now a booming business. Around 600,0000 mainland Chinese go abroad to seek higher quality medical services and drugs every year.[39]

First Time Abroad

But this increasein tourism also had some negative effects. Although the situation has increased a lot, there used to be ample press coverage about the improper behavior of some Chinese travelers, and in 2013, a foreign ministry official said that half of the cases handled by Chinese embassies abroad were directly related to irresponsible tourist behavior.[40] Foreign hotels and restaurants complain about older generation Chinese tourists who spit in public or waste too much food. A plane flying from Zurich to Beijing had to turn back because two Chinese passengers were fighting, and there were a number of incidents where passengers tried to open airplane emergency exits.[41] And a Chinese middle-school student famously scribbled his name on a 3500-year-old Egyptian temple.[42] The owner of the hotel in Amsterdam mentioned above observed that his three-star hotel is on a picturesque harbor with traditional Dutch boats, and that Chinese tourists sometimes climb onto the decks to take photos, and may even open the shutters and go below. Complaints from boat owners forced him to erect a three-meter fence between his hotel and the harbor.

Incidents like these gave Chinese tourists a bad reputation. Within China, these incidents were discussed extensively, often on social media, where feelings of shame and a sense that the Chinese nation had lost face dominated the debate. The government tackled the problem by pointing out the need for civilized and polite behavior, even distributing brochures to familiarize tourists with Western culture and courtesies. Roots of this kind of misconduct can be also partially traced back to the Cultural Revolution. For ten years, many schools and universities remained closed, and professors were ousted from their positions. This left an entire generation without adequate education. Another reason for this increase of stories about improper behavior is of course also connected with the sudden uptick in travel numbers.

Although Chinese citizens today are more internationally oriented, many have never set foot outside China. When my Chinese adventure began in 2004, the country was still fairly closed, with Westerners considered a kind of alien species. During one of my first visits to a Yichun hairdresser, a total stranger entered the barbershop to touch my blond hair and verify that it was real. He had never seen a Westerner, let alone felt his hair. Perfect strangers invited me for lunch or dinner, and shy young people wanted to try out their English-language skills. Posing for pictures with foreigners was common, especially for Chinese from outside the big cities; I estimate that there are hundreds of pictures of me circulating all around China. My children still attract attention. After the birth of my son in Tai'an, nurses from adjacent operating rooms rushed out to have a glimpse of the Chinese-European newborn.

As with anywhere, cultural differences can cause misconceptions and a lack of understanding. A few years ago, while on a flight from Beijing to Brussels, I noticed an elderly Chinese couple behaving strangely. Not only did the woman go to the toilet every fifteen minutes, she kept pacing the aisles; furthermore, their loud conversation visibly irritated the other passengers. The couple, who only spoke Chinese, seemed to be trying to start a conversation with anyone who would listen. In the baggage hall, I saw them clutching their passports, clearly in distress about where to go. I told them to follow me, that I would take them past customs and to the exit. Relieved, they thanked me profusely and told me they were visiting their son who had studied in Belgium and now had a job there. It was their first time outside of China. After their happy family reunion, their son told me how much trouble he had gone through to arrange their visa and how he had feared that something would go wrong. The older man said they were panicked about finding their luggage, and mentioned how nervous his wife was at being on her first flight. This drove home the fact that travel is not only for the wealthy on organized tours, and that the prospect of seeing family can cause sleepless nights for everyone involved.

Demanding Consumers

Tourism, globalism, increasing individualism, online shopping, and the greater variety of available products have all made Chinese consumers more sophisticated. When Western brands entered the Chinese market for the first time, they had to create brand awareness as quickly as possible. Chinese bought Western products because they were Western and also of better quality than Chinese products. Chinese consumers often used products unconventionally. For example, people unused to the taste of wine might mix it with cola. I attended banquets where wine was served in small beer glasses and drunk bottoms up. Guests at other banquets drank brandy and cognac from the appropriate glasses, but would fill them to the brim. Companies once spent time and resources educating the Chinese in the use of unfamiliar products, but today's Chinese consumers understand and actively seek out sophisticated products and services.

Consumers are also rapidly becoming more selective, purchasing from overseas anything not locally available. After our neighbors renovated their Shanghai apartment, they ordered brand-new furniture online from the United States. It's also the reason why cross-border e-commerce is growing enormously, which was in 2019 a staggering $1.8 trillion business.[43] China is expanding the scope for cross-border e-commerce because it can be more easily tracked and taxed, especially when compared to gray-market *daigou* purchases. It also better protects consumers from fake or shoddy goods. So because of the size of the retail market, and the fact that Chinese consumers are buying globally, more and more Western companies already pay closer attention to Chinese preferences than they do to Western ones. For example, Chanel started already in 2015 with a global pricing strategy that offers its products at the same price all over the world.[44] The company knows that Chinese consumers will compare Chanel products online to find the best international price.

The young urban population in particular is the driving force behind this new wave of consumption. Just like their Western counterparts, Chinese youngsters are much more familiar with consumer goods than are their parents. But as a rule of thumb they are anxious to try everything and are not as brand loyal as Western consumers. And even the untapped market is enormous. A top Coca-Cola executive told me there are still five hundred million Chinese who have never drunk Coke in their lives.

This also leads to inconsistencies in buying behavior. My wife won't hesitate to pay substantially for new shoes from some luxury brand, and then show equal enthusiasm at a local farmers' market where she'll spend ten minutes bargaining for a piece of fruit. Watching this makes me a little embarrassed, but she argues that haggling is normal, even expected. Chinese consumers also expect an array of new products to appear regularly in the market. That's why some companies launch certain new products first in China and only then in the rest of the world. If customers see only slight differences in quality, they will think nothing of changing brands. In terms of the consumer goods market, China's development path diverged completely from that of the West; nevertheless, theirs is sophisticated and extremely complex.

Cultural aspects are also important. Thus, despite China's many cars, sales of children's car seats lag, because Chinese parents are often still convinced that holding their children on their laps is safer. China is also a growing wine market, but this has mostly applied to red wine. Historically white wine has had virtually no traction in China—all wine was referred to as "red wine," *hong jiu*. White wine was often called *bai jiu*, "white wine," awkwardly translated into the same name as the most famous Chinese alcohol. This was thus not appealing, since Chinese consumers assumed that it tasted the same.

But in price and quality, Chinese brands are increasingly competing with Western products. Although goods from the West still enjoy a higher status, "Made in China " is losing its stigma. Since Xi Jinping has become president, Chinese pride and patriotism have been surging. Sophisticated consumers also increasingly opt for newly emerging premium brands instead of traditional ones. Having something unique and stylish has become more important than buying another flashy Gucci bag.

This partly explains whysome consumers are favoring homegrown products. The Chinese smartphone manufacturer Huawei is surfing this wave. A combination of patriotic consumer purchases because of the U.S.–China trade war—in which Huawei plays a central role—and the fact that the company was one of the first to roll out 5G technology–based phones, favored sales of the Huawei product, while hurting Apple's iPhone. In 2019, Huawei sold 140 million phones in China, a jump of 35 percent over 2018. The same year Apple's Iphones sales decreased by 22 percent to 27.5 million.[45] Times are changing rapidly. I still remember vividly how when the iPhone 4 was released in Beijing in 2010, the store had to hire extra security guards to handle the crowds inside and the lines outside. Even later, customers could only purchase the iPhone 4S on order, not at the store itself.

But despite Chinese brands becoming qualitatively as good as their Western counterparts, their glamour factor is still a lot lower. Especially for products introduced by Western brands, such as chocolate and chewing gum, foreign companies still enjoy a higher reputation. Brands with historical and cultural background, such as luxury watches and bags, continue to do well.

Because of all these fast-changing trends large multinationals face several major problems in China. Not only do they need to find new ways to overcome a slowdown of the Chinese economy, but at the same time they need to manoeuver geopolitical tensions. When there was an outcry in Western media of alleged forced labor used in the cotton industry in Xinjiang beginning 2021, and several major western brands expressed concern, Chinese consumers grew more nationalistic and started to boycott brands like H&M (BBC. 2021. Xinjiang cotton: Western clothes brands vanish as backlash grows. www.bbc.com/news/world-asia-china-56533560.amp). Increasingly important, they must track Chinese consumers' rapidly changing preferences, while also coping with growing local competition. As the CEO Asia of Nike told me, in China he needs to fight his Western competitors like Adidas, local competitors like Li-Ning, and be on his toes for geopolitical tensions. For some brands, this is a difficult task. Although giants such as Procter & Gamble and L'Oréal continue to dominate, their market share decreases constantly as local brands adapt faster. In 2019, China and Hong Kong had nine luxury brands in Deloitte's "Global Powers of Luxury Goods Top 100" listing of the world's hundred largest luxury goods companies.[46] This is, for instance, more than France with seven companies. The Chinese cosmetics brand Herborist, which distinguishes itself by using traditional Chinese herbs and medicine, not only unveiled a flagship store on the prestigious Avenue de l'Opéra in Paris in 2015, it also matches its Western competitors in price.[47] The greater presence of Chinese brands in the domestic arena has thus intensified competition in other industries. Between 2008 and 2017, the market share of foreign firms dropped by 17 percent in pet foods and 13 percent in both video games and passenger vehicles.[48]

And it's just a matter of time before Chines brands start to compete more and more internationally also. To shake off the "Made in China" stigma, Chinese companies are also creating a more international image, advertising in other countries even if their products are not available there. This is not so much to create awareness among international consumers as to show the Chinese that local brands have become global players.

Case in point: during the 2012 Olympic Games in London, public transportation buses sported advertisements for Yili, despite the fact that this dairy brand wasn't available in the United Kingdom.[49] But in this way Yili showed thousands of Chinese tourists that the brand had "made it." Yili, was also shown in the televison series *The Big Bang Theory*.[50] The series wasn't broadcast in China, but no matter; millions of Chinese tune in on streaming sites.[51] In 2018, the Chinese corporation Wanda bought advertising space on billboards around the soccer fields where teams competed in World Cup matches in Russia. And product placement in Hollywood films and television series serves the same purpose. That the strategy is successful, I can confirm myself. I once attended a lavish government banquet in Qian'an where a guest opened a bottle of Moutai rice wine, announcing proudly that he had bought it at Charles de Gaulle

Airport in Paris. He could have bought it in any Chinese liquor store—but this one was from Paris, so it was special.

As Chinese consumers are willing to pay extra for products whose quality they can trust, another—perhaps surprising—result is that China is becoming the champion of consumer rights. For decades, China has been notorious for knockoffs, but now companies are using QR codes, mobile apps, and third-party services to build consumer confidence in the origin and authenticity of the goods they sell, from luxury handbags to bags of frozen beef mince. China has also launched also a larger anti-counterfeit campaign, including through an AI bot that analyzes data to detect sellers who are offering fake goods. E-commerce giant Alibaba, reported that it saw a 67 percent drop in problem sales across its platforms in 2018. In addition, the campaign also has led to the closure of almost 4300 counterfeit-goods workshops in China.[52]

Consumption as an Economic Engine

After decades of deprivation and planned-economy rationing, this is the age of Chinese consumption. It is fully encouraged by the central government, which sees the middle class as an engine of economic growth. But it is at the same time also hindered by China's weak social safety net. Families save money for health emergencies and possible unemployment, which means that many keep their spending pragmatic and their purchases budget-appropriate. China's current underdeveloped social security system still puts the brakes on its consumption patterns, but a more comprehensive and efficient system might free Chinese purses. The same goes for the *hukou*, or registration, system, which, reformed, would allow family members to accompany migrant workers to the cities. After all, city dwellers spend more than their rural counterparts.

Although sales numbers indifferent sectors remain strong and growth continues, Chinese consumers have also somewhat become more cautious over the last years. Not to mention the effects of COVID-19, possible reasons include the U.S.–China trade war, China's anti-corruption campaign, the country's slower economic growth, and the fact that the tastes of the rich are moving away from the ostentatious. As mentioned before car sales took a hit where for the first time since the 1990s, sales dropped in 2018 and 8 percent in 2019. Unsurprisingly American car manufacturers' decline in sales was close to disastrous. China is the second biggest market in the world for Ford, which has faced declining sales there since 2017; 2018 and 2019 were especially challenging, with decreases of

37 and 26 percent, respectively.[53] General Motors sold 15 percent fewer cars in 2019, but China is still the biggest market in the world for GM, which sold 3.09 million cars there in 2019.[54] The German car manufacturers fare better. Volkswagen kept the declining sales under control, while Audi and Porsche sold even more cars in 2019.[55]

Whatever the future holds, it's abundantly clear that Chinese consumer behavior will help shape the global economy. China is already one of the world's most complex and sophisticated markets and, for many companies, the largest growth market. This trend will increase. More important, this evolution is happening much faster in China than in any other country. Chinese consumers are already the biggest shoppers abroad, and increasing numbers of Chinese vacation overseas. Foreign companies are increasingly switching their local production toward local consumption rather than export as before. "Made in China, for China" is becoming more and more a reality. The growth of the Chinese middle class, consumption as a status symbol, and the increase in tourism are all factors that will impact, not only the Chinese economy, but the world as a whole.

Notes

1. McKinsey. 2013. Mapping China's middle class. www.mckinsey.com/industries/retail/our-insights/mapping-chinas-middle-class. Accessed March 6, 2018.
2. McKinsey. 2019. China luxury report 2019. www.mckinsey.com/~/media/mckinsey/featured%20insights/china/how%20young%20chinese%20consumers%20are%20reshaping%20global%20luxury/mckinsey-china-luxury-report-2019-how-young-chinese-consumers-are-reshaping-global-luxury.ashx. Accessed December 4, 2020.
3. Business Insider. Retail sales will drop 5,7% this year because of the pandemic. www.businessinsider.com/worldwide-retail-sales-will-drop-due-to-pandemic-2020-6?r=DE&IR=T. Accessed December 12, 2020.
4. McKinsey. 2019. China luxury report 2019. www.mckinsey.com/~/media/mckinsey/featured%20insights/china/how%20young%20chinese%20consumers%20are%20reshaping%20global%20luxury/mckinsey-china-luxury-report-2019-how-young-chinese-consumers-are-reshaping-global-luxury.ashx. Accessed December 4, 2020.
5. Alizila. 2019. Where China's biggest consumption growth is happening. www.alizila.com/china-consumption-growth-lower-tier-cities. Accessed December 4, 2020.
6. Morgan Stanley. 2018. Bullish in China's lower-tier cities. www.morganstanley.com/ideas/china-lower-tier-cities. Accessed December 4, 2020.

7. McKinsey. 2019. China luxury report 2019. www.mckinsey.com/~/media/mckinsey/featured%20insights/china/how%20young%20chinese%20consumers%20are%20reshaping%20global%20luxury/mckinsey-china-luxury-report-2019-how-young-chinese-consumers-are-reshaping-global-luxury.ashx. Accessed December 4, 2020.
8. Bloomberg. 2020. Apple's $44 billon China market threatened by Trump WeChat ban. www.bloomberg.com/news/articles/2020-08-12/apple-s-44-billion-china-market-threatened-by-trump-wechat-ban. Accessed December 31, 2020.
9. The Verge. 2020. All Apple stores in China have reopened. www.theverge.com/2020/3/13/21177964/apple-stores-china-reopened-coronavirus-covid-19. Accessed September 6, 2020.
10. The Balance. 2019. Apple's retail stores around the world. www.thebalancesmb.com/apple-retail-stores-global-locations-2892925. Accessed February 3, 2020.
11. CNN. 2020. China's car sales fell 8% in 2019 and the slump is entering its third year. https://edition.cnn.com/2020/01/13/business/china-car-sales/index.html. Accessed October 4, 2020.
12. CNBC. 2019. China annual auto sales fall for first time in about two decades with more pain on the way. www.cnbc.com/2019/01/03/china-annual-auto-sales-fall-for-first-time-in-about-two-decades.html. Accessed October 21, 2020.
13. Shine. 2017. China becomes Maserati's largest market with greatest contribution from Levante. www.shine.cn/biz/auto/1710275532. Accessed March 5, 2019.
14. *Chinadaily*. 2020. Mercedes-Benz prospers as best-selling premium brand. https://www.chinadaily.com.cn/a/202001/13/WS5e1bb876a310cf3e3558407b.html. Accessed December 21, 2020.
15. *Chinadaily*. 2019. What's in store for malls in China? www.chinadaily.com.cn/a/201901/11/WS5c380388a3106c65c34e3e65.html#:~:text=There%20are%20around%204%2C500%20shopping,shopping%20centers%20within%20the%20year. Accessed November 4, 2020.
16. CGTN. 2020. China becomes world's biggest movie market, war epic "The Sacrifice" aims to be next big hit. https://news.cgtn.com/news/2020-10-20/China-becomes-world-s-largest-film-market-as-more-big-releases-loom-UIT5ztWPfO/index.html. Accessed December 4, 2020.
17. Reuters. 2019. China 208 movie box office revenue growth slows. www.reuters.com/article/us-china-film/china-2018-movie-box-office-revenue-growth-slows-idUSKCN1OV19X. Accessed October 24, 2020.
18. Supchina. 2020. Movie screens in China go dark amid coronavirus. Again. https://supchina.com/2020/03/27/movie-screens-in-china-go-dark-amid-coronavirus-again/. Accessed April 16, 2020.

19. *Forbes*. 2019. Box office: 'Avengers: endgame' topped 'Avatar' thanks to China, not America. www.forbes.com/sites/scottmendelson/2019/08/08/avengers-endgame-infinity-war-avatar-marvel-iron-man-black-panther-last-jedi-star-wars-spider-man-pikachu-mulan-china-box-disney-office/#6e5ee3f37943. Accessed March 4, 2020.
20. *Newsweek*. 2020. Hollywood has long played by China's rules—will a new cold war derail that? https://www.newsweek.com/hollywood-has-long-played-chinas-ruleswill-new-cold-war-derail-that-1518947. Accessed December 31, 2020.
21. *The Washington Post*. 2015. Stephen Colbert's "Pander Express" is a brilliant takedown of how Hollywood sucks up to China. www.washingtonpost.com/news/wonkblog/wp/2015/10/10/stephen-colberts-pander-express-is-a-brilliant-takedown-of-how-hollywood-sucks-up-to-china. Accessed April 18, 2019.
22. CGTN. 2020. Chinese tourists made 169 million outbound trips in 2019: report. https://news.cgtn.com/news/2020-02-29/Chinese-tourists-made-169-million-outbound-trips-in-2019-report-OtIYWsZmOQ/index.html.
23. *The Korea Times*. 2019. Number of foreign tourists to Korea up 15% in 2018. www.koreatimes.co.kr/www/culture/2019/01/141_262527.html. Accessed May 4, 2020.
24. *The Diplomat*. 2020. With plane load of Chinese visitors, Thailand kicks off attempted tourism revival. https://thediplomat.com/2020/10/with-plane-load-of-chinese-visitors-thailand-kicks-off-attempted-tourism-revival/#:~:text=In%202019%2C%20nearly%2011%20million,a%20Chinese%20tourist%20from%20Wuhan. Accessed December 30, 2020.
25. PXCom. 2018. Europe: Chinese tourism to be higher than ever in 2018. https://pxcom.media/en/blog/europe-chinese-tourism-2018/. Accessed May 13, 2019.
26. *Global Times*. 2020. Lack of Chinese tourists to Europe may lead to 10n euro loss: analyst. https://www.globaltimes.cn/content/1195235.shtml. Accessed December 4, 2020.
27. *The Telegraph*. 2019. The unstoppable rise of the Chinese traveler—where are they going and what does it mean for overtourism? www.telegraph.co.uk/travel/comment/rise-of-the-chinese-tourist. Accessed May 4, 2020.
28. China outbound travel & tourism market. Chinese tourists account for 21% of global travel spending in 2018. www.cottm.com/news-center/news/chinese-tourists-account-21-global-travel-spending-2018. Accessed April 20, 2020.
29. Vogue Business. 2018. Study: Chinese shoppers to make up 46% of luxury goods purchases in 2025. www.voguebusiness.com/consumers/chinese-consumers-luxury-purchases-growth-bain. Accessed December 2, 2020.

30. Bain&Company. 2019. What's powering China's market for luxury goods? www.bain.com/insights/whats-powering-chinas-market-for-luxury-goods/. Accessed July 12, 2020.
31. Bloomberg. What's "Daigou" and what's it to Gucci and Beijing? www.bloomberg.com/news/articles/2019-01-28/what-s-daigou-and-what-s-it-to-gucci-and-beijing-quicktake. Accessed March 4, 2020.
32. McArthurGlen. 2017. McArthurGlen increases shopping experience in Roermond. www.mcarthurglen.com/da/press/mcarthurglen-increases-shopping-experience-in-roermond-by-adding-more-than-50-new-shops. Accessed February 4, 2019.
33. Union Pay. 2020. List of countries/regions accepting Unionpay cards. https://m.unionpayintl.com/wap/en/serviceCenter/cardUsingInstructions/1437.shtml. Accessed December 23, 2020.
34. Bain&Company. 2019. What's powering China's market for luxury goods? www.bain.com/insights/whats-powering-chinas-market-for-luxury-goods/. Accessed July 12, 2020.
35. California Hotel & Lodging Association. HLA. 2018. Hotel Profile: Hilton Huanying. https://chla.mynewscenter.org/hilton-huanying/. Accessed April 20, 2020.
36. BBC. 2019. Thomas Cook brand sold to Club med owner Fosun for £11 m. www.bbc.co.uk/news/amp/business-50267453. Accessed December 5, 2020.
37. McKinsey. 2018. Chinese tourists: Dispelling the myths. www.mckinsey.com/~/media/McKinsey/Industries/Travel%20Transport%20and%20Logistics/Our%20Insights/Huanying%20to%20the%20new%20Chinese%20traveler/Chinese-tourists-Dispelling-the-myths.ashx. Accessed May 12, 2020.
38. *Chinadaily*. 2019. Chinese tourists take to Antarctica in a big way. www.chinadaily.com.cn/a/201901/12/WS5c395cb3a3106c65c34e4092.html. Accessed April 13, 2020.
39. Asia Actual. 2020. China encourages local manufacturing of foreign medical devices. https://asiaactual.com/blog/china-encourages-local-manufacturing-of-foreign-medical-devices/ Accessed December 20, 2020.
40. *Chinadaily USA*. 2013. Chinese tourists aren't that bad. https://usa.chinadaily.com.cn/epaper/2013-08/20/content_16907531.htm. Accessed April 5, 2018.
41. *The Straits Times*. 2015. Chinese tourist faces charges for opening plane door. www.straitstimes.com/asia/east-asia/china-tourist-faces-charges-for-opening-plane-door. Accessed January 3, 2019.
42. *Chinadaily USA*. 2013. Chinese tourists aren't that bad. https://usa.chinadaily.com.cn/epaper/2013-08/20/content_16907531.htm. Accessed April 5, 2018.

43. Vogue Business. 2020.China's cross-border e-commerce, or Haitao, grows on search for exclusivity and thrift. https://www.voguebusiness.com/consumers/china-cross-border-ecommerce-haitao-exclusivity-thrift%3famp. Accessed December 29, 2020.
44. *Global Times*. 2015. Chanel cuts mainland prices. https://www.globaltimes.cn/content/913074.shtml. Accessed July 4, 2019.
45. Reuters. 2019. Huawei snatched marker share from Apple, local rivals in China in 2019. www.reuters.com/article/us-china-smartphone/huawei-snatched-market-share-from-apple-local-rivals-in-china-in-2019-idUSKBN1ZR2CH. Accessed February 2, 2020.
46. Deloitte. 2019. Global powers of luxury goods 2019. www2.deloitte.com/content/dam/Deloitte/ar/Documents/Consumer_and_Industrial_Products/Global-Powers-of-Luxury-Goods-abril-2019.pdf. Accessed April 12, 2020.
47. Jahwa. 2020. Herborist. www.jahwa.com.cn/en/herborist. Accessed March 21, 2019.
48. ChinaPower. 2020. How dominant are Chinese companies globally? https://chinapower.csis.org/chinese-companies-global-500/. Accessed January 4, 2021.
49. *The Atlantic*. 2012. Here's the bizarre Chinese Olympics ad campaign that's baffling England. www.theatlantic.com/international/archive/2012/07/heres-the-bizarre-chinese-olympics-ad-campaign-thats-baffling-england/260442. Accessed March 4, 2019.
50. Dairy Reporter. 2013. Mengniu brand value plummets in 2012 as the Yili brand soars. www.dairyreporter.com/Article/2013/01/18/Mengniu-brand-value-plummets-in-2012-as-the-Yili-brand-soars. Accessed July 16, 2019.
51. *Fortune*. 2015. Why Chinese censorship couldn't stop "Bing Bang Theory" fans. https://fortune.com/2015/07/30/chinese-censorship-big-bang-theory. Accessed March 4, 2019.
52. OYZ. 2020. The unlikely new champion of consumer rights: China. https://www.ozy.com/the-new-and-the-next/the-unlikely-new-champion-of-consumer-rights-china/406392/. Accessed December 23, 2020.
53. CNBC. 2020. Ford's vehicle sales in China tumble 26.1% in 2019. www.cnbc.com/2020/01/13/fords-vehicle-sales-in-china-tumble-26point1percent-in-2019.html. Accessed May 4, 2020.
54. Xinhuanet. 2019. China still General Motors' biggest market. www.xinhuanet.com/english/2019-02/07/c_137803334.htm. Accessed December 2, 2020.
55. Xinhuanet. 2019. Volkswagen China delivers down 2.8 pct in first nine months. www.xinhuanet.com/english/2019-10/21/c_138490540.htm. Accessed March 3, 2020.

CHAPTER 7

The Chinese Online Tsunami

Qian'an is a Tier 4 city with a relatively large middle class, but there were few Western products for sale there before 2008. There was no shopping mall selling international brands, and residents knew little of what modern China's metropolises had to offer. The explosive growth of the steel and cement sectors had improved the lives of many locals, but they had trouble spending their new wealth. Now, in March 2013, however, my wife was closing her luxury children's clothing shop, opened only three years before. It had done well at the outset, but sales of designer kids' clothes had been declining, making it hard to stay profitable.

Although Qian'an's steel-related companies were often larger than their Western counterparts, their business networks were still primarily local. They had no need to seek foreign markets or create a more global network. Many business owners struck it rich overnight, but couldn't conceal the fact they had little to no education and limited knowledge about the world outside their own small part of it. Many of my Qian'an friends felt they were living in a gilded cage. Within that cage, they could afford almost anything, but once they left the city, they felt insecure and unsophisticated.

There were many reasons to assume that a local store selling high-quality children's clothes could achieve success, especially since it would save many in the city's middle class a trip to Beijing. My wife had a sound business plan. She purchased the latest fashions in the south of China, in

S. Agten, *Adventures in the Chinese Economy: 16 Years from the Inside*,
https://doi.org/10.1007/978-981-16-1167-4_7

the Pearl River Delta, which is home to huge textile wholesale markets, which sold internationally well-known brands cheaply. Then she shipped them to Qian'an and sold them at a huge profit. The business flourished so much that in 2011, a year after she established her shop in Qian'an, she opened a second store in her hometown, Tai'an, a Tier 3 city, where the same concept worked equally well.

From 2012, however, sales started to decrease. Not only were there fewer customers in her shops, but those bought less. The situation kept deteriorating, and both stores started to lose money. So, in 2013, my wife decided to close down both stores. How did this happen so fast? The main reason was the exploding popularity of e-commerce, especially the success of Alibaba, the Chinese company that spearheaded this evolution. Virtually overnight, hundreds of thousands of brick-and-mortar shops were struggling to stay afloat.

Besides forever changing the face of retail, the rise of Alibaba is also directly related to China's explosion in internet usage. That the internet dramatically revolutionized the country is undeniable. In modern China—much more than in the Western world—the internet is an absolutely essential part of daily life. Online shopping, digital payments, thousands of different smartphone apps, the huge amount of social media activity, livestreaming, online education medical consultation, and the tremendous number of online videos all illustrate how interwoven with China's everyday life the internet is.

This evolution took place at an unprecedented speed. According to the China Internet Network Information Center, a branch of the country's Ministry of Industry and Information Technology, in 2005 there were 111 million internet users.[1] Fifteen years later, China's internet population had reached 850 million, the largest in the world and more than Europe and the United States combined.[2] In fact, 21 percent of all the internet users worldwide are in China.[3] And compared to the United States where internet penetration sits at 95 percent, China still has a lot of untapped potential as the same penetration rate stands at only 59 percent.[4]

Because of its size, the Chinese internet sector operates according to very different market rules than do Western internet sectors; furthermore, it has a big influence on internet companies throughout the world.

Since the Chinese internet is vastly different than that of the Western world, most domestic internet companies and their products or services are not known abroad. And just as in the West, in China, a number of millionaires also have the internet to thank for their fortunes. The government actively promotes internet usage, since it advances integration—and control—in China. After all, the internet lowers certain barriers within the complex entity the country still is. The result is that from commerce to governance, from journalism to routine communication, much of Chinese life is increasingly virtual and digital. That the internet is strongly established and an essential part of daily life is evident by the widespread availability of wi-fi. Nearly every big-city restaurant or café has free wi-fi; those that don't are seen as archaic. Asking for the wi-fi password before ordering food or drinks is for most customers a matter of routine. Scanning a QR code and ordering online at the table of the restaurant itself instead of asking for a waitress, is becoming the norm.

Few would have predicted, however, that the internet would play such a prominent role in today's China. After all, it was almost universally seen as integral to democracy and freedom of speech and, by its very nature, would be impossible to limit. Former U.S. President Bill Clinton echoed the beliefs of many when he crowed that the internet was opening up the world. "There's no question China has been trying to crack down on the internet," he said. "Good luck. That's sort of like trying to nail Jell-O to the wall."[5] How wrong he was. The Chinese government has reinvented this new technology with its own interests in mind, deploying an army of hardware engineers and software specialists to turn the internet into one large and controllable medium.

This is the most famous aspect of China's internet, but it only tells part of the story. The Chinese government also supported the economic sectors that originated around the internet so that they could grow, flourish, and compete head-on with foreign companies. And lastly—but with increasing importance—the Chinese internet is used for purposes of control, such as gathering feedback and monitoring public opinion.[6]

Censorship

Outside China, the Chinese internet is viewed negatively, especially when it comes to censorship and blocking foreign websites. One of the best-known aspects of internet censorship is the so-called Great Firewall, which blocks information viewed as undesirable by the regime. The Chinese government has invested heavily in the construction of this Great Firewall, and it is actually only a part of the much larger Golden Shield project, which oversees all information that flows into and around China.[7]

The project's purpose is not, as often mistakenly assumed, to obtain complete control over Chinese citizens; it is more to channel information so that the country's social stability is not compromised. In addition, the CCP wants to avoid the internet being used to organize and coordinate political activities that could jeopardize its leadership. It seeks to banish direct criticism. The project's total cost is unknown, but estimates run to billions of dollars, with more than two million people permanently employed to monitor opinion and censor internet content.[8]

Beside this, there are hundreds of thousands of others in the private and public sectors involved, including many Western companies providing technical support. The best-known victims of the Great Firewall are YouTube, Google, Twitter, Instagram, and Facebook—all websites that cannot be accessed directly in China. Like a digital Berlin Wall, the Great Firewall has divided the internet into two worlds: the domestic internet, whose websites load quickly and openly easily, and the global internet, with a number of websites harder to access or blocked altogether.

Western media often assume that the Chinese internet user is completely shielded from the outside world. That is not true. Internet companies that adapt Chinese legislation and have servers within China's national borders are freely accessible. Yahoo is available to all, but its competitor Google was blocked in 2002,[9] and in 2006 temporarily introduced Google.cn, a censored version that complied to the Chinese law.[10]

By the end of 2018, some ten thousand domain names were still blocked in mainland China.[11] And despite any Western outcries, U.S. companies like Apple and Microsoft even help China censor the net so that they can gain access to China's millions of potential customers.[12] The government is especially concerned about websites that can reach large numbers of people and spread news and rumors instantaneously—as seen in the 2011 Middle East revolutions.

Media sites like those of the *New York Times*, *Wall Street Journal*, *Washington Post*, and *South China Morning Post* are also inaccessible because they publish news the government considers potentially destabilizing. Then authorities may react instinctively, like killing the wasp after it stings. In 2012, when the *New York Times* wrote that former premier Wen Jiabao's extended family had accumulated a fortune of no less than $2.7 billion, the website of the newspaper was blocked.[13]

But despite the existence of censorship, most foreign websites are freely accessible. For the rest, people use a virtual private network (VPN) connection as a detour to blocked websites, albeit at a much slower speed. In the past, VPN usage was widespread, but the new cybersecurity law that came into force in 2017 has clarified the rules. The use of VPN is not illegal in China, but the Chinese government has explicitly described who can use it and what for. In general, companies can legally use VPNs as long as they purchase services from those authorized to sell them. Individuals can use a VPN for personal purposes.[14]

But this doesn't prevent internet censorship from being a thorn in the eye of foreign companies. Surveys of Western companies operating in China have shown that navigating internet restrictions such as the Great Firewall is an enormous challenge. For some foreign companies with servers outside China, the firewall can be an operational nightmare—I learned this from personal experience—with access to websites or company servers being very slow.

Because the government tries to exercise control over the flow of information, users employing secure VPN connections can find simple operations hard to manage. Especially in the evening, it can be impossible to send e-mails via VPN. During big municipal or national events such as the annual party conferences in Beijing and international conferences that host foreign heads of state, the internet speed often slows to an absolute minimum. It's clear during those periods that "someone" is doing "something" on the internet. But as mentioned, companies that have their servers located within China enjoy much faster internet and easy accessibility. The new cybersecurity law provides increased scrutiny of the information flow, as well as stipulating that any company that collects personal information within Chinese borders must store this information in the country.[15]

The Internet Makes Life Easier

But just as in the Western world, the internet has benefited the average citizen. As mentioned above, with the widespread availability of wi-fi and the strong mobile telecommunications network, the internet is a permanent presence for many Chinese. When we were still living in Beijing, I regularly participated in day trips to the "Wild Wall," or the unrepaired, undervisited parts of the Great Wall located 100 miles outside of the city in sparsely populated areas. Although the wall winds over mountain peaks—yielding stunning views—mobile phones still have excellent service. Whether at northern ski resorts or in apartment elevators, using smartphones is rarely a problem. Chinese commuters watch online videos on subway rides and download music on highways. Even in Tibet, still one of the world's most inaccessible regions, I had few problems using my smartphone to surf the internet.

On one hand, then, Chinese internet users enjoy the commercial and social benefits of the internet; on the other hand, the regime controls its "abuse," arguing political necessity. In fact, the Chinese government optimizes the internet to create a wide support for its national policy.

With respectable—if not the world's fastest—internet speed, as well as accessibility and abundant availability online for everything the Chinese consumer needs, the vast majority of Chinese internet users see censorship and the Great Firewall as a non-issue. Baidu and Youku Tudou work as fast as their Western counterparts Google and YouTube. For my wife, colleagues, and friends, the internet is a vital tool that simplifies everyday life. All of them are active on social media, they buy enormous amounts of products online, can quickly follow trends and evolutions, and handle financial matters much more easily than we do in the Western world. Although my wife and her friends speak English, they don't often surf foreign websites, because Chinese social media present international news the same way the foreign channels do. In other words, the Great Firewall is a problem for foreigners living and traveling in China, not for local Chinese. Foreigners complain about internet speed and the unavailability of websites, which is exactly why the Great Firewall is so notorious abroad. But as noted, that is only part of the picture.

Although the number of available online tools has reached phenomenal proportions, this wasn't always the case. As in many other sectors, when the Chinese internet revolution was taking off, companies sought to copy successful Western formulas. The local market wasn't very competitive, so they saw no need to create innovative products. Copycats of foreign success stories such as Facebook, Twitter, and YouTube were flooding the Chinese market

Back then, the market was completely unregulated and populated by unsophisticated users willing to try anything new. Moreover, Chinese companies involved in copying Western products faced few repercussions. Even the most blatant copycats had little to fear. Since bringing a new product to market takes time and money, assessing public interest was critical. Even successful products would attract hordes of competitors, especially in China's flexible, fast-moving market and copying a time-tested formula was the obvious choice.

In China, the government's strict monitoring of new internet services also partly explains why the copycats were successful and why foreign companies had trouble obtaining a foothold in the Chinese internet sector. As in the West, the Chinese tech companies are fierce, aggressive, innovative competitors, as well as being financially strong companies that respond rapidly to new trends. In addition, Western companies never focused on localizing and adapting to the Chinese market. China's internet companies and other startups excelled in optimizing, marketing, and improving products and ideas that were made in America.[16]

That's why car-hailing company Didi Chuxing beat Uber, for instance, and eventually acquired the Chinese operation of the company in 2016. Didi Chuxing worked from the start with taxi drivers instead of individual car owners, cooperated better with local governments, and introduced payment systems better adapted to the Chinese user.[17] Didi Chuxing has 400 million registered users and delivers 25 million rides a day—my family are regular users—roughly twice as many as Uber and all the other global sharing apps combined.[18] And Didi Chuxing is just one of several large ride-hailing firms operating in the country.

Of the giants that dominate the Chinese internet sector, Alibaba, Tencent, and Baidu are traditionally the best-known in the West. Those three companies (collectively known as BAT) are comparable to Facebook, Apple, Microsoft, Google, and Amazon (collectively known as FAMGA). Then there is also the acronym TMD which stands for Meituan Dianping (food delivery), Toutiao (news and information), and Didi Chuxing. These three companies are rising stars and also have multi-billion valuations.

Not so long ago the United States dominated the list of most valuable tech companies in the world. But in 2020, there were four Asian companies in this list, among which Alibaba and Tencent which occupied the sixth and seventh places.[19] Baidu, Alibaba, and Tencent all started as copycats, but in many ways they have overtaken their Western role models. Baidu, the Google of China, is the top search engine, while Alibaba is the e-commerce leader. Tencent is the dominant player in social media. In the tech start-up world, the omnipresent Alibaba and Tencent can make or break others in the market. Some venture capital companies refuse to invest in promising start-ups because then they directly compete with one of these three.[20] Nearly all the top players in the home delivery and car-sharing markets are backed by Tencent or Alibaba. Crucial to understand is that, unlike Western internet companies, Chinese companies engage in constant guerilla warfare across a broad spectrum, each having built an incredibly diverse ecosystem that spreads its tentacles over all sectors.

Founded in 2000 by Robin Li and Eric Xu, Baidu is now world's fourth-most visited website and is a search engine for other websites, music, and photos.[21] Baidu offers over 57 web services, including Baidu Maps, Baidu Wangpan (cloud storage), and Baidu Baike (online encyclopedia).[22] Baidu used to be as highly esteemed as Alibaba and Tencent, but lost its shine because it failed to introduce good mobile services, and it was boycotted after a cancer patient died as a result of advertised medical treatment o Baidu.[23]

Alibaba is listed on the New York Stock Exchange, where its market capitalization passed $500 billion in January 2018.[24] In valuation, Alibaba leaves companies like Boeing or McDonald's far behind. For some time in 2018 and 2019 founder Jack Ma was the richest person in China.[25] His story is legendary in China, because he started his business as a former English teacher in a Hangzhou apartment as recently as 1999.[26]

Alibaba operates various platforms, including online retail (Tmall and TaoBao), payment services (Alipay), B2B web portals (Alibaba.com, 1688.com) and cloud computing (Aliyun).[27] At the pace these internet companies are growing, it's always hard to keep up with relevant data, but in 2018 in terms of Gross Merchandise Value (GMV) Alibaba dwarfs Amazon with $768 billion versus $239 billion.[28] In the same year, Alibaba had more than 650 million active shoppers on its e-commerce platforms,[29] compared to Amazon's 310 million.[30] Looking at these numbers, Alibaba is by far the world's largest e-commerce company.

After its 1998 founding in Shenzhen, Tencent was in 2017 the first Asian company to top $500 billion in value.[31] The company offers just about everything, including mobile gaming, software development, e-commerce, and instant messaging. It is known for QQ, a desktop messaging service, and even more for WeChat, which started as a Chinese answer to WhatsApp, but has now morphed into something much bigger. Explaining WeChat to Westerners, I invariably say: "Oh, it's like WhatsApp—only better!" China's most common use of the internet is for entertainment purposes, and Tencent generates a large part of its income from online gaming.[32] The Chinese gambling sector topped the global ranking with revenue of $40 billion in 2040, just a bit more than the runner up, the United States.[33]

WeChat

We cannot discuss the Chinese internet without mentioning the absolute killer app, WeChat, which Tencent launched in 2011 for mobile messaging, and which has rapidly become a global sensation.[34] To claim that China and the Chinese economy can no longer do without WeChat is no exaggeration. In mid-2020 WeChat had 1.2 billion users worldwide, and it's still growing.[35] It's one of the largest online communities in the world, like Facebook, YouTube, WhatsApp, and QQ, like other Tencent products. But WeChat's big difference from its competitors is that it's like a multi-purpose Swiss knife. Aside from being a tool for communication, it is among others as a social network and a booking and online payment system. In other words, WeChat combines Twitter, WhatsApp, Facebook, Paypal and more, providing a vast variety of functions. Almost everything is possible via WeChat. Users can communicate through free messages and phone calls; they can also play games, order meal deliveries, book taxis or ride-sharing cars, buy train, flight, or movie tickets, shop online, top up phone or bank balances, pay utility bills, donate to charities, and on and on—paying for everything with the app. WeChat has successfully harnessed the increasing popularity of integrated services, where one smartphone app leaves modern consumers with everything at their disposal. Friends who dine together will routinely book the restaurant and the taxi via WeChat, and can also pay each other back on the app (there's even a bill-splitting service for those who want to go Dutch). Already during the Chinese New Year period of 2016, WeChat started to handle more payments than PayPal in a whole year.[36] The red holiday gift envelopes, or *hong bao*, that families traditionally exchange in person could from then on be transferred over WeChat also.

WeChat is also the preferred communication tool in the business world. In the past, potential business contacts exchanged cards; today, they just scan QR codes and add each other as WeChat friends. I know from my own experience that even contracts and nondisclosure agreements are being sent by WeChat instead of e-mail. Anyone who doesn't use WeChat barely exists in China. WeChat also illustrates that in terms of digital innovation, Chinese companies have taken the lead over their Western competitors. The CEO of Facebook, Mark Zuckerberg, understands WeChat's value and influence. With Facebook planning to transform into a platform focused on private messaging, Zuckerberg admitted he should have listened to earlier advice about learning from WeChat.[37] Facebook's chances of success in China are limited, not because it is blocked—as is assumed as the only reason in the West—but because it is seen as old-fashioned and uninteresting.

China also plays a pioneering role in other areas of social media. There are an enormous number of sophisticated social media channels that have developed rapidly and in unique ways to become the best the internet has to offer. The Great Firewall has protected them from Western competitors, which means they could focus on adapting to the local market. Most Chinese social media sites are much larger than those in the Western world. The microblogging site Sina Weibo, for instance, with its more than 500 million users in 2019, is almost twice as large as Twitter.[38] Toutiao, a news and information content platform powered by artificial intelligence, is an upcoming giant. By mid-2020, it had already more than 270 million monthly active users.[39] The controversial Douyin, a platform for short videos, known as TikTok in the West, is arguably the first Chinese app with a global user base. In 2020 it had grown to 800 million active users worldwide (150 million in China) and is nowadays perhaps the most discussed social media app in the world.[40]

Chinese social media users are also the world's most active, with social networking and social media penetration hitting 87.2 percent in 2018. Compared to those in other countries, Chinese users are more active and have more accounts—an average of 2.65 per person—where they can engage in instant communication or public discussions, read blogs, view short videos, and so on.[41] I have seen for myself that daily international news or events are shared and commented on more quickly on Chinese social media sites than on their Western equivalents. When something happens in the Western world, my wife often knows the details before I do. News is being spread and discussed so quickly that official news follows the social media, not vice versa.

Window to the World

The main reason why social media are so immensely popular is actually a direct consequence of government control. Because Chinese citizens are highly critical of state-controlled media, social media are an ideal platform to share news. Despite censorship, the information exchange happens so quickly that checking content isn't always a watertight process. The growing individualism of the population also plays an important role. Parents are traditionally deeply involved in their children's lives, while in the small apartments and densely populated cities, privacy can be hard to find. Social media offer a new channel to millions of Chinese citizens who were never supposed to reveal their feelings and personal ideas. Now they use social media for unabashed and virtually unrestrained expressions of their individual opinions and feelings about a wide range of facts and events. The internet provided a new sense of community for Chinese citizens, most of whom lacked robust civil-society organizations. In addition, the government also left some room for criticism via social media. Officials realize that times have changed and the general population needs a certain outlet. Simply put: as long as there is no organized movement that poses an actual (or perceived) threat to those in power, criticism is permitted.

Microblogs such as Sina Weibo don't just offer the public a new channel to voice their opinions, they started to serve as a platform for complaints and expressing daily concerns. Heated social problems such as the various food scandals, persistent environmental pollution, and corruption receive extensive comments. When in 2011, a Chinese producer of air purifiers hinted in advertisements that many of its customers were government officials, a wave of criticism erupted on various blogging sites.[42]

In the same year, a high-speed train derailed in the coastal city of Wenzhou, killing 40 people and injuring 172. Government officials banned journalists from investigating, directing them to use only the official information. But when local residents photographed workers burying the wreckage instead of examining it for evidence, the photos went viral and angry online voices accused the government of hiding the truth, not seeking the cause. As a result, an official investigation ensued that led to at least fifty-four officials facing disciplinary action.[43]

Officials who violate rules or don't exhibit exemplary behavior are also publicly criticized on social media. As a result of President Xi Jinping's anti-corruption campaign, which encourages citizens to take pictures of officials enjoying overly luxurious banquets or behaving inappropriately, many authorities truly fear the power of social media.

But while the Chinese people explored diverse ways to use the internet, the leadership began to develop a taste for the powers it offered, such as a better understanding of citizens' concerns and new ways to shape public opinion. Yet as the internet increasingly became a vehicle for dissenting voices, government control increased. President Xi Jinping may embrace the social media that liveblog his visits and other videos, but since his presidency started in 2012, there has been a palpable determination for authorities to move beyond deleting posts and passing regulations. Not only politically but also socially, there is more control. In 2014, WeChat was forced to close twenty million accounts involved with prostitution.[44] And in 2019 Freedom's House annual global assessment of internet freedom, identified the Chinese government as the worst student in the class.[45]

But despite this censorship and control, it's undeniable that the internet has given Chinese citizens a greater window on the world. Not only is China integrating more fully into the global economy, but its citizens now also possess the technological means to gain instant access to the world around them. They are quickly becoming global citizens, and often know much more about the Western world than the West knows about them. In addition to Chinese superstars, who often have tens of millions of followers, international celebrities are being followed as well. Consumers in all corners of the country go online to search for the latest fashions in Europe, compare bargains on Amazon with the various Alibaba platforms, and book cheap airline tickets for their international trips. The internet's rapid development created a more demanding Chinese consumer, who is willing to pay more for better quality and spend more time comparison shopping. Because foreign products in China still often fetch premium prices, and because the fear remains that buyers will purchase counterfeit goods instead of genuine articles, consumers buy more and more products that are directly shipped from abroad to their homes in China. China is still a society that requires trust to be *earned*, which makes word-of-mouth advertising or peer references more important than they are in the West. For consumers, obtaining information and the advice of friends and family members is crucial when buying something. This also explains the enormous popularity of social media and chat rooms, channels that companies need to take very seriously when selling in China.

E-Commerce

For the Chinese consumer the world has become one big marketplace. Nearly 75 percent of China's 850 million internet users shop online.[46] Shoppers placing orders one day can receive them the next—or sometimes even later that afternoon. This makes China the world's largest e-commerce market. In 2019 China contributed more than half to the global $3.5 trillion e-commerce market.[47] The same year online retail sales in China totaled more than 34 percent of total retail sales which is three times as big as the U.S. market where online sales accounts for 11 percent.[48] As mentioned this is mainly thanks to Alibaba and its affiliates, which almost singlehandedly developed the e-commerce market from virtually nonexistent fifteen years ago into the world's largest today. Alibaba's U.S. IPO has also changed the international landscape and created two e-commerce poles: Alibaba in China and Amazon in the United States.

The power of the Chinese consumer and the e-commerce market is demonstrated dramatically every November 11, known as Double 11 (referring to month and day) or Singles' Day. This was started in 1993 as an anti-Valentine's Day, a celebration of singledom, and a salute to China's serious male gender imbalance. After being adopted by Alibaba in 2009, it has become a national online shopping frenzy, when just about everything can be obtained at a discount (Chinese characters have strong visual significance; Double 11's four upright lines are thought reminiscent of single people).[49] During the 2020 Double 11—which now stretches actually over a 11-day period—online sales totaled $115 billion USD. The various Alibaba platforms alone generated a turnover of over $74 billion,[50] which dwarfs the totals for the U.S. shopping days Black Friday, Cyber Monday, Thanksgiving Day, Amazon Prime Day, the Wednesday before Thanksgiving, and the U.S. Singles' Day combined.[51]

The reason for the success of Chinese e-commerce is directly related to the great diversity within China. After all, e-commerce can reach consumers that live anywhere, and these may have very different wants and needs, depending on their disposable income. The growth of e-commerce shuttered many brick-and-mortar stores, like my wife's, and created a totally new form of consumer behavior. Consumers compare more thoroughly than they did before, they wait for discounts before making their purchases, and have become champions of showrooming: they look at products in a store but buy them online via their smartphones, often just a few minutes later. This "new retail" as a means to blend online and offline shopping experiences and integrate more technology into each stage of the retail supply chain, has become, even more so than in the West, crucial for the Chinese retail market. That's also the reason why e-commerce giants like Alibaba and JD.Com have opened brick-and-mortar stores too. At the same time there is a lot of vertical integration going on with expansion into smart production and supply chains which in return create more efficiencies. Also the use of livestream hosts and bloggers has become critical to generate sales.

Digital advertising has reached new heights. In 2018, spending on digital advertising in China reached $65.4 billion—approximately 23.1 percent of the global total.[52] Harnessing the power of China's media influencers is key for both Chinese and foreign brands. Social media influencers, known as *wanghong*, are likewise being used to appeal to audiences. In 2017 for instance, Burberry collaborated with influential Chinese fashion blogger Mr. Bags to sell a limited-edition bag on Wechat, which sold out within ten minutes.[53]

In the field of New Retail, China is an absolute forerunner. The first Amazon Go store opened to the public in 2018, but three years earlier Alibaba opened its first Hema supermarket in China.[54] In 2020 there were more than 320 Hema stores, and Alibaba plans to have 2000 across China[55] (for comparison, in the same year there were 26 Amazon Go stores).[56] The Hema stores are a cashless fine-dining supermarket chain which combines e-commerce, restaurant—like fresh seafood to be cooked and consumed inside—supermarket and distribution center. Customers can stroll around the store, smartphone in hand, select products of choice and have them conveniently delivered in half an hour within a 3-mile radius. We sometimes go there for lunch, and my wife uses their app regularly and orders almost everything online to get it delivered at home. Chinese streets are also packed with the delivery couriers on their e-scooters racing through narrow alleys to deliver meals, groceries, or packages ordered online. I have had more than one close call nearly colliding with a delivery person's scooter. In 2018, more than fifty billion packages were delivered in China, accounting half of the world's total.[57] The online food delivery services market alone—basically controlled by Meituan Dianping—was in 2017 worth around $37 billion.[58] This, of course, is adding to China's environmental concerns, and the impact of this business on the environment is one of the most hotly debated issues of late.

Meanwhile, official statistics state that 98 percent of China's internet users are actually mobile users—they go online using smartphones or tablets.[59] Unlike in Western countries, where people first experienced the internet on a PC, Chinese consumers—especially those born after 1985—switched to smartphones much faster. This also explains China's enormous sales of smartphones. Until ten years ago, it was rare to see a smartphone on the street. Today, there are more than 700 million smartphone users which in 2019 bought 366 million smartphones. Globally one in four smartphones is being sold in China, which makes China already since 2012 the biggest smartphone market.[60] To lift domestic integration even higher, the Chinese government had set the goal of having a billion people using the mobile internet in a few years. Even my in-laws, at their respectable age, now use their smartphones as if they were tech-savvy children.

Not surprisingly, China is also the world's largest producer of smartphones. This means that Chinese tech companies focus much more on hardware, software, and services for smartphone users than they do for PC users. In modern China, the smartphone is indispensable for daily life. Social media have gone completely mobile, as have shopping, services, payments, and communication. Now that more than 80 percent of all online purchases take place over a mobile device, China has become the first "mobile-first" commerce nation globally.[61] Because of ever-improving network coverage in the Chinese countryside and increasingly 5G connections, the future of mobile shopping looks brilliant. My wife and her friends now use only their smartphones. Computers have been discarded.

And also here foreign smartphone manufacturers are losing against local competitors, As of mid-2019, Huawei held a 36 percent share of the market, while other Chinese companies Vivo, Oppo, and Xiaomi combined for another 50 percent. The top foreign player is Apple with around a six percent share.[62]

Chinese customers don't think in terms of online or offline; for them, the model is mixed. Companies that don't respond to these trends risk losing out. Moviegoers now mostly buy their tickets online, for example. Additional services, such as booking seats, using GPS, and receiving detailed information about nearby restaurants and parking, are offered. It's worth noting that for most people these additional services are not considered add-ons, but the bare minimum. The British luxury retailer Burberry offers customers the opportunity to surf its website in-store. There are digital mirrors and touchpoints available allowing customers to share their experiences instantly on social media. Faster internet and websites that adapted to mobile shopping also enable new forms of mobile payment.

So also in terms of online payments, China is booming like no other country. It also dwarfs the United States completely. And different than other countries the use of credit card in China is sporadic. In 2019 about

81 percent of smartphone users in China will use mobile payments this year, compared to just 27 percent in the United States.[63]

The Chinese mobile payment market is dominated by two players, Alipay and WeChat. Because of its connection to Alibaba, Alipay has evolved from a payment system into a one-stop portal for payment solutions, which is also the main reason why it's much more advanced than PayPal, for instance. In addition to online shopping and payments, Alipay users can also transfer money via the system and pay bills, consult bank balances, make investments, and change money, all via their smartphones. Alipay offers these services in a very integrated and user-friendly way, making all transactions possible with one click. Jack Ma's Alipay is significantly more advanced than anything else globally available. In mid-2020, Alibaba's Alipay had 1,3 billion annual active users worldwide. It processes $17 trillion worth of transactions in one year[64] which is an astonishing 25 times more than PayPal.[65] Both WeChat and Alipay record the staggering amount of about 700 million transactions per day.[66] China has simply become an almost cashless society, something that I actually enjoy very much.

In recent years, the Chinese internet has become more politicized and more restrictive. From the government's perspective, the mobile internet's rapid expansion offers tremendous advantages in terms of governance. That's also why it's not unlikely that China will become the first officially cashless society. If everything is being done by smartphone, the government can obtain almost a complete digital overview of every citizen's travel habits, conversations, purchases, and so on. But to Chinese netizens, the trade-off is worth it.

Notes

1. *Chinadaily*. 2006. China internet users hit 111 million in 2005. https://www.chinadaily.com.cn/english/doc/2006-01/18/content_513396.htm. Accessed February 3, 2019.
2. Visual Capitalist. 2020. Which countries have the most internet users? https://www.visualcapitalist.com/countries-with-most-internet-users. Accessed December 24, 2020.
3. World Economic Forum. 2019. Most people on the internet live in this country. www.weforum.org/agenda/2019/06/most-people-on-the-internet-live-in-this-country. Accessed October 4, 2020.

4. Visual Capitalist. 2020. Which countries have the most internet users? https://www.visualcapitalist.com/countries-with-most-internet-users. Accessed December 24, 2020.
5. *The New York Times*. How China walled off the internet. 2018. www.nytimes.com/interactive/2018/11/18/world/asia/china-internet.html. Accessed March 12, 2019.
6. Hoover Institution. 2018. How Chinese authorities and individuals use the internet. www.hoover.org/research/how-chinese-authorities-and-individuals-use-internet. Accessed February 2, 2019.
7. *The Guardian*. 2018. The great firewall of China: Xi Jinping's internet shutdown. www.theguardian.com/news/2018/jun/29/the-great-firewall-of-china-xi-jinpings-internet-shutdown. Accessed March 21, 2020.
8. *The Guardian*. 2018. The great firewall of China: Xi Jinping's internet shutdown. www.theguardian.com/news/2018/jun/29/the-great-firewall-of-china-xi-jinpings-internet-shutdown. Accessed March 21, 2020.
9. *The Guardian*. 2010. How Google censors its results in China. www.theguardian.com/technology/2010/jan/13/how-google-censors-china. Accessed April 2, 2019.
10. *The Guardian*. 2018. The great firewall of China: Xi Jinping's internet shutdown. www.theguardian.com/news/2018/jun/29/the-great-firewall-of-china-xi-jinpings-internet-shutdown. Accessed March 21, 2020.
11. *Newsroom*. 2019. China's censors block Newsroom.co.nz www.newsroom.co.nz/2019/06/12/630727/china-blocks-newsroomconz. Accessed March 3, 2020.
12. *Wired*. 2019. US companies help censor the internet in China, too. www.wired.com/story/us-companies-help-censor-internet-china. Accessed April 5, 2020.
13. *The Guardian*. 2012. New York Times blocked by China after report on wealth of Wen Jiabao's family. www.theguardian.com/world/2012/oct/26/new-york-times-china-wen-jiabao. Accessed May 23, 2019.
14. TechNadu. 2020. How to use a VPN in China without breaking the law. www.technadu.com/how-to-use-vpns-in-china-without-breaking-the-law/18492. Accessed January 1, 2021.
15. Center for Strategic and International Studies. 2020. Who benefits from China's cybersecurity laws? www.csis.org/blogs/new-perspectives-asia/who-benefits-chinas-cybersecurity-laws. Accessed December 4, 2020.
16. TheStreet. 2019. Chinese tech firms are increasingly being copied by U.S., not just copying. https://www.thestreet.com/technology/china-not-the-world-s-tech-copycat-anymore-14636273. Accessed November 4, 2020.
17. Forbes. 2016. Three lessons from Uber's defeat in China. www.forbes.com/sites/helenwang/2016/08/12/3-lessons-from-ubers-defeat-in-china/#2a26fe9a69cb. Accessed April 4, 2019.

18. *Wired*. 2018. Didi Chuxing took on Uber and won. Now it's taking on the world. www.wired.co.uk/article/didi-chuxing-china-startups-uber. Accessed March 2, 2019.
19. U.S. News. 2020. The most valuable tech companies in the world. https://money.usnews.com/investing/stock-market-news/slideshows/most-valuable-tech-companies-in-the-world. Accessed December 23, 2020.
20. *The Wall Street Journal*. 2015. Kingmakers of China's internet: Baidu, Alibaba and Tencent. www.wsj.com/articles/kingmakers-of-chinas-internet-baidu-alibaba-and-tencent-1445451143. Accessed November 4, 2019.
21. Gadgets Now. 2020. 10 most popular websites in the world. www.gadgetsnow.com/slideshows/10-most-popular-websites-in-the-world/baidu/photolist/74077561.cms. Accessed April 10, 2020.
22. *Website Magazine*. 2020. Baidu vs. Google: A comparison. www.websitemagazine.com/blog/baidu-vs-google-a-comparison. Accessed January 2, 2021.
23. Quartz. 2019. China's favorite food delivery service is now worth more than its biggest internet search firm. https://qz.com/1648807/bat-no-more-meituan-dianping-is-now-worth-more-than-baidu/. Accessed April 5, 2020.
24. *South China Morning Post*. 2018. Alibaba joins Tencent in the exclusive US$500 billion market value club. www.scmp.com/business/companies/article/2130497/alibaba-joins-tencent-exclusive-us500-billion-market-value-club. Accessed November 3, 2019.
25. Business Insider. 2019. Alibaba cofounder Jac Ma is the richest man in China—Here's how he spends his $38 billion net worth. https://www.businessinsider.com/how-alibaba-founder-jack-ma-makes-and-spends-his-billions-2019-11?r=DE&IR=T. Accessed May 5, 2020.
26. Alibaba Group. 2020. History. www.alibabagroup.com/en/about/history. Accessed December 5, 2020.
27. Investopedia. 2020. Who are Alibaba's main competitors? www.investopedia.com/articles/markets/042716/baba-who-are-alibabas-main-competitors.asp. Accessed May 21, 2020.
28. *Jing Daily*. 2019. Amazon vs. Alibaba: Everything you need to know about the two biggest e-tailers. https://jingdaily.com/amazon-vs-alibaba-everything-you-need-to-know-about-the-two-biggest-e-tailers. Accessed October 19, 2020.
29. Business Insider. 2019. Alibaba, the $435 billion Chinese shopping giant, is gunning for Amazon in Europe. www.businessinsider.com/alibaba-is-gunning-for-amazon-in-europe-2019-8?r=DE&IR=T. Accessed June 3, 2020.

30. nChannel. 2019. Amazon statistics. www.nchannel.com/blog/amazon-statistics. Accessed November 4, 2020.
31. *South China Morning Post*. Tencent is first Asian company to top US$500 billion in value, joining Apple and Facebook. www.scmp.com/business/companies/article/2120712/tencent-breaches-us500b-valuation-shares-rally-above-hk41460. Accessed December 12, 2020.
32. CNBC. 2019. Tencent profit beats market as analysts predict stock will climb back above $500 billion in value. www.cnbc.com/2019/08/14/tencent-earnings-preview-gaming-wechat-pay-to-drive-profits.html. Accessed January 4, 2020.
33. Newzoo. 2020. Top 10 countries/markets by game revenues. http://newzoo.com/insights/rankings/top-10-countries-by-game-revenues. Accessed March 11, 2020.
34. Techinasia. 2018 History of WeChat. www.techinasia.com/history-of-wechat. Accessed August 5, 2020.
35. *South China Morning Post*. 2020. weChat now has over 1.2 billion users worldwide. www.scmp.com/abacus/news-bites/article/3084358/wechat-now-has-over-12-billion-users-worldwide. Accessed December 5, 2020.
36. The Drum. 2016. WeChat had more mobile transactions over just Chinese New Year than PayPal had during 2015. www.thedrum.com/news/2016/02/09/wechat-had-more-mobile-transactions-over-just-chinese-new-year-paypal-had-during. Accessed January 21, 2019.
37. *South China Morning Post*. 2019. Mark Zuckerberg says he should have listened to earlier advice about learning from WeChat. www.scmp.com/tech/apps-social/article/2189449/mark-zuckerberg-says-he-should-have-listened-earlier-advice-about. Accessed March 20, 2020.
38. Impact of Social Sciences. 2020. Weibo—How is China's second largest social media platform being used for social research? https://blogs.lse.ac.uk/impactofsocialsciences/2020/03/26/weibo-how-is-chinas-second-largest-social-media-platform-being-used-for-social-research/. Accessed December 5, 2020.
39. Statista. Number of monthly active users (MAU) of the leading news apps in China as of March 2020. https://www.statista.com/statistics/910787/china-monthly-active-users-on-leading-news-apps/. Accessed May 31, 2020.
40. Oberlo. 2020. 10 TikTok statistics you need to know. www.oberlo.com/blog/tiktok-statistics#:~:text=TikTok%20was%20launched%20in%20September,worldwide%20(Datareportal%2C%202020. Accessed November 1, 2020.

41. Ecommerce Strategy China. 2019. Insights into China's social medial networks 2019. www.ecommercestrategychina.com/column/insights-into-chinas-social-media-networks-2019. Accessed December 4, 2020.
42. *The New York Times*. 2011. The privileges of China's elite included purified air. www.nytimes.com/2011/11/05/world/asia/the-privileges-of-chinas-elite-include-purified-air.html.
43. *The Guardian*. 2018. The great firewall of China: Xi Jinping's internet shutdown. www.theguardian.com/news/2018/jun/29/the-great-firewall-of-china-xi-jinpings-internet-shutdown. Accessed March 27, 2020.
44. *Time Magazine*. 2014. 20 million Chinese WeChat accounts closed for links to prostitution. http://time.com/2851900/china-wechat-prostitution. Accessed November 4, 2020.
45. *The Diplomat*. 2019. China's internet freedom hit a new low in 2019, and the world could follow. https://thediplomat.com/2019/11/chinas-internet-freedom-hit-a-new-low-in-2019-and-the-world-could-follow/. Accessed March 3, 2020.
46. Chinadaily Hong Kong. 2019. Number of online shoppers in China hits 610 million. www.chinadailyhk.com/articles/62/250/44/1551506282401.html. Accessed February 4, 2020.
47. Alizila. 2019. China is world leader in e-commerce, new retail innovation: emarketer. https://www.alizila.com/china-is-world-leader-in-ecommerce-new-retail-innovation-emarketer/. Accessed July 1, 2020.
48. Business Insider. 2020. Retail sales will drop 5.7% this year because of the pandemic. www.businessinsider.com/worldwide-retail-sales-will-drop-due-to-pandemic-2020-6?r=DE&IR=T. Accessed December 23, 2020.
49. Medium. 2018. A history of Alibaba's double-eleven singles day. https://medium.com/@chewweichun/a-history-of-alibabas-double-eleven-singles-day-775b7108af. Accessed June, 24, 2019.
50. CNBC. 2020. Alibaba, JD set new records to rack up record $115 billion of sales on Singles Day as regulations loom. www.cnbc.com/2020/11/12/singles-day-2020-alibaba-and-jd-rack-up-record-115-billion-of-sales.html. Accessed December 23, 2020.
51. Business Insider. 2018. Black Friday and Cyber Monday set records—But compared, they still only made up half of Alibaba's Singles Day online sales. www.businessinsider.com/black-friday-cyber-monday-vs-singles-day-sales-2018-12. Accessed April 4, 2019.
52. ChinaPower. 2020. How dominant are Chinese companies globally? https://chinapower.csis.org/chinese-companies-global-500/. Accessed January 5, 2021.
53. ChinaPower. 2020. How dominant are Chinese companies globally? https://chinapower.csis.org/chinese-companies-global-500/. Accessed January 5, 2021.

54. Indigo Digital. 2019. The future of retail: 9 ways Alibaba is redefining retail stores. www.indigo9digital.com/blog/futureofretailalibaba. Accessed September 4, 2020.
55. Chemlinked. 2020. A look into Alibaba new retail wonder Hema Xiansheng's expansion in China. https://market.chemlinked.com/industry/a-look-into-alibaba-new-retail-wonder-hema-xianshengs-expansion-in-china#:~:text=Alibaba%20"New%20Retail"%20store%2C,consumers%20with%20higher%20spending%20power. Accessed December 23, 2020.
56. Grocerydive. 2020. Amazon plans more Go Grocery stores. www.grocerydive.com/news/amazon-plans-more-go-grocery-stores/581046/. Accessed December 5, 2020.
57. Xinhuanet. 2019. How can China deliver 50 billion packages every year? www.xinhuanet.com/english/2019-09/17/c_138397454.htm. Accessed September 3, 2020.
58. *South China Morning Post*. 2017. Dinner at your door: inside China's US$37 billion online food delivery services market. www.scmp.com/business/companies/article/2111163/dinner-your-door-inside-chinas-us37-billion-online-food-delivery. Accessed March 4, 2020.
59. Forbes. 2018. China now boasts more than 800 million internet users and 98% of them are mobile (infographic). www.forbes.com/sites/niallmccarthy/2018/08/23/china-now-boasts-more-than-800-million-internet-users-and-98-of-them-are-mobile-infographic. Accessed December 3, 2020.
60. Statista. 2020. Smartphone market in China—Statistics & facts. https://www.statista.com/topics/1416/smartphone-market-in-china/#:~:text=In%202019%2C%20smartphone%20shipments%20in,volume%20of%20global%20smartphone%20shipments. Accessed December 3, 2020.
61. Alizila. 2019. China is world leader in e-commerce, new retail innovation: emarketer. https://www.alizila.com/china-is-world-leader-in-ecommerce-new-retail-innovation-emarketer/. Accessed July 3, 2020.
62. ChinaPower. 2020. How dominant are Chinese companies globally? https://chinapower.csis.org/chinese-companies-global-500/. Accessed January 5, 2021.
63. Alizila. 2019. China is world leader in e-commerce, new retail innovation: emarketer. https://www.alizila.com/china-is-world-leader-in-ecommerce-new-retail-innovation-emarketer/. Accessed July 9, 2020.
64. China Internet Watch. 2020. Alipay. www.chinainternetwatch.com/tag/alipay/#:~:text=It%20has%20more%20than%201.3,than%202%2C000%20partner%20financial%20institutions. Accessed December 31, 2020.
65. Statista. 2020. PayPal's annual payment volume from 2012 to 2019. www.statista.com/statistics/419783/paypals-annual-payment-volume/. Accessed December 4, 2020.

66. Third Bridge. 2020. China's 2020 digital payment industry—WeChat Pay vs Alipay. www.thirdbridge.com/chinas-2020-digital-payment-industry-wechat-pay-vs-alipay/. Accessed December 23, 2020.

CHAPTER 8

Made in China 2.0 and Beyond

In November 2014, I was on a business trip in the historic city of Hangzhou, a two-hour train ride away from Shanghai. A former dynastic capital of China, the city is known for the scenic beauty of West Lake and its many ancient sites. Marco Polo called it "beyond dispute the finest and the noblest city in the world,[1]" and it now hosts millions of tourists annually.

Hangzhou is also now the headquarters of the Alibaba group, and, being in the neighborhood, I wandered inside the building. I was stunned. Silicon Valley culture was evident everywhere. Young entrepreneurs were walking around in sneakers and jeans, start-ups of all sizes had offices in the building, and ping-pong tables and treadmills were everywhere. There were even special rooms to hold parties.

Alibaba's headquarters are similar to Googleplex or Yahoo's Sunnyvale Campus, modern buildings fully equipped with the latest gadgets. The success of Alibaba gave birth to a whole tech ecosystem and network of start-ups and software companies in Hangzhou, which now revolves around the high-tech sector. In the past, the city housed small and medium-sized enterprises that focused on exports. Now there are venture capital firms, high-tech and software centers, and companies that focus on big data, virtual reality, and artificial intelligence. Hundreds of technology companies now call the city home, including Didi Chuxing.

S. Agten, *Adventures in the Chinese Economy: 16 Years from the Inside*,
https://doi.org/10.1007/978-981-16-1167-4_8

In the past, Hangzhou's young graduates wanted to work for state-owned companies or foreign multinationals; today, they go job-hunting at technology firms. The story goes that Hangzhou women used to seek potential husbands at the local steel giant, Hanggang, but today are looking for someone who earns his living at Alibaba.

Investment in R&D

Alibaba, Tencent, Baidu, Ant Financial, Didi, JD.com, Xiaomi, Meituan Dianping, and other Chinese tech companies with multi-billion dollar valuations have emerged as new economic and tech giants, and some of them are starting to conquer the world with new products and superior services.

The main reason why these companies have become market leaders is their dedication to innovation through research and development (R&D). China's economy is increasingly focused on technology, which will have an immeasurable impact on the global economy. This trend has been going on for years now. In 2014 already, a survey of foreign executives found that two-thirds of them regarded their Chinese competitors as equally or even more innovative.[2]

Chinese companies used to be called "fast followers": they copied foreign products and adapted them to the Chinese market. In recent years, however, they have embarked on the path of innovation. In some sectors, real innovation comes almost entirely from China. The country is now reaping the benefits of investments in the past and from a long-term policy that prioritized scientific and technological development after the country's current economic liberalism got under way. Like almost everything else in China, big government is the catalyst for this focus on innovation.

China's investment in R&D and innovation was prompted by the changing economic situation. Since its opening up, China has become the world's factory and developed a huge manufacturing capacity, producing nearly all conceivable goods on razor-thin margins. As noted earlier, cheap labor, raw materials, unused land, and flexible environmental laws were the country's main competitive advantages. Based on these, in only four decades, China rose to become the world's second biggest economy, ranking just behind the United States. Now, however, prices are rising for materials and labor. Moreover, the government is cracking down on environmental abuses, and breaking China's laws has consequences.

In order to remain globally competitive, China has had to develop a domestic R&D sector, making science and technology an integral part of its economic growth. Being successful in China is one thing; becoming a global player is reserved only for companies that can offer real added value.

China simply wants to evolve from "Made in China" to "Designed in China," from imitation and production to innovation. This is a natural course in any country's economic development. It was the path followed by Japan in the 1980s and South Korea in the 1990s. And the broad generalizations about copying and innovation that the West makes about China today were once leveled at Japan and Korea. The difference is that China is innovating at a much faster rate. This is partly because a lot of innovation is technological, which by its nature moves faster, but more so because the country has been better integrated into the global economy thanks to its high volume of investment and its gigantic domestic market. The Chinese government sees innovation as a long-term strategy that guarantees that the country can maintain its political and social stability, as well as its position as a global economic superpower.

Decades-long investment in education are paying off also. Despite continuing problems as described in a previous chapter, in 2016, almost five million Chinese university students graduated from the STEM (Science, Technology, Engineering, and Mathematics) fields.[3]

Chinese engineers and scientists are in demand at both domestic and international tech companies. The quality of the top universities has also improved enormously, with some competing with the best universities in the West. In its 2017 global rankings, *U.S. News & World Report* listed Tsinghua University in Beijing, called the Chinese MIT, as the world's best school for engineering and computer sciences.[4] And prestigious Chinese universities are spreading their influence worldwide. More and more Chinese researchers are publishing in international scientific journals: in 2016 for instance China overtook the United States as the number one publisher of scientific publications.[5]

Beyond offering high-quality education, however, top Chinese universities have dramatically increased their research budgets and stepped up collaborations with foreign universities. Foreign institutions once hesitated to accept Chinese students, fearing theft of intellectual property and espionage, but despite what often is reported in the media, today this should be less of a concern—partly because these Chinese universities often rank as high or higher than do their foreign counterparts.

Open innovation is also on the rise, with companies and universities eager to work together. In fact, it's often foreign universities and multinationals that spearheaded these collaborative arrangements to gain greater access to new talent and research. Examples are numerous. In 2016, for instance, Tsinghua University and the University of Washington—with a $40 million donation from Microsoft—opened the Global Innovation Exchange, a new technological campus located in Washington State and set to be a catalyst for innovation.[6]

China's spending on R&D totaled $33 billion in the year 2000, which had grown to $468 billion by 2018, an annual average increase of 17 percent, while U.S. average spending on scientific R&D grew 4.3 percent a year during roughly the same period.[7] In 2018, the United States spent $582 billion on R&D[8] and was still the undisputed leader in this, but runner-up China is closing the gap rapidly.

China's Thousand Talents Plan, launched in 2008 provides benefits and start-up packages in order recruit high-level Chinese scientists and experts educated or residing overseas and lure them back to China.[9] And that this strategy works, I can prove myself. One of my best friends in Shanghai is Dr. Jing wu Zang got his Ph.D. abroad, returned to China in 2012 under the Thousand Talents Plan scheme. In 2016 he founded the now Nasdaq listed biotech I-Mab Biopharma, of which he is still the Chairman. In just four short years he made the company into a Chinese clinical stage company with a globally competitive pipeline, which at the end of 2020 valued more than $3 billion.

Need for Innovation

Innovation is driven not only by government efforts and enormous funding, but by fierce competition selling to the growing Chinese middle class. Companies realize that only innovation can lock in new customers for them. In the domestic market, Chinese companies compete with Western companies to lure consumers away with products of equal or better quality. Chinese consumers have also become more sophisticated. Western products still enjoy high status, but design and functionality have become more important than ever. Consumers are also looking for a variety of alternatives and enhanced quality. Combined with ever-improving domestic technology, this trend creates a lot of room for development and growth, not only within China but also abroad. Long-term investments in R&D are not merely worthwhile for many companies.

China has gone from being a market too big to ignore to one in which companies must innovate constantly if they are to survive.

PwC's 2018 'Global Innovation Study' found that 145 Chinese companies were among the top 1000 R&D spenders in the world, a considerable jump from just 25 companies in 2012.[10]

Many pragmatic Chinese CEOs are personally dedicated to innovation. Once, the impetus came from the government; today, business leaders recognize that innovation is the key to long-term success. Furthermore innovation is thriving as never before in the private sector in China. Some jewels have emerged. Lenovo, the world's largest PC producer and a major manufacturer of smartphones, has a total of 46 laboratories and research centers across China, Japan, and the United States.[11] Huawei has increased its annual R&D budget from $480 million in 2004[12] to $19.3 billion in 2019,[13] a 40-fold increase in just 15 years. Compared to a handful of workers in 2005, Huawei's campus in Shenzhen now employs more than 30,000 employees.[14] And the investment paid off—as of 2019, the company held more than 85,000 patents worldwide.[15]

In 1995, BYD or "Build Your Dreams" was a battery producer with 20 workers[16]; today, the group produces hybrid and electric cars using an exclusive battery technology. A pioneer in electric vehicles and leader in energy storage, the company employs more than 220,000 people[17] and was in 2019 the world's second biggest electrical vehicle producer.[18] The company, which is 25 percent owned by super-investor Warren Buffett[19] also developed the world's first electric bus. Between 2010 and 2019, BYD sold 50,000 buses in three hundred cities worldwide.[20]

Foreign companies are increasingly aware of China's R&D capabilities. In the 2005 PricewaterhouseCoopers Strategy's annual Global Innovation 1000 Study, there were only eight Chinese companies. In 2014 there were already 114.[21] In 2009 of the Fortune 500 companies worldwide, over 400 had launched R&D centers in China.[22] Four years later Multinationals operated more than 1600 R&D centers in China.[23]

Most foreign companies investing in R&D in China are not looking only to integrate the local facilities into their global ecosystem, they also want to adapt their products more smoothly to the local market; being "in China, for China" has become more important than ever. Some companies also develop products and services in China and roll them out globally later. For instance, Airbus's opened its second global innovation center in Shenzhen in 2019. That makes complete sense because in 2018 more than 20 percent of Airbus commercial aircraft entered Chinese market which at that time was served by 1700 Airbus aircraft.[24]

Chinese companies and investors are also integrating themselves more in the Western world originally to gain better access to Western expertise. The Chinese dairy company Yili has set up an R&D center that collaborates with the Wageningen University in the Netherlands, a world center in dairy research, in studying dairy products and food safety.[25] And Baidu from its side, opened in 2014 an artificial intelligence center targeting deep learning in Silicon Valley with a total investment of $300 million.[26] Attracting Silicon Valley talent and top executives is also a common strategy among Chinese companies.

And then there are of course also investments and acquisitions abroad to try to gain access to new technologies and markets. These investments done by Chinese Venture Capitalists and companies targeted deep tech sectors important to global competitiveness such as artificial intelligence, robotics, autonomous vehicles, virtual reality and gene editing.[27]

Lenovo paying $1.3 billion in 2005 for IBM's Personal Computer Division seemed curious at the time, but it was in fact the start of all kinds of investments by Chinese firms.[28] Between 2005 and 2020, Chinese firms and funds invested $187.8 billion in the United States; $21.9 billion of this was in tech sectors.[29]

The U.S.–China trade war and greater scrutiny under the Trump administration of Chinese venture investments have reversed this trend completely, but in the past companies such as Tencent, Alibaba, and Huawei have made countless overseas investments and acquisitions, especially in promising technology companies. They have taken majority stakes in, among others, developers of online games and e-commerce websites, but have also invested in the financial sector and, over the past few years, in AI, blockchain, and big data companies. It's interesting to see that Tencent from its side has acted more as a pure financial investor, and till 2019 invested in nearly 46 "unicorns" (companies valued at more than $1 billion) globally. Alibaba on the other hand tries to integrate all the companies it has invested in into its own ecosystem.[30]

Patents and Intellectual Property (IP)

All these R&D investments have drastically increased the number of Chinese patents to astronomical numbers. In 2007 China filed 161,000 patent applications or just 8.5 percent of the global total.[31] But in 2016 China reached a milestone as the China's National Intellectual Property Administration processed 1.3 million patent applications, or 42.8

percent of all applications in the world, or twice as many applications as in the United States.[32] In 2017 the World Intellectual Property Organization (WIPO) announced that two Chinese technology companies were the top filers of international patent applications: Huawei and ZTE.[33] It's clear that China is driving the international patent applications to a record height. A new milestone was achieved in 2019 when China became the top filer for international patents. With 58,990 applications filed via WIPO's Patent Cooperation Treaty (PCT) System, China ended the U.S. reign as the biggest filer, a position held by the latter each year since the PCT began operations in 1978.[34] This evolution means clearly that foreign companies selling and/or producing in the Chinese market must increasingly take Chinese patents into account.

Committed to be a world leader in 5G. ZTE in 2020 has in total more than 5000 5G patents, and in total 34,000 granted patents worldwide.[35] Lenovo now has more than 6500 patents under its name.[36] Alibaba is pushing heavily into the blockchain field and became in 2020 the top global blockchain patent holder with 212 out of 3924 blockchain-related patents in the world.[37]

The underlying story is that once Beijing has identified a scientific field or sector as significant for economic development and or national security, it is willing to make a huge investment that may not generate economic returns for years. This commitment is carried out at bureaucratic, economic, academic, and civic levels by rallying the resources of state and society. Talented researchers are enticed with promotions and their own laboratories. Private companies, entrepreneurs, and investors are encouraged with tax breaks, direct subsidies, and other state cooperation. China's rise is as much about science and technology as trade and geopolitics. Beijing understands that better than anyone.

Any mention of R&D will bring up the typical Chinese problem of protecting intellectual property rights. After all, China is well-known as a major copycat country. But since the Chinese government is heavily committed to innovation, it also realizes that not amending its historically weak intellectual property laws will create problems in the long run.

Chinese companies themselves have exerted heavy pressure on the legal system to ensure that intellectual property (IP) legislation allows them to benefit from their inventions. Although in some areas, the regulations are still relatively weak, there is already a significant improvement. In terms of IP litigation and prosecution, the caseload of Chinese courts has grown rapidly. In 2019 no less than 475,000 IP cases were being concluded before Chinese courts.[38]

To cope with the growing number of lawsuits in Beijing, authorities have already in 2014 set up special IP courts in Shanghai and Guangzhou.[39] In fact, China has experienced tech infringements of all sizes, which illustrates also the enormous competition in the market. Because of the lower cost of a lawsuit in China than, for instance, in the United States, there are of course a lot more court cases there.[40]

Finally, some people are convinced that foreign firms are not getting a fair shake in China's courts. In reality, foreign companies fare just as well in enforcing IP rights in trial as privately owned Chinese firms. A 2016 study found that between 2006 and 2011, foreign companies brought over 10 percent of patent infringement cases in China and won over 70 percent of those cases. With these numbers, it is no wonder that China has become a popular place for foreign companies to carry out IP litigation.[41]

Stronger laws are also visible in China's e-commerce sector, which was once flooded with copycat products. In 2019, a new law made e-commerce players like Alibaba and JD.com responsible for the products being sold under their sizable cyber-umbrellas. This forced them to strengthen their efforts to banish copycats from their platforms.[42]

Even the flourishing online video market shows a clear trend toward increased IP protection. In the past, customers could easily find a range of, for example, pirated Hollywood blockbusters, Korean soap operas, HBO television series, and BBC documentaries on the internet, and even more often on the street—out of canvas bags or even established shops. Sometimes American films or series appeared on Chinese video platforms before they did on American ones. However, things have changed dramatically. Youku Tudou, which used to be the China's most famous online video platform, and in 2013 covered about a third of the market always had a vast selection, started to bar pirated versions from its platform seven years ago. The company found that carrying banned material meant losing not only Chinese advertising but also international partnerships.[43]

Equally important is that today's consumers want higher quality and are willing to pay for it. Many young people, instead of settling for pirated versions, now choose to watch movies in high definition, since these play better on mobile phones.[44] My family saw the shift ourselves when we visited Beijing's famous YaXiu Market, once a mecca for pirated DVDs and counterfeited designer clothes, sunglasses, and luxury watches sold across glass countertops in well-appointed shops. Yaxiu (sometimes spelled phonetically as Yashow) was a first stop for foreign tourists and even Chinese consumers honing their bargaining skills. Now, however, the building has been converted into a luxurious shopping center selling only original products. Copycats are literally being banished from the streets.

Chinese Silicon Valley

Just as in Silicon Valley, China's attention to innovation and technological development has created a thriving ecosystem of start-ups, incubators, and venture capital firms. Thousands of ambitious start-ups play a crucial role in transforming an economy from one that relies on production and exports to one grounded in technology and services. The number of start-ups and new companies has increased spectacularly, with an all-height boom in a two-month period in 2015 when around 4.5 million new businesses were established in China.[45] This translates to more than 10,000 start-ups a day during that period. Of course, most of them won't survive and many are empty shells, but in China, quality is drawn from quantity. Especially in the Chinese technology sector, there is a critical mass of expertise, talent, and financial resources available, with major consequences for the rest of the world.

These start-ups are spread all over the country in a still-fragmented market, but in the tech sector, several cities clearly have the potential to grow into a Chinese Silicon Valley. Beijing, Shanghai, Shenzhen, and similar places possess not only the needed venture capital but numerous talented entrepreneurs convinced of technology's ability to solve everything: "If you can think it, you can do it," as one emerging entrepreneur put it. Beijing, Shanghai, and Hangzhou were responsible for more than 30 percent of global growth in venture capital investment during 2010–2012 and 2015–2017. They are also home to 75 percent of China's unicorns.[46]

For the past few years I have been heavily involved in the start-up scene as a mentor at Chinaaccelerator, one of the country's biggest accelerators, investing in seventy start-ups annually. Increasingly, I see young Western entrepreneurs launch their start-ups immediately in China instead of abroad. They believe that the ecosystem and market is livelier and that things move faster in China than in the West. China is an excellent testing ground for their products, services, or business models because the market picks up new trends incredibly fast. This enables them to rapidly adjust to what the market wants.

Shenzhen, in the south of China, is the world's electronics factory and thus excellent testing ground for hardware companies. What 30 years ago was a small fishing village across the water from Hong Kong is now one of China's biggest center of innovation. 90 percent of the world's electronics come from Shenzhen, including toys, televisions, air conditioning units, mobile phones, and drones.[47] Besides this know-how there is also a huge amount of brainpower available, as every year six million students come from all over China to the Greater Bay Area—Shenzhen at its heart—looking for jobs and opportunities.[48]

And then there is an entire network of companies that produce the wide range of components needed for electronic devices. Many of the world best and greatest technology companies call Shenzhen home, such as telecom giants Huawei en ZTE, Tencent, BYD, biotech specialist BGI, robot kit maker Makeblock, and the world's largest drone maker DJI.[49] In 2017 three innovative sectors—internet, biotechnology and telecom-contribute to over 40 percent of Shenzhen's economic output.[50] Given the enormous innovative drive, it's not an exaggeration to say that even Silicon Valley looks to Shenzhen for inspiration.

Beijing's Zhongguancun Science Park is home to more than 9000 high-tech companies and as many as 80 tech start-ups are born there every day.[51] Lenovo has its headquarters and some of its R&D facilities there, and Baidu and Xiaomi, the smartphone and Internet of Things giant, have also set up shop here. The ecosystem draws further support from nearby research institutes, universities, incubators, and multinationals, most of which have regional head offices in the vicinity.[52] Beijing has more than 122,000 dollar millionaires, so there are plenty of angel investors and a lot of venture capital available.[53] As the financial capital of China, Shanghai also boasts tremendous available venture capital and is especially notable for innovation in the field of the life sciences. Zhangjiang Hi-Tech Park, only a few kilometers from where I live, is called the Pharma Valley of China because of its hundreds of pharmaceutical companies and life-science start-ups.

Like many other sectors, the Chinese tech landscape is also characterized by deadly competition. Illegal copying of new products or competitors' exploitation of innovative ideas remains a problem. In the Western world, a good idea attracts a number of imitations, but in China there is almost no limit to what can happen when a vision for a start-up emerges. Competition is extremely fierce to see the least. A newly launched app that hasn't been downloaded a few million times within months has missed its start. Chinese venture capital companies also play increasingly important roles. Chinese venture capital boom started in 2014 and topped in 2018 with a total of $105 billion for that year alone, which was almost as much as in the United States.[54] 2019 however was globally a challenging year for venture capital investments, when total investments dropped from $302 billion in 2018 to $258 billion. But especially China took a big hit.[55] For European companies, all this adds some intriguing layers, since big tickets are now not only found in the United States, but increasingly also in China. Especially for the European healthcare sector, China offers major opportunities—for example, there is a huge demand for better medicines and treatments. This technology can be found in Europe, and as such attracts Chinese capital.

Success Stories

Chinese tech companies are now making global waves with an increasing amount of success stories, although the tech entrepreneurial scene in China is still young and as such there isn't yet a strong generation of experienced tech entrepreneurs. In June 2019 China surpassed the United States for the first time, when 206 of the 494 unicorns worldwide were located in China (versus 203 in the United States).[56]

For a long time the long-term success stories of Baidu, Alibaba, and Tencent were the only real reference points for tech start-ups. And that's partly the reason why People like Alibaba's Jack Ma, Tencent's Ma Huateng (also known as Pony Ma), and Xiaomi's Lei Jun are very much present in the media, personifying the success of the self-made Chinese tech entrepreneur and acting as role models for many graduates. The same way Westerners know the stories of Bill Gates and Steve Jobs, both of whom dropped out of university and chose their own paths, every Chinese person knows about Jack Ma, who had the dream of connecting Chinese companies with foreign markets via the internet and founded Alibaba in his little Hangzhou apartment. Jack Ma can rightly be called China's first internet entrepreneur and is often compared to Steve Jobs because of his visionary ideas.

Chinese innovation also works differently than in the West. Companies use a pragmatic innovation model; they go to the market quickly to test and commercialize new products rather than perfecting them before launch. In this way, they get constant customer feedback and can adjust their ideas to market requirements. Not only have Tencent or Alibaba in this way already overtaken their Western competitors, but other companies are also challenging traditional Western domination. Xiaomi, a company that started as a smartphone producer in 2010, is one such example. And as so many Chinese tech companies, also Xiaomi got initially inspired by one of the Western competitors. In their case it was Apple, which could be seen by the first Xiaomi smartphones who looked very similar as iPhone. Four years after its inception however, the company was valued at $45 billion, immediately making it the world's most valuable start-up at that time. In the same year, it also became the world's third-largest producer of smartphones, and was in total more valuable than Uber.[57]

One of the main reasons for Xiaomi's initial success was that it succeeded in producing a smartphone that is equal in quality but half the price of the competition. When the newest model, the MI2, was launched online in 2012, the first batch of 50,000 smartphones sold out within three minutes. Xiaomi distinguished itself from its competitors as it never planned to make money on hardware; its main goal was to sell applications and online services. And as so many Chinese tech companies Xiaomi also branched out to other products and dug deeper into the ecosystem and basically turned into an Internet of Things company. It has created more than 50 models of smartphones, several tablets, laptops, headphones, smart scales, a smart heated jacket, kettles, all kinds of bags, surveillance cameras, and a bunch of devices for a smart home like smart speakers and various electric screwdrivers.[58] As such the company has changed its image from a producer of cheap smartphones to an innovative company with affordable products. In 2020 Xiaomi became Western Europe's third-largest smartphone seller, and announced that 55 percent of its revenues came from markets outside China.[59] And like Apple, Xiaomi has a host of loyal users who spread the message and faith in the brand.

In China's financial sector, TechFins, or tech giants disrupting finance, have also challenged traditional banks, and did so long before their Western counterparts followed the same trend. Any major upheaval is thanks mainly to Baidu, Alibaba, and Tencent, which bring all kinds of facets together on one platform aimed at hundreds of millions of smartphone users. Tencent's WeChat is basically on every Chinese smartphone.

For its part, Baidu has access to a huge amount of data that it can leverage in a whole range of industries, including the financial sector.

And that is where Alibaba comes in. Traditionally, Chinese customers had difficulties getting loans because banks couldn't assess risk—China never developed a credit card habit. But Alibaba collects enormous amounts of data from its customers, who purchase nearly everything online, and has the means to assign credit risk scores. The Chinese government is still a shareholder in the vast majority of Chinese banks, but when a private banking sector started to develop, Alibaba, Baidu, Tencent, and JD.com all obtained their own banking licenses.[60] Alibaba was perfectly placed to build on its own payment systems and financial platforms, Ant Financial has been particularly successful here and challenged the traditional banks in every way possible. As part of the Alibaba group, it now operates some of the key financial service businesses in the Chinese market. For example, Alipay not only handles transactions on Alibaba's Taobao and Tmall e-commerce platforms, but has also expanded to supporting mobile payments in stores and restaurants, a trend that has taken off in recent years. Then there is also Yu'e Bao, a giant fund started in 2013 and overseen by Ant Financial. In 2019 588 million users of Alipay invested amounts of as little as one yuan in the fund, and as such grew at one point in time into the world's largest money market fund.[61]

"If data were petroleum in the artificial intelligence era, then China would be Saudi Arabia," the Chinese venture capitalist Kai-Fu Lee, former president of Google China, has memorably observed.[62] The sheer mass of data and technology available makes China the perfect experimental and implementation ground for everything data-related. AI is already widely deployed in China. Overcrowded cities, huge traffic jams, long lines, and old-fashioned procedures caused frustration and wasted time and money, but technology provides new ways to deal with these problems.

An executive of the Ping An insurance company told me that 70 percent of all car accident payments are handled the day after the crash. Drivers take pictures of the damage and load them onto an app, and the AI-driven Ping An system takes care of the damage assessment and payment. In 2019 the world's most valuable AI unicorn, China's SenseTime focuses on computer vision and deep learning.[63] SenseTime is a market leader in almost all vertically integrated industries, including smart cities, smartphones, mobile internet, online entertainment, automobile, finance, retail, education, real estate, and so on.

Artificial Intelligence is also at the core of Meituan Dianping, which hit a $100 billion valuation during the corona pandemic.[64] The company is best known for food delivery, restaurant reviews, hotel booking, movie tickets, and so on. This service plays to the Chinese consumer who craves convenience and has little patience. More than 350 million people across 2800 cities used Meituan Dianping to carry out around $34 billion worth of transactions in just six months in 2018, which comes to 1783 services every second.[65] Harnessing its user-consumption data such as records of interests and price sensitivity, the company can recommend other consolidated services across its broad spectrum of offerings. To optimize delivery, Meituan uses a Smart Dispatch system that calculates 2.9 billion route plans every hour. This allows the company's 600,000 electric bike riders to pick up and drop off up to ten orders at a time in the most efficient way possible.[66]

Chinese companies are also extremely customer-focused. In a market of 1.3 billion, they truly put customers' needs first. One such example is Pinduoduo, the leading Chinese app for social e-commerce, and in 2017 the fastest growing app in the history of the Chinese internet.[67] One would think that start-up competition against e-commerce giants Alibaba and JD.com equals suicide, but Pinduoduo proved a success story. Pinduoduo users are predominantly female, live in Tier 3 or 4 cities, and are bargain hunters who can assemble enough WeChat friends to order items in bulk from manufacturers and skip the middleman. Anyone logging on WeChat Moments (the app's social networking function) to share with friends can get the deal.

As agriculture is an integral part of Pinduoduo's business—in 2019 600,000 merchants sold farm produce through its platform, which translates into 12 million farmers who supplied fruits and vegetables—the company started to develop a long-term agritech commitment.[68] Agriculture is one of the least digitized sectors in China,[69] so innovation plays a critical role in the multifaceted food sector, precisely because the problems are so significant and so widespread. From farm to kitchen table, and throughout the entire food supply chain, some start-ups gather systemic data that consumers can consult via online marketplaces.

Drones are increasingly being used in all parts of life. Since a year or so our family starts to rent drones to take pictures during our holidays, which has become really easy as they are easily available to rent out. That is no surprise either; China is set to become an industry leader and change the aviation world forever. The Shenzhen-based technology company

DJI had over 70 percent of the global market share for the consumer drone industry in 2017.[70] The company utilizes a complete supply chain integration as well as a sophisticated manufacturing pipeline and logistical support. That and its blistering pace of innovation means that no company based in the West has the tools to compete. Mobility-focused DJI seeks to redefine a next-generation logistical network and reinvent the way dense population centers and dispersed rural communities move people, goods, and services.

Innovation starts to manifest in other ways also. Some companies have innovated by restructuring their organizations. Though most companies use traditional models and, like Chinese society as a whole, are oriented top-down, companies such as Xiaomi and the household appliance giant Haier have introduced completely new structures. Haier is a pioneer with its flat, decentralized organization, which promotes the entrepreneurial spirit of its employees.[71] Xiaomi and Haier also make good use of their online platforms, where they collect feedback from their customers, something that could help many Western companies understand their markets better.

It's for all to see that Chinese society has embraced a wide range of technological advances for the simple reason that they make life better and living more convenient. The shortage of workers and demands for better-quality products has driven the need for factory automation. Cleantech solves environmental pollution problems, while biotech introduces new and better medicines to the market, which in turn reduces the cost of caring for the aging Chinese population. The use of facial recognition and AI at cash registers—called "smile to pay"—lessens the need for cash or even mobile phones.

In many fields, China is now an advanced technological society. So it's little wonder that the first edition of the famous Consumer Electronics Show (CES) outside the United States, was held in Shanghai in 2015.[72]

The COVID-19 pandemic also showed how in vaccine development and the life sciences space China had made great strives forward. Among others, not only Western pharma giant Pfizer and the biotech Moderna's vaccines showed good safety and efficacy results, two Chinese companies—Sinovac and Sinopharm—developed its own vaccines, despite though achieving less efficacy.[73]

Problems

Despite all those success stories, China still has major obstacles on its path to innovation. On the Global Innovation Index, which ranks companies worldwide for innovation capabilities, China was number 14 in 2019.[74] Considering that forty years ago China was still a developing country, this is, in all respects, a huge achievement. Worldwide surveys routinely show that China scores well in education, university research, general infrastructure, and patent development. But there is still work to be done, especially in the areas of stronger IP legislation, more efficient use of public funds, and improving the ecosystem in general. In respect to ecosystems Silicon Valley was not built in a day either. Only after Professor Frederick Terman encouraged students to start their own businesses in the 1930s, and then in 1951 helped create the Stanford Industrial Park (now Stanford Research Park), did it start to take shape as the hub of innovation it is today.[75]

The Chinese Silicon Valley will also have to mature, although that evolution is likely to happen much faster. China still does not lead in "classic" science or frontier innovation and inventing radical new technologies. The country might be the second biggest spender on R&D, but in 2017, it still imported six times more IP than it exported ($29 billion versus $5 billion).[76]

In the field of patents, there are problems also. Despite the huge amount of patents, quantity doesn't always represent quality. According to Bloomberg roughly 91 percent of Chinese design patents, 61 percent of utility patents, and 37 percent of invention patents granted in 2013 had been discarded by 2017.[77]

China is very good, however, at creating new business models, improving technologies, and adapting them to the Chinese market. But despite China's allocating huge resources and energy to innovation and creativity, its political system restricts intellectual freedom. This is especially true in the educational system. From my own experience, I know that Chinese students are smart and generally have had a good education, but that doesn't mean that they can immediately put any creative or critical thinking into practice. The emphasis is still too much on memorizing and too little on critical analysis, which, of course, is something the Chinese government wants to keep in its place.

Another specific problem is the *hukou* system. Migrants living in Beijing, Shanghai, or Shenzhen may launch start-ups, but these internal registration rules mean they cannot buy houses there or send their children to good local schools. Consequently, the likelihood that they can remain and incubate in the country's most innovative cities is limited.

What China does have, of course, is critical mass in the form of its enormous population. "Made in China" may not always be "Designed in China"—yet—but the Western world must get used to seeing more and more Chinese tech players striding the global stage with products and services equal or even superior to Western quality. With its commitment to innovation, research, and development, China is once again demonstrating its huge capacity to reinvent itself.

The effects of this technological evolution and focus on innovation cannot be overestimated. The whole of Chinese society—including myself—is gripped by it. Just looking at my own children, born and now being raised in China, drives home how technology and innovation have become the new normal. To give just one example, my son sees electric cars as standard, and most young Chinese assume their first auto purchase will be an electric one. A whole new generation of well-educated, tech-savvy Chinese living fully in the modern world will set new international standards through their spending and economic power.

Notes

1. Visit Hangzhou. 2020. Marco Polo. www.visithangzhou.com/cmarter4b3a.html?doc=998&node=1031. Accessed December 4, 2020.
2. Information Technology & Innovation Foundation. 2019. Is China catching up to the United States in innovation? Pg. 9. www2.itif.org/2019-china-catching-up-innovation.pdf. Accessed March 5, 2020.
3. Forbes. 2017. The countries with the most STEM graduates. www.forbes.com/sites/niallmccarthy/2017/02/02/the-countries-with-the-most-stem-graduates-infographic. Accessed April 4, 2020.
4. Sixth Tone. 2017. www.sixthtone.com/news/1001057/tsinghua-named-worlds-best-engineering%2C-computer-science-school. Tsinghua named world's best engineering computer science school. Accessed October 5, 2019.
5. Nature. 2018. China declared world's largest producer of scientific articles. www.nature.com/articles/d41586-018-00927-4. Accessed August 6, 2019.
6. Electrical & Computer Engineering. 2017. UW and China's Tsinghua University launch groundbreaking global innovation exchange. www.ece.uw.edu/spotlight/uw-and-chinas-tsinghua-university-launch-groundbreaking-global-innovation-exchange. Accessed January 19, 2020.

7. Forbes. 2020. China is closing the gap with the U.S. in R&D expenditure (infographic). www.forbes.com/sites/niallmccarthy/2020/01/20/china-is-closing-the-gap-with-the-us-in-rd-expenditure-infographic/#590f64865832. Accessed October 5, 2020.
8. Science. 2020. China again boosts R&D spending by more than 10%. www.sciencemag.org/news/2020/08/china-again-boosts-rd-spending-more-10. Accessed December 3, 2020.
9. *Nature*. 2018. China's plan to recruit talented researchers. www.nature.com/articles/d41586-018-00538-z. Accessed February 4, 2020.
10. ChinaPower. 2020. How dominant are Chinese companies globally? https://chinapower.csis.org/chinese-companies-global-500/ Accessed January 6, 2021.
11. Lenovo. 2021. Our company. www.lenovo.com/be/nl/lenovo/our-company. Accessed January 4, 2021.
12. *Journal of Business & International Marketing*. 2007. Huawei technologies corporation: from local dominance to global challenge? https://pdfs.semanticscholar.org/795b/9862474d89d13116d5d313e471c0a6d045f2.pdf. Accessed January 2, 2021.
13. *Global Times*. 2020. Huawei R&D spending surpasses that of each of 25 provinces in China. www.globaltimes.cn/content/1199647.shtml. Accessed December 4, 2020.
14. Business Insider. 2019. We got a tour of Huawei's sprawling Shenzhen campus, home to the Chinese tech giant at the eye of a global security storm. www.businessinsider.com/we-went-to-huaweis-shenzhen-campus-where-30000-staff-live-and-work-2019-2%3famp. Accessed January 3, 2021.
15. *Global Times*. 2020. Huawei R&D spending surpasses that of each of 25 provinces in China. www.globaltimes.cn/content/1199647.shtml. Accessed December 4, 2020.
16. BYD. 2020. BYD milestones. www.byd.com/cn/en/BYD_ENAboutByd/CompanyIntro_mob.html;jsessionid=9IbM6LHKJlkXdmNtHJAcpSJhreL2io6bcgw7bvw4VKBjVrhUEJOP!1923592976!1208301761. Accessed December 4, 2020.
17. Forbes. 2020. BYD. https://www.forbes.com/companies/byd/?sh=4e4f402c3526. Accessed January 5, 2021.
18. *Chinadaily*. Top 10 best-selling electric vehicle makers. https://global.chinadaily.com.cn/a/202002/17/WS5e49c4c0a310128217277e35.html. Accessed December 5, 2020.
19. Investor's business daily. 2020. Here's why this Warren Buffet-backed electric car stock is surging. https://www.investors.com/news/electric-car-stocks-rise-led-by-byd-china-signals-subsidies-stable-2020/. Accessed December 5, 2020.

20. Inside EVs. 2019. Accessed March 4, 2019. BYD produced 50,000 electric buses in nine years. https://insideevs.com/news/342760/byd-produced-50000-electric-buses-in-nine-years. Accessed March 6, 2020.
21. PricewaterhouseCoopers. 2014. The 2014 global innovation 1000. http://boletines.prisadigital.com/the2014globalinnovation1000.pdf. Accessed March 6, 2019.
22. Fujitsu Research Institute. 2010. Foreign companies accelerating R&D activity in China. www.fujitsu.com/jp/group/fri/en/column/message/2010/2010-05-13.html. Accessed April 22, 2019.
23. *China Business Review*. 2015. Foreign company R&D: In China, for China. www.chinabusinessreview.com/foreign-company-rd-in-china-for-china/. Accessed March 5, 2019.
24. Wings Herald. 2019. Airbus opened an aviation development center in China. www.wingsherald.com/airbus-opened-an-aviation-development-center-in-china. Accessed May 5, 2020.
25. *Chinadaily*. 2014. Yili sets up R&D center in Europe. www.chinadaily.com.cn/business/2014-02/26/content_17305903.htm. Accessed March 5, 2018.
26. Fierce Wireless. 2014. Baidu's Silicon Valley center targets deep learning. www.fiercewireless.com/tech/baidu-s-silicon-valley-r-d-center-targets-deep-learning. Accessed March 5, 2019.
27. CNBC. 2020. How the US–China trade war has starved some Silicon Valley start-ups. www.cnbc.com/2020/01/31/chinese-venture-capitalists-draw-back-silicon-valley-investments.html. Accessed June 5, 2020.
28. Forbes. 2016. How Lenovo became the largest PC-maker in the world. www.forbes.com/sites/jnylander/2016/03/20/how-lenovo-became-the-largest-pc-maker-in-the-world. Accessed November 5, 2019.
29. American Enterprise Institute. 2021. China global investment tracker. www.aei.org/china-global-investment-tracker/. Accessed January 4, 2021.
30. Thelowdown. 2020. Tencent's global investment empire. https://thelowdown.momentum.asia/tencents-global-investment-empire/. Accessed January 4, 2021.
31. ChinaPower. 2020. Is China leading in global innovation? https://chinapower.csis.org/china-innovation-global-leader/. Accessed January 5, 201.
32. ChinaPower. 2020. Are patents indicative of Chinese innovation? https://chinapower.csis.org/patents/. Accessed January 5, 2021.
33. World Intellectual Property Organization. 2018. China drives international patent applications to record heights; demand rising for trademark and industrial design protection. www.wipo.int/pressroom/en/articles/2018/article_0002.html. Accessed December 5, 2019.

34. World Intellectual Property Organization. 2020. China becomes top filer for international patents in 2019 amid robust growth for WIPO's IP services, treaties and finances. www.wipo.int/pressroom/en/articles/2020/article_0005.html. Accessed November 5, 2020.
35. ZTE. 2020. ZTE ranks global top with 2561 families of 5G declared standard-essential patents to ETSI. www.zte.com.cn/global/about/news/20200228e1.html. Accessed January 5, 2021.
36. Lenovo. 2021. Our company. www.lenovo.com/be/nl/lenovo/our-company. Accessed January 4, 2021.
37. Technode. 2020. Alibaba is the top global blockchain patent holder. https://technode.com/2020/07/03/alibaba-leads-global-blockchain-patent-but-china-lags-behind-us-and-s-korea/. Accessed October 19, 2020.
38. Mondaq. 2019. Chinese courts concludes over 475,000 IPR cases. www.mondaq.com/china/trademark/936768/chinese-courts-concludes-over-475000-ipr-cases-in-2019. Accessed March 5, 2020.
39. *The Diplomat*. 2018. China's progress on intellectual property rights (res, really). https://thediplomat.com/2018/01/chinas-progress-on-intellectual-property-rights-yes-really. Accessed March 6, 2019.
40. *The Diplomat*. 2018. China's progress on intellectual property rights (res, really). https://thediplomat.com/2018/01/chinas-progress-on-intellectual-property-rights-yes-really. Accessed March 6, 2019.
41. *The Diplomat*. 2018. China's progress on intellectual property rights (res, really). https://thediplomat.com/2018/01/chinas-progress-on-intellectual-property-rights-yes-really. Accessed March 6, 2019.
42. *South China Morning Post*. 2019. Here's how China's new e-commerce law will affect consumers, platform operators. www.scmp.com/tech/apps-social/article/2180194/heres-how-chinas-new-e-commerce-law-will-affect-consumers-platform. Accessed March 5, 2020.
43. Reuters. 2013. Once piracy heavens, China's internet video websites turn police. www.reuters.com/article/us-china-internet-video-idUSBRE9B414Z20131205. Accessed January 21, 2018.
44. MarketingToChina. 2014. The Chinese video platforms finally reject piracy. http://marketingtochina.com/chinese-video-platforms-finally-reject-piracy. Accessed June 4, 2018.
45. China.org. 2015. China's startup boom: 7 new firms every minute. www.china.org.cn/business/2015-06/09/content_35775291.htm. Accessed February 12, 2018.
46. ChinaPower. 2020. Is China leading in global innovation? https://chinapower.csis.org/china-innovation-global-leader/. Accessed January 5, 2021.
47. World Economic Forum. 2017. The astonishing rise of Shenzhen, China's gadget capital. https://www.weforum.org/agenda/2017/11/inside-shenzhen-china-s-gadget-capital/. Accessed April 11, 2020.

48. Information Age. 2018. Shenzhen, China: The next Silicon Valley? www.information-age.com/shenzhen-next-silicon-valley-123471169/. Accessed April 4, 2020.
49. Medium. 2018. Shenzhen: The tech capital of the world. https://medium.com/wonk-bridge/shenzhen-the-tech-capital-of-the-world-7b1a0469c39f. Accessed November 4, 2020.
50. Medium. 2018. Shenzhen: The tech capital of the world. https://medium.com/wonk-bridge/shenzhen-the-tech-capital-of-the-world-7b1a0469c39f. Accessed November 4, 2020.
51. *South China Morning Post*. 2018. Zhongguancun: Beijing's innovation hub is at the centre of China's aim to become a tech powerhouse. www.scmp.com/tech/start-ups/article/2172713/zhongguancun-beijings-innovation-hub-centre-chinas-aim-become-tech. Accessed December 4, 2020.
52. *South China Morning Post*. 2018. Zhongguancun: Beijing's innovation hub is at the centre of China's aim to become a tech powerhouse. www.scmp.com/tech/start-ups/article/2172713/zhongguancun-beijings-innovation-hub-centre-chinas-aim-become-tech. Accessed December 4, 2020.
53. WorldAtlas. 2020. Cities with the most millionaires. www.worldatlas.com/articles/cities-boasting-the-most-millionaires-around-the-globe.html. Accessed January 4, 2021.
54. Bloomberg. 2019. China's venture capital boom shows signs of turning into a bust. www.bloomberg.com/news/articles/2019-07-09/china-s-venture-capital-boom-shows-signs-of-turning-into-a-bust. Accessed January 3, 2021.
55. *Fortune*. 2020. China tech's venture capital boom is going cold. www.fortune.com/2020/01/22/china-tech-venture-capital-boom-goes-cold/amp/. Accessed January 4, 2021.
56. Quartz. 2019. A new Chinese ranking of global unicorns puts China ahead of US for the first time. www.qz.com/1732991/chinas-hurun-list-says-china-has-more-unicorns-than-us/amp/ accessed February 4, 2020.
57. *Daily Mail*. 2014. Xiaomi becomes world's most valuable tech start-up: Chinese smartphone manufacturer is now valued at $45 BILLION. www.dailymail.co.uk/sciencetech/article-2891532/Xiaomi-worlds-valuable-tech-start-Chinese-smartphone-manufacturer-valued-45-BILLION.html. Accessed August 5, 2020.
58. Mi Community. Xiaomi's path to success. All u need to know about the unbelievable journey! 2019. https://c.mi.com/thread-2126517-1-0.html. Accessed December 5, 2020.
59. Fortune. 2020. China's Xiaomi becomes Western Europe's third-largest smartphone seller. www.fortune.com/2020/11/25/xiaomi-third-quarter-results-largest-western-europe/amp/. Accessed January 4, 2021.

60. China Banking News. 2019. China's big four tech giants collectively amass 40 financial licenses despite de-financialization drive. www.chinabankingnews.com/2019/11/03/chinas-big-four-tech-giants-collectively-amass-40-financial-licenses/. Accessed October 5, 2020.
61. *The Wall Street Journal*. 2019. More than a third of China is now invested in one giant mutual fund. www.wsj.com/amp/articles/more-than-a-third-of-china-is-now-invested-in-one-giant-mutual-fund-11553682785. Accessed December 2, 2020.
62. YiCai Global. 2018. China is to data what Saudi Arabia to oil, Kaifu Lee tells AI forum. www.yicaiglobal.com/news/china-is-to-data-what-saudi-arabia-is-to-oil-kaifu-lee-tells-ai-forum. Accessed May 22, 2020.
63. Forbes. 2019. Meet the world's most valuable AI startup: China's Sensetime. www.forbes.com/sites/bernardmarr/2019/06/17/meet-the-worlds-most-valuable-ai-start-up-chinas-sensetime. Accessed October 5, 2020.
64. Techcrunch. 2020. China's food delivery giant Meituan hits $100B valuation amid pandemic. www.techcrunch.com/2020/05/25/chinas-food-delivery-giant-meituan-hits-100b-valuation-amid-pandemic/amp/. Accessed January 4, 2021.
65. Fastcompany. 2019. The 2 most innovative companies in the world today are changing how hundreds of millions of Asian consumers buy food, book hotels and (a lot) more. www.fastcompany.com/90298866/meituan-grab-most-innovative-companies-2019. Accessed July 22, 2020.
66. Fastcompany. 2019. The 2 most innovative companies in the world today are changing how hundreds of millions of Asian consumers buy food, book hotels and (a lot) more. www.fastcompany.com/90298866/meituan-grab-most-innovative-companies-2019. Accessed July 22, 2020.
67. Walkthechat. 2018. Pinduoduo: A close look at the fastest growing e-commerce app in China. https://walkthechat.com/pinduoduo-close-look-fastest-growing-app-china. Accessed November 11, 2020.
68. Techcrunch. 2020. Why Alibaba rival Pinduoduo is investing in agritech. www.techcrunch.com/2020/12/16/pinduoduo-agritech/amp/. Accessed January 4, 2021.
69. McKinsey. 2017. Digital China: Powering the economy to global competitiveness. https://www.mckinsey.com/~/media/McKinsey/Industries/Technology%20Media%20and%20Telecommunications/High%20Tech/Our%20Insights/Digital%20China%20Powering%20the%20economy%20to%20global%20competitiveness/MGI_Digital-China_Executive-summary_Dec-2017.pdf. Accessed January 4, 2021.
70. World Economic Forum. 2018. 3 reasons why China is the global drones leader. www.weforum.org/agenda/2018/09/china-drones-technology-leader. Accessed May 15, 2020.

71. Corporate rebels. 2018. The world's most pioneering company of our times. https://corporate-rebels.com/haier. Accessed September 7, 2020.
72. China Bridge. 2015. CES Asia 2015. https://cbichinabridge.com/ces-asia-2015. Accessed January 4, 2018.
73. BBC. 2020. What do we know about the China's coronavirus vaccines? www.bbc.com/news/amp/world-asia-china-55212787, BBC. 2021. Chinese officials says local vaccines 'don't have high protection rates'. www.bbc.com/news/world-asia-china-56713663. Accessed April 8, 2021.
74. World Intellectual Property Organization. 2019. Global Innovation Index (GII) 2019. www.wipo.int/global_innovation_index/en/2019. Accessed November 4, 2020.
75. Business Insider. 2020. Animated timeline shows how Silicon Valley became a $2.8 trillion neighborhood. www.businessinsider.com/silicon-valley-history-technology-industry-animated-timeline-video-2017-5?IR=T. Accessed January 5, 2021.
76. McKinsey Global Institute. 2019. China and the world: Inside the dynamics of a changing relationship. https://www.mckinsey.com/featured-insights/china/china-and-the-world-inside-the-dynamics-of-a-changing-relationship. Accessed November 21, 2020.
77. Bloomberg. 2018. China claims more patents than any country. Most are useless. www.bloomberg.com/news/articles/2018-09-26/china-claims-more-patents-than-any-country-most-are-worthless. Accessed February 4, 2020.

CHAPTER 9

Better Unhappy Rich Than Poor

In the austere Maoist China of the 1960s, the Communist Party completely controlled economic, political, social, and cultural life. It set the economic cornerstones with the planned economy, determined which citizens were allowed to study at what universities, and ultimately decided how much food was available for each family. But its control didn't stop there. Citizens were often forced out on the streets to perform good deeds such as cleaning buses or cutting strangers' hair. The Party wanted to match its enormous impact on society with control of private lives. An elderly colleague at Yichun University told me that until the late 1990s, authorities exercised strict oversight of students' day-to-day activities. For example, female students had their monthly periods monitored, and, as she put it: "If they did not get them on time, they'd better make sure they came as soon as possible."

Even as recently as 2004, when I was living in Yichun, I witnessed the Party's influence on daily routines. Certain citizens were made responsible for the neighborhood and cleared the streets in winter. In groups of ten, they started working before dawn. When my in-laws married in 1984, they needed the local government's permission—which was also required for divorce. International travel was almost impossible.

A planned economy is just that—completely and comprehensively planned. The government dictated who produced what, and how much

S. Agten, *Adventures in the Chinese Economy: 16 Years from the Inside*, https://doi.org/10.1007/978-981-16-1167-4_9

or how many. Until the 1990s, younger university graduates were immediately transferred to state-owned companies and paid predetermined salaries. No one complained; choice was literally a foreign concept. This economic and social influence led to a all-encompassing unity. Chinese citizens were expected to follow certain rules, have well-defined jobs, and lead the lives the Party dictated. Westerners may also remember seeing pictures of the blue or gray Mao uniforms nearly everyone wore. My in-laws still display a photo of them proudly posing in the fashion of the day.

Growing Individualism

In the China of 2020, the world is completely different. Economic liberalization has triggered a tsunami of developments with far-reaching social consequences. The Chinese government no longer interferes in the daily lives of its citizens as it used to—and citizens would not accept that anyway. The current consumer society, with its broader range and wider choice of products, not to mention increased tourism, better mobility, and, of course, the internet, has made Chinese citizens more international and increasingly demanding.

Individual freedom has grown dramatically and China's growing individualism manifests itself in specific ways. Being different—always viewed as hostile by authoritarian regimes—was dangerous back in the days of Maoist standardization. Today, the pendulum is swinging to the other side. In general, societies that champion individuals have variety, and showing personal freedom is socially acceptable, even encouraged. Among a population of 1.3 billion, Chinese also find it necessary to differentiate themselves from the masses to express their unique personalities, which is why social status, power, and money are so important. After all, these are the most direct ways to show that society is no longer one giant unified body. Many Chinese feel that nothing is more important than the online sharing of pictures of their latest trip abroad, a new purchase, or dinner at some fancy restaurant. Others collect art to show the world how special they are.

The reality is that those who think they're special and can prove it have all the advantages in China. Being wealthy or powerful, of course, brings benefits around the world, and significantly so in China. Far from being egalitarian, China is a class-based society of the purest kind, and everyone is trying to move up. The distinction between haves and have-nots is widely accepted as part of the new, economically liberal China, where exclusiveness is always appreciated. When I went to open a bank account at a new China Merchants Bank office in 2015, I was politely informed that the office was for VIP customers only. Did I have $1.4 million for the minimum balance required? I suddenly felt very poor. Some sports fitness complexes have annual membership fees of around ten thousand dollars. And private schools screen both children and parents for their "appropriateness," which usually means wealth and status.

Increasing individualism and the desire to express one's own personality and wealth also mean that new products and services in China quickly find their way into the market. Having something that few others have is an excellent way to distinguish yourself. The abundance of new products gives young people with means of every opportunity to express their individualism, and the possibilities they find in major cities in terms of modernity, social life, and cultural events are in no way inferior to Western urban centers. International events such as rock festivals, marathons, exhibitions, sports competitions, contemporary or classical music concerts, fashion weeks, fringe theater, pop-up shops, and so on all take place in major Chinese cities. Every day there is something for everyone. Above all, Shanghai is about to take on London or New York.

Big Chinese cities have a vibrant nightlife. Since China has a real food culture, some restaurants are open around the clock. In my younger years in Beijing, I regularly went to the hippest clubs, where alcohol flowed in excess. Alcohol consumption is widespread; people throw their drunken friends into taxis to be taken home here just like everywhere else in the world. Beijing or Shanghai might be good for those seeking a second youth. There are lively clubs, including well-known gay and lesbian establishments, that regularly feature international DJs. Drug use is also on the rise. Despite China's strong-arm approach and increasing crackdowns in clubs and bars, the government estimated that there were 2,5 million drug users in the country at the end of 2016 while the actual number is probably much higher and rising.[1]

As entertainment booms, so does the world of show business. In addition to Chinese stars filling the stages of Chinese cities, foreign artists make regular appearances, although not without conflict. Icelandic singer Bjork shouted out "Tibet, Tibet" at the end of a concert in Shanghai in 2008,[2] while Elton John caused a stir when in 2012 when he dedicated on stage his Beijing performance to the artist and political dissident Ai Weiwei.[3] And when the Rolling Stones toured China in 2014, the authorities for some reason removed their song "Honky Tonk Woman" from the set list of numbers, Mick Jagger said.[4]

Other stars are less controversial. Maroon 5, Katy Perry, and Taylor Swift have all performed in Chinese cities without incident; I also remember attending a Bob Dylan concert in Beijing. Once we saw groups of giggling young women in front of an upscale Beijing hotel and discovered that David Beckham—an absolute superstar in China—and his wife Victoria were in town. Because soccer is both popular and lucrative, top European teams tour China and compete in a series of games each year. I saw Barcelona, Manchester United, and Bayern Munich play in Beijing. English teachers may be surprised at a teen's astonishing knowledge of European cities until they realize all these urban centers have soccer teams.

NBA basketball is also hugely popular. More than six hundred million people watched some kind of NBS programming over the 2017–18 season, while the NBA has 25 marketing partners in China.[5] NBA teams come to China every year and compete against each other, or against local teams, to the delight of the crowds. But this popularity has a price. When in 2019, Daryl Morey, the general manager of the Houston Rockets (where Yao Ming was a star player), tweeted his support for Hong Kong protesters, Chinese companies such as NBA digital partner Tencent, sportswear giant Li-Ning, Shanghai-Pudong Development Bank, and the NBA's network broadcaster CCTV 5 all threatened and announced to suspend ties with the team. As a result the NBA needed to apologize.[6] This left NBA players and executives scrambling to choose between defending a private individual's right to free expression and capitalizing on the lucrative sponsorship deals the NBA enjoys in China, all the while worrying about their future in the world's biggest market.

But global players have long understood that international events cannot afford to stay away from China. Since 2004, Shanghai has hosted a Formula One race,[7] and five years later it became the first Asian location of the Association of Tennis Professionals World Tour Masters 1000.[8] As China's live events market was booming in 2019, with revenues close to $3 billion, Western showbiz flocked to china too. In the same year Cirque du Soleil launched its permanent residence show in Asia, for which it selected Hangzhou. After the corona lockdown in China, it was one of only two Cirque productions operating worldwide.[9] *Disney on Ice* also performs every year in different cities in China,[10] and in 2016 Disneyland Shanghai was opened which in its first year welcomed 11 million visitors.[11] Since 2003, the Miss World competition has held its finals eight times on the subtropical island of Hainan.[12]

In addition to increasing internationalization, the desire for modernity is reflected in other forms. While young people still respect traditional Chinese holidays, Western holidays are increasingly hip. Modern Chinese citizens believe they must adapt to international standards, sometimes via their wallets. Beijing and Shanghai have annual Christmas markets, inspired by German examples, and restaurants offer special menus not only throughout the Yuletide season but also during Halloween. More and more Chinese children don costumes for school activities, and the combined holiday and nutritional value of pumpkins has made China the world's largest producer.[13] Perhaps most surprising to those in the West, in a country that once criminalized religion, I have seen a growing numbers of couples choose the fashionable option of getting married in church. Many Chinese celebrate Valentine's Day on February 14th, and so-called Chinese Valentine's Day on the seventh day of the seventh lunar month, which varies. This tells of a mortal and a fairy-turned-weaver girl who are separated by her goddess mother but meet once a year by crossing the Milky Way over a bridge of magpies. Some international holidays or events are much more popular in China than abroad, such as Children's Day, introduced by the United Nations in 1954,[14] and International Women's Day, always important even in the Maoist era.

Chinese youth is also experiencing a real sexual revolution—71 percent of the young respondents to a 2014 survey admitted having had sexual relationships before marriage, which would have been considered actually illegal as recently as 1997.[15] This leads to more abortions and sexually transmitted diseases. Despite sexual education be incorporated into primary as middle-school curricula in 2011, this education by authoritarian parents and conservative schools—because study, after all, is the only goal of school—leaves much to be desired. So it's not easy to raise awareness about contraception, also because restrictions on advertising sex-related products, including condoms, were only lifted in 2014.[16]

Because of this and advertisements portraying abortion as an easy, painless solution, birth control pills are not widely used, unlike in Western countries. Abortion clinics are widely available, and terminating pregnancies is a matter of course. I remember a twenty-two-year-old student in Yichun casually mentioning that she had already had four abortions. A few of my wife's former classmates have also had several each. The National Health and Family Planning Commission estimates that in 2017 nine million abortions were performed.[17]

Generational Conflicts

But the desire for modernity also causes conflicts. While varying degrees of the generation gap exist everywhere, China's rapid, revolutionary change from a Maoist planned economy to a technologically advanced consumer society has made this gap is more of a chasm. Nevertheless, strong family ties remain. Many Chinese teenagers are stuck between the traditional values they grew up with and the modern world they now live in. They still have a sense of duty to their parents and recognize the many genuine sacrifices that elders make for their children. Today's Chinese teenagers have the world on a comparative silver platter: they can say what they feel, work where they like, marry or stay single, have children or buy a dog. Their parents faced tremendous pressure from government and family, and their lives were never their own. The sheer volume of choice overwhelms many families, not to mention financial pressures unheard of in a planned economy. Parents are often happy to drastically reduce their own standard of living to help their children, which is partly because they rely on their children to care for them in their old age. China is a graying society with an underdeveloped social safety net. Most children feel responsible for their parents, allowing them to move into their homes, or transferring them money every month.

China's culture of strong family ties and parental respect creates additional pressure and can take extreme forms. I know a sixty-year-old woman whose life is almost completely determined by her eighty-four-year-old mother. A friend told me of someone who had been supporting his mother, father, sister, and niece since he was twenty-one, but still didn't want his mother to hear he went swimming in a hotel pool, because she thought it was too dangerous. Especially among the post-1980s generation, children know their parents' old-fashioned notions no longer apply in modern China, but they find it difficult to free themselves from parental influence and the associated problems.

Unlike Westerners, who are raised to think and act more independently, Chinese grow up hearing much more about (and from) their parents and older people in general. Grandparents usually decide on their grandchildren's education, often because the grandparents are raising these children in the provinces while the parents work in one of China's big cities, where their lives are governed by the *hukou* registration system. And when the parents themselves take responsibility for their children's education, dads are often absent, because they are away earning money.

I see many Chinese teenagers with "two faces," a modern one for their friends and a traditional, dutiful one for their families. My wife has always been a free spirit and probably a prime example of everything Chinese children should not be. But, with her parents in Tai'an, she is calm and reserved, buying them whatever they would not buy for themselves. She sees this as her duty. The growing emotional distance between the two worlds also causes young people to hide things from their parents. One colleague's mother took a three-hour train ride to take care of her grandson when he had a cold, convinced that she could look after him better than her daughter could. Now, this colleague no longer informs her parents when her son is sick. A lesbian friend in Beijing hides her sexual orientation from her family in her provincial hometown; she and her girlfriend traveled to Australia to get married. Considering how easy it is to track someone's every step on social media, the fact that her parents know nothing of her personal life is quite an achievement!

Stress Factors

Chinese society is a unique combination of traditional values, modern influences, and technological progress. This complexity leads to daily stress. Most Chinese are flexible and pragmatic, but the lack of clear rules creates insecurity. The Western world may complain of stress at work and pressure in general, but this is nothing compared to what the Chinese citizen has to endure privately and in the workplace. In China's megacities, commuters often wait in long lines to board crowded buses and subways. Business days can be long and intense. In Qian'an, it was normal to work from six o'clock in the morning until eight in the evening, even on weekends, after which many would return to a small living space shared with their parents. In China, privacy is a rare and valuable asset, and not having it takes a psychological toll.

Living in a rapidly developing, economically fast-growing society also brings other pressures. Convenience and easy availability of products and services are positives of urban life, but big cities, especially Chinese cities where the population numbers ten to twenty million, can be exhausting. You are never alone in China. Just setting foot outside the door means being confronted with honking cars, electric mopeds weaving through traffic, and crowds on the sidewalk. Once when a friend called tech support from her seventh-story Beijing apartment, the traffic noise below was so loud, she was asked if she was playing with toy trains. Chinese cities are awake day and night: there is never any peace. Those living near construction sites are exposed to noise even on nights and weekends, and it seems that every apartment is being renovated again and again. Citizens connect many of the country's social problems directly with the large population and related competition. Chinese people need to develop a high level of mental resilience to withstand all this.

This accumulation of pressure on the citizen is called *chi ku*, which, translated literally, means "eat the bitterness." The English may be famous for keeping stiff upper lips, but the Chinese excel at biting through life's bitterness, setting aside all comfort, and adapting to circumstances to achieve their goals. *Chi ku* figures in all layers of society and shapes the lives of many. University students may live eight in a room that measures a dozen square meters. Our nanny, well-schooled in *chi ku*, lives with her husband and daughter in a tiny rented apartment so as to save enough to help her daughter buy her own house. Many shopkeepers also eat bitterness, staying open from early morning until late at night, while also living in back rooms where the children do homework and the women hand wash the laundry.

Businesspeople often spend more evenings in restaurants or tea houses networking or negotiating contracts than at home with their families. Those traveling home during the Chinese New Year must also be prepared for *chi ku*. I have taken several holiday trains or buses, but now I avoid the masses as much as possible. The word "masses" is to be understood literally, because once a year at this time, China grinds to a complete halt economically, while nearly the entire population is set in motion. During the Chinese New Year 2019, travelers made around three billion trips across the country, making this the world's largest population migration.[18]

China's transport infrastructure is very well developed, but it should not surprise anyone that during the planet's largest movement of people, connections are in short supply. Bus and train stations are overcrowded with travelers carrying suitcases, boxes, and large plastic totes with zippers. People sometimes stand in line for days during the Chinese New Year to get train tickets to their hometowns, often thousands of miles away—and for some, the holiday ends without them ever leaving the station, and destined to return the next year. *Chi ku* in abundance. In 2010, it took two days for my wife and I to drive our car the four-hundred-mile journey to her birthplace Tai'an, normally an eight-hour journey, including stops along the way. After that, we decided to never again travel by car during Chinese New Year. A former colleague needs to take three bus and train trips to reach his parents' isolated mountain village.

Most Westerners take for granted things like affordable quality education, abundant nature and green spaces, clean air, safe food, and (in Europe) cheap but excellent health care services. They will agree that money does not necessarily make people happy. In China, it's different. In many ways, the financial pressure and the need to earn more are much greater than in the Western world. Home ownership is valued very highly, but with housing in the big Chinese cities as expensive—or sometimes even more expensive—as in big U.S. cities, and comparatively lower salaries, purchasing a home is a considerable burden for many Chinese. A bigger, more expensive house means more privacy and more greenery; higher salaries also provide good (foreign) education instead of cheap public education, as well as safe food in the form of imported products, and international clinics for better health care. The vast majority of the population are firmly convinced that one can buy happiness. "In today's China, it's better to be rich and perhaps unhappy than poor and certainly unhappy," a good friend of my father-in-law says.

Financial status is critical in China, where the main goal of some 1.3 billion people is to improve their own lives and those of their children. Entrepreneurship is seen as of paramount importance in enabling one to lead a financially secure, good life, and the Chinese are among the world's most enterprising people. Those who have "made it" are role models to whom entire generations look up. It's not hard to understand why Chinese society is so competitive.

Decay of Values and Norms

This celebration of financial success means that although the Communist Party may technically run the country, capitalism is king. Just as the Chinese champion individualism to offset the uniformity of the past, unrestrained materialism is a backlash against former decades of scarcity. Things are improving now rapidly, but excesses were common. And where there were excesses, there was also corruption—within the government and in all strata of society. In the series of food scandals, corrupt officials bear as much blame as careless companies. The big environmental problems were not just the result of lax laws unenforced by corrupt officials—companies that channel polluted water into rivers are equally responsible.

Western companies must also accept their share of responsibility. "Made in China" has had a bad reputation in the West, but let's not forget that there are numerous multinational companies in China that have benefited from the system and have increased their profits accordingly. It is hypocritical to blame only Chinese companies, as is often done. Any company that set up shop in China knew—or finds out very quickly—what to expect and had the option of shutting down if faced with corruption or immoral behavior. But the opposite has happened. In a bid to enter the Chinese market in 2016, Facebook seemingly developed a message censorship system.[19] Foxconn, the manufacturer of iPhones, was guilty of labor law violations that could have easily been avoided if Apple had monitored its employees' working conditions. No company is forced to follow non-ethical standards, but many had chosen this path as the easiest way to succeed.

The average Chinese citizen wasn't entirely innocent either. From personal experience, I know that many Chinese businessmen found compliance with ethical standards irrelevant to success. Whenever I asked friends whether corruption should generally be contained, they unanimously answer, "Yes!" If I then asked if they would be just as corrupt if they had the chance, many have the same response. Again, things have changed dramatically but the Chinese considered those with authority or responsibility illegally profiting from the use of their influence to be perfectly normal.

In daily life, one rarely faced corruption, but everyone knows that in special cases a so-called *hong bao* (envelope with money) or a present used to work wonders. One of my best students in Yichun earned a considerable extra income by borrowing company officials' identity cards and taking their compulsory English exams for them. A few days before the birth of our son in Tai'an, my in-laws thought it advisable to invite the gynecologist to dinner. I was puzzled, but they explained that this would ensure a smoother delivery. When a friend took his driving test, he gave the teacher a pair of slippers and cigarettes before he got into the car, which he felt would significantly increase his chance of passing. In the business world, the problem was even much bigger. Not only were there corruption and conflicts of interest at the top, but some employees also had lucrative side jobs.

In Qian'an, where all these practices were taken to the extreme, companies had incredible difficulty managing their staff. Many low-skilled workers literally tried everything to supplement their incomes. Workers in steel companies responsible for loading and unloading trucks often demanded a small additional amount from the truck driver to guarantee faster service. Drivers who did not pay sometimes waited for hours. Workers on the weighbridges sometimes drove trucks over the scales twice or registered the same freight twice and sent the steel company two bills. This "bonus" was shared between the workers and the transport company. Warehouse managers and salesmen also had their own ways of earning more. The owner of a large steel company once told me he just accepted his employees' earning additional income in such ways, casually telling me, "They take everything they can get their hands on."

Morality Crisis

The cocktail of extreme competition, increasing individualism, entrepreneurial spirit, dreams of quick money, and systemic corruption has led to an increasingly acute problem in society: self-centered and sometimes immoral behavior was increasing by the day. Even at school, young people learned that the end justified the means. Sometimes Chinese society seemed to consist of individuals who wanted to gain maximum individual power and freedom at the expense of others. Thirty years of the one-child policy raised children with an "after me, the deluge" mentality—children who cared little about the world beyond themselves. Parents may have had the best intentions, but a whole generation of citizens has de facto grown up as the centers of their own worlds. This was probably unavoidable, since most had two parents and four grandparents clearing their paths and solving their problems. But these only children were poorly prepared for everyday life, especially since education is more theory than practice.

Rapid urbanization has also played a role. After all, many traditional social structures have been lost, in part, because many villages were held together by strong social control and traditional morality. Today, those villages are disappearing. Their residents are housed in new apartment blocks in towns and cities where anonymity and individualism prevail.

Between 2000 and 2010, nearly 900,000 Chinese villages were deserted or displaced by new infrastructure or city expansion. "The DNA of our culture is in the villages," Professor Li Huadong of the China

Traditional Village Protection and Development Research Centre says. "If our villages are destroyed, Chinese people will cease to be Chinese.[20]"

My experience has taught me that ethics and honesty have been better preserved in the countryside and in smaller cities than they have in large urban centers. The rapid transition from a state-controlled society to one with much more individual freedom is leading citizens to seek a new generally accepted moral code. This led to many discussions on social media, and the general opinion seems to be that China still has a long way to go to establish a new set of moral and ethical standards, fit for its rapidly changing image. Even after sixteen years in the country, I am still once in a while frustrated by the sometimes staggering level of self-centered behavior of people around me. This can include elemental issues of courtesy or manners such as smoking in smoke-free areas, talking loudly on buses or in public places, listening to movies on phones without headphones, or cutting in instead of waiting in line with everyone else.

Especially in traffic, Chinese often took the adage "my car, my freedom" literally. People would block whole lanes or even whole roads to run errands, they'll stopped their cars to talk to others on the street and let the traffic pile up behind them, or they would simply park in the middle of the road and get out. When we lived in Beijing, our neighbors were among the richest people in China—one was a well-known movie star, another had a business empire of restaurants and movie theaters. One day, a resident dissatisfied with the building's maintenance services blocked the entrance to the underground parking garage to force the management company's hand, unconcerned that he was preventing his neighbors from parking their Maseratis, Ferraris, and Aston Martins.

Overall, the Chinese remain passive confronted with such occurrences. Responding to antisocial behavior is not rooted in their culture. Fei Xiaotong, a pioneer in Chinese anthropology, studied Chinese society for nearly sixty years. In his famous book *From the Soil: The Foundations of Chinese Society*, he discusses Chinese morality and ethics in the 1940s and calls the high degree of selfishness the greatest fault of the Chinese people.[21] As an example, he described Chinese citizens simply throwing their garbage out of their windows. And this also happened to me once; after parking my car in front of a house in Qian'a one night, I woke to find it covered with kitchen waste.

Guanxi

Of the many stories questioning modern morality in China, two have dominated the media and lodged themselves in Chinese collective memory. In Nanjing, in 2006, a young man named Peng Yu helped an elderly woman who had fallen in the street. He took her to hospital, waited with her to make sure she had not been harmed by her fall, and even paid for her medical treatment. Later, the woman and her family sued Peng for causing her injuries. The judge agreed, on grounds that no innocent person would ever help a total stranger.[22] The court verdict caused a media firestorm, but Chinese society learned its lesson—before lending a hand, think twice.

In fact, people may have recalled this story five years later in connection with the tragic case of Yueyue, a two-year-old girl in Foshan who was hit by a van in a busy market street. The driver took off, crushing her again beneath his rear wheels, while passersby simply ignored her as she lay severely injured in the street. Then she got hit again by a truck. It took several minutes before a woman finally stopped to help the girl.[23] Recorded by traffic cameras, this was later seen by millions of people (including me) on Tudou Youku, the Chinese YouTube, provoking public anger and outraged national debate.

But while many found fault with the judge or the passersby, within the context of traditional Chinese culture, these controversial reactions were not surprising. Even today in China, people tend to only trust their small network, or *guanxi*, of family, friends, acquaintances, and business associates. Everyone who does not belong must look out for themselves. "If it's not your thing, you should not interfere" is perhaps the best description of this mindset. Therefore, the compassionate Peng Yu could not count on the judge's mercy. This makes ostrich-like behavior and indifference widespread in Chinese society. Parents who struggle with a stroller on a staircase should expect no help. On a highway, I once saw a serious traffic accident just twenty meters in front of my car. Three passengers had been flung out of their car and lay bleeding in the street as dozens of vehicles raced past them. Only one other driver and I stopped to help.

On the other hand, the idea of *guanxi* ensures that Chinese people build an extensive network of good and true friends. Human relations are more important than contracts, and China has not always enjoyed a good reputation in negotiations with Western companies. But for those who want to make truly profound friendships—very difficult for foreigners who stay only a few years—a world of great hospitality, sincerely warm personal feelings, and seemingly endless help opens up. For real friends, no effort is too much. I have a very close friend who told me that I belong to a select group of three people for whom he has a rule—that he will come anywhere in China within twenty-four hours if we need urgent help. For him, this principle is absolute.

But *guanxi* also has a downside. My father-in-law opened a restaurant at a young age, but had to close it soon afterward because he always let his friends eat for free. He did not think it appropriate to let them pay. Since *guanxi* works reciprocally, it is good to have it, but better not to return it. *Guanxi* can also work negatively. After all, people can be replaced and lose their positions and power, which makes *guanxi* almost useless and, in some cases, may cause problems. Those who do have *guanxi* usually don't show it too much, precisely because it is such a valuable commodity, whose creation and care requires much effort.

A lack of morality isn't limited to incidents on the streets; it has morphed into organized crime, such as child trafficking, a problem since the 1980s. Official figures are hard to come by, but in 2015 it was estimated that annually 20,000 children were being abducted.[24] Children are most often sold for adoption but some are forced to work as beggars for criminal gangs. Sometimes their own parents sell them, for a myriad of reasons. Whatever the story, it is big business as a boy could be sold for up to $16,000.[25]

A controversial 2014 case involved a Chinese obstetrician who was found guilty of abducting and selling seven babies. The doctor had persuaded parents to give up their children, telling them that their infants were critically ill and would soon be dead anyway. Instead, she sold them to child traffickers.[26] The fact that the doctor—a confidante and counselor—had sold these babies caused tremendous outrage. This has also led to an increase in anxious, watchful parents. When our children were still very little, in public places my wife and I never let them out of our sight in public places.

Big Brother and Big Government

Over the past forty years, China has transformed from a society with excessive control to one with significantly more freedom. As mentioned earlier, now people can lead their own lives, can travel internationally, and enjoy international culture and products. However, despite the great liberal stride forward from 1980s till now, ostensibly to combat corruption and to smooth the path for great economic reforms and projects, that once-celebrated openness is being restricted again. We are not talking about going back to austere Maoist times, but it's clear to see that more control is being exerted again.

When beginning 2018, the Communist Party amended the constitution to end the two-term limit for presidents, Western observers viewed this as a move to make Xi Jinping—for all intents and purposes—an emperor. In China, however, most people saw it differently. I heard many saying that a leader can achieve more in three terms than in two, immediately clarifying that "three terms is enough, but not four." It seems that a lot of Chinese could agree with the move, as long as it doesn't mean a return to the old days of total control. But China is certainly moving—at least for now—back toward a more rigid system. Under Xi, censorship is being reinforced, and crackdowns on dissidents and NGOs are increasing. Stability is more important than ever as internationally China is growing, the world is becoming less stable, the economy slows and the country searches for new balance.

As mentioned China is all digital now, and as such has also tightened surveillance primarily to ensure that everybody obeys the law. According to research in 2020, half of the 770 million cameras in use globally, are installed in China. And 18 out of the top 20 most surveilled cities are in China[27]—while London was in third place. Combined with artificial intelligence and facial recognition software, these cameras create a vast surveillance system, now used to conduct seemingly innocuous tasks, such as monitoring visitors at tourist sites and conducting security checks at airports, and for more invasive purposes, like predictive policing and helping carry out the country's policies.[28] However It's only a small step from there toward stricter control in every way possible, of course.

To the West, another dystopian detail is the establishment of the so-called Social Credit System, which monitors the behavior of government officials, foreign and domestic corporations, and even private citizens. According to the Chinese government, the motivation is to fight corruption and fraud and to rebuild public trust, given its food scandals, pollution, etc. But Western critics see this as a thinly disguised surveillance operation that will track dissidents and violate privacy on a science fiction-level scale. This leads to global outcries that Big Brother is everywhere and reinforces the idea that the Chinese government is all about control. The truth however is much more complicated than that. Nor is a credit system a Chinese invention. Every Westerner has been exposed to it for years already. Anyone who shops on Ebay has a rating on shipping times and communication. Data brokers the timely manner in which one pays its debts, giving customers a score that's used by lenders and mortgage providers, while Uber drivers and passengers both rate each other.[29]

As yet, in China there's no one social credit system. There are local government systems in place on the one hand, and corporate systems on the other. But these are not coordinated at all. The future however might be different, China's social credit system expands the idea of credit checks to all aspects of life: caught jaywalking, don't pay a court bill, play your music too loud on the train—you could lose certain rights, such as booking a flight or train ticket, etc.[30]

But although it's true that technology plays a much larger role in daily life, and control via machines keeps growing, most Chinese willingly sacrifice privacy in return for more security and stability. My Chinese friends do not want the government to have total control, but they see the value of a system that can cull societal rotten apples. Given China's long history of counterfeit products, food scandals, and wide-ranging cheating and fraud that has caused so much damage to Chinese society, this attitude is not surprising. For them, cameras prevent crazy driving, traffic jams, and crime, while the Social Credit System may bring down corrupt local officials. In other words, Chinese citizens are not against more government control as long as they can see a clear advantage and it doesn't cross certain boundaries. Whether these boundaries will in fact be crossed remains to be seen. China's government may have already built the world's largest mass surveillance system, but its citizens appear ready to impose some limits. There are talks of a law that would be China's first ban on the mandatory use of facial recognition technology on private citizens.[31]

And the days of punishing good Samaritans may be waning too. Philanthropy and volunteering are on the rise. Every year, I see more and more charity events being organized. In particular, the 2008 Sichuan earthquake, which killed more than 87,000 and left nearly 5 million homeless, led to a shift in the Chinese attitude toward helping those outside their *guanxi* network. The number of foundations in China shot up, from 1331 in 2008 to more than 6300 in 2018. In 2016, China introduced its first charity law, which promises tax benefits to charitable organizations and emphasizes transparency.[32] Many rich entrepreneurs are focusing on social initiatives to make China a better place to live. Following the example of American counterparts like Bill Gates, they want to give something back to the society that enabled them to realize their own Chinese dream. The truth is that, often because of personal experiences, many Chinese entrepreneurs want to contribute to the country they love. Jack Ma as the most generous and donated both in 2014 and 2015 $2.2 billion.[33] Most entrepreneurs chose to donate to educational institutions, by setting up scholarships, establishing schools, and donating material for students and teachers to enjoy better facilities. Poverty reduction is another area in which rich entrepreneurs choose to donate their money.

Another development is modern China's growing interest in corporate social responsibility. In the great public debate about food safety, pollution, and social problems, Chinese companies are being criticized by their customers for the societal harm they do. It is clear to these large organizations that making a global statement means taking social responsibility. They see, too, that many Western consumers expect multinationals to make positive contributions to society, to work on sustainable development and social responsibility, and to do business fairly. From 1991 to 2005, Chinese companies issued just 22 CSR reports. In 2006–2009, the total rose to nearly 1600.[34] But in the first 10 months of 2019 alone that number had risen to more than 1900.[35] Chinese companies thus increasingly recognize that taking corporate social responsibility is necessary if they are to shake off their reputation for being "fast followers" in the global economy.

Notes

1. *Sixth Tone*. 2018. The truth about China's unknown millions of drug users. www.sixthtone.com/news/1001599/the-truth-about-chinas-unknown-millions-of-drug-users. Accessed October 5, 2019.
2. *The Guardian*. 2008. Bjork's Shanghai surprise: a cry of 'Tibet!'. www.theguardian.com/world/2008/mar/04/china.musicnews. Accessed May 5, 2019.
3. *The Guardian*. 2012. Elton John dedicates Beijing show to Ai Weiwei. www.theguardian.com/world/2012/nov/26/elton-john-dedicates-show-ai-weiwei. Accessed February 21, 2018.
4. *The Guardian*. 2014. Rolling Stones told not to play Honky Tonk Women at Shanghai gig. www.theguardian.com/music/2014/mar/13/rolling-stones-honky-tonk-women-shanghai-gig. Accessed March 5, 2019.

5. Forbes. 2019. Inside the NBA's push to make basketball the world's most popular sport. www.forbes.com/sites/shlomosprung/2019/03/04/nba-china-ceo-derek-chang-takes-us-inside-nbas-push-to-make-basketball-worlds-most-popular-sport/?sh=1258dfdb51b0. Accessed November 5, 2020.
6. *Independent*. 2019. NBA in groveling apologies after China suspends broadcasts of Houston Rockets games over Hong Kong 'freedom' tweet. www.independent.co.uk/news/world/asia/houston-rockets-hong-kong-protests-china-nba-tencent-apology-twitter-a9146211.html. Accessed March 5, 2020.
7. Formula 1. 2015. The Chinese Grand Prix—did you know? www.formula1.com/en/latest/features/2015/4/the-chinese-grand-prix---did-you-know-.html. Accessed April 4, 2019.
8. Rolex Shanghai Masters. 2021. Event information. https://en.rolexshanghaimasters.com/event-info. Accessed January 4, 2021.
9. *Sixth Tone*. 2020. The show must go on: how Cirque du Soleil survived China's lockdown. www.sixthtone.com/news/1006086/the-show-must-go-on-how-cirque-de-soleil-survived-chinas-lockdown. Accessed January 5, 2021.
10. *That's Guangzhou*. 2016. The wonderful world of Disney on ice! Is coming to Guangzhou. www.thatsmags.com/guangzhou/post/15749/the-wonderful-world-of-disney-on-ice-is-coming-to-guangzhou. Accessed May 5, 2019.
11. *CNBC*. 2017. Shanghai is becoming the most profitable Disneyland park in the world: analyst. www.cnbc.com/2017/06/16/shangahi-is-becoming-the-most-profitable-disneyland-park-in-the-world.html. Accessed March 5, 2019.
12. *Chinadaily*. 2018. Sanya to host Miss World 2018. www.chinadaily.com.cn/a/201810/11/WS5bbf09b0a310eff303281dbc.html. Accessed April 8, 2019.
13. Thomson Reuters. 2017. Pumpkin production doubled in a decade. Who's winning this race? https://blogs.thomsonreuters.com/answerson/pumpkin-production-doubled-decade-whos-winning-race/. Accessed August 11, 2019.
14. United Nations. 2021. World Children's Day 20 November. www.un.org/en/observances/world-childrens-day#:~:text=World%20Children%27s%20Day%20was%20first,worldwide%2C%20and%20improving%20children%27s%20welfare. Accessed April 2, 2020.
15. *BBC*. 2016. China's high-speed sexual revolution. www.bbc.com/news/magazine-35525566. Accessed November 15, 2019.
16. *Sixth Tone*. 2018. Left in the dark on contraception, young Chinese seek abortions. www.sixthtone.com/news/1002188/left-in-the-dark-on-

contraception%2C-young-chinese-seek-abortions. Accessed March 5, 2020.
17. *Sixth Tone*. 2018. Left in the dark on contraception, young Chinese seek abortions. www.sixthtone.com/news/1002188/left-in-the-dark-on-contraception%2C-young-chinese-seek-abortions. Accessed March 5, 2020.
18. *CNN*. 2019. World's largest annual human migration now underway in China. https://edition.cnn.com/travel/article/lunar-new-year-travel-rush-2019/index.html. Accessed March 5, 2020.
19. *The New York Times*. 2016. Facebook said to create censorship tool to get back into China. www.nytimes.com/2016/11/22/technology/facebook-censorship-tool-china.html. Accessed November 4, 2020.
20. *The Telegraph*. 2013. China's villages vanish amid rush for the cities. www.telegraph.co.uk/news/worldnews/asia/china/10470077/Chinas-villages-vanish-amid-rush-for-the-cities.html. Accessed June 22, 2019.
21. Professor Fei Xiaotong. The Chinese University of Hong Kong. http://www.cuhk.edu.hk/ipro/991022-4.htm. Accessed December 5, 2020.
22. *Sixth Tone*. 2017. What a tragic traffic accident incident says about Chinese social ethics. www.sixthtone.com/news/1000343/what-a-tragic-traffic-incident-says-about-chinese-social-ethics. Accessed March 29, 2019.
23. *The Guardian*. 2011. Toddler left dying after hit and run prompts soul searching in China. https://www.theguardian.com/world/2011/oct/17/toddler-hit-and-run-china. Accessed March 6, 2019.
24. *BBC*. 2020. China abduction: Parents find son snatched in hotel 32 years ago. https://www.bbc.com/news/world-asia-china-52717670. Accessed January 5, 2021.
25. *BBC*. 2015. The father searching for his abducted son. https://www.bbc.com/news/magazine-31814295. Accessed January 3, 2021.
26. *BBC*. 2014. China doctor jailed for selling babies to traffickers. www.bbc.com/news/world-asia-china-25723863. Accessed January 6, 2021.
27. Comparitech. 2020. Surveillance camera statistics: which cities have the most CCTV cameras? www.comparitech.com/vpn-privacy/the-worlds-most-surveilled-cities/ Accessed October 22, 2020.
28. *Fortune*. 2020. The world's largest surveillance system is growing—and so is it's backlash. https://fortune.com/2020/11/03/china-surveillance-system-backlash-worlds-largest/ Accessed January 7, 2021.
29. *Wired*. 2019. The complicated truth about China's social credit system. www.wired.co.uk/article/china-social-credit-system-explained. Accessed January 4, 2021.
30. *Wired*. 2019. The complicated truth about China's social credit system. www.wired.co.uk/article/china-social-credit-system-explained. Accessed January 4, 2021.

31. *Fortune*. The world's largest surveillance system is growing—and so is it's backlash. https://fortune.com/2020/11/03/china-surveillance-system-backlash-worlds-largest/. Accessed December 4, 2020.
32. *Sixth Tone*. 2018. The destructive earthquake that gave China's charities new life. https://www.sixthtone.com/news/1002250/the-destructive-earthquake-that-gave-chinas-charities-new-life. Accessed March 4, 2020.
33. China Development Relief. 2020. Philanthropy by Chinese entrepreneurs: the trends over the past decade. https://chinadevelopmentbrief.cn/reports/philanthropy-by-chinese-entrepreneurs-the-trends-over-the-last-decade/. Accessed January 4, 2021.
34. Collective responsibility. 2018. CSR in China: from follower to leader. www.coresponsibility.com/csr-china-follower-leader/. Accessed November 4, 2020.
35. CSR-China. 2019. The GoldenBee CSR report honor roll 2019 released. http://en.csr-china.net/a/knowledge/CSRNews/2019/1226/500.html. Accessed March 5, 2020.

CHAPTER 10

Qian'an: From Zero to Hero (and Back)

In September 2008, I moved to Qian'an in Hebei Province, a city 125 miles east of Beijing, to set up a new joint-venture company, which included building and then managing a new cement factory. The first time I traveled to Qian'an to meet our future Chinese joint-venture partner, he was flanked by senior officials from the local government. This was a clear sign of how entwined government and business are in China. Developing a constructive relationship with the local government, always a business partner, is an absolute requirement. Since the plans for the joint-venture partnership were still in the initial phases and no contract had yet been signed, the government had rolled out the red carpet for the foreign investors and waxed poetic about the advantages of investing in the city. An investment by a foreign company would not only create more jobs and generate more tax revenue, it would also boost the city's image.

After the effusive greeting, the extensive reception committee took me on a grand tour. The first thing I noticed was that everything in the city revolved around prestige and power. After visiting a huge, hypermodern steel plant, we went to the local museum to see a 3-D movie giving an overview of the city's history, a source of great pride to the local officials. After lunch, there was an official reception at the town hall, where one of the four vice mayors warmly expressed his hope that we would soon be able to sign an official joint-venture agreement with our partner and complete the investment. If we needed any governmental assistance, we

S. Agten, *Adventures in the Chinese Economy: 16 Years from the Inside*, https://doi.org/10.1007/978-981-16-1167-4_10

had only to ask. Nothing was impossible. To finish the day, he invited me for an extravagant banquet. Clearly, our planned investment was fully supported by the local administration, who would do everything in their power to get our company to Qian'an.

Small and Local

I lived in Qian'an for three years and worked there for another two. The city is characterized by heavy industry, lots of air pollution, and almost everything else that modern China no longer wants to be associated with. It's a Tier IV city and had fewer than eight hundred thousand inhabitants in 2018,[1] just a small town to most Chinese. People from international cities like Beijing or Shanghai avoid living or working there, because the population still clings to its traditional habits, observes its own time, and depends on the local *guanxi* network of friends and acquaintances. "It's not what you know, but who you know" is the rule. Laws and regulations are loose concepts. In most cases, the local government—not the court system—acted as the ultimate judge, determining what was right and wrong, allowed or forbidden. Foreign visitors are rare, and seen by locals as an oddity. On the popular website TripAdvisor, where people post reviews of hotels and places of interest, a German businessman described the city as a place best avoided. A Chinese traveler wrote that one should only visit the city if one had no other choice. The Great Wall, which winds through the mountains, was—for many—Qian'an's only highlight.

Like hundreds of other Chinese cities, Qian'an is almost entirely dependent on one economic sector. A good illustration of this is Datang, also known as Sock City because it accounts for almost 30 percent of the world's sock production.[2] For its part, Qian'an was a giant steel hub. As much steel is being produced in Qian'an as in the whole of Germany, not exactly a small sector player. Astonishingly, Qian'an developed this industry from scratch starting in the year 2000. Before then, only one state-owned enterprise, the Shougang Group, was allowed to produce steel. From 2000 on, however, private companies joined the game, which created the kind of dynamic and frenzied environment only possible in China. Enormous steel plants were built virtually overnight. Local farmers who owned land rich in iron ore transformed their farmlands into mines. Some made their fortunes in a matter of weeks. Shougang Group employees resigned their jobs and used their expertise to set up their own steel mills. Huge money flows developed to financially support the capital-intensive steel sector.

When I moved to the city in 2008, there were already ten huge steel plants and several smaller steel companies producing steel and its derivatives. Constructed in five years over seventy-seven square miles, they kept expanding. Even during the 2009 financial crisis, local government was encouraging new, larger production lines. This newly acquired wealth completely transformed Qian'an. On several occasions I was told that the city had entered the top fifty of China's most prosperous Tier IV cities in 2011, something of which locals were particularly proud. As the newly rich, growing middle class demanded better homes, new apartment buildings kept sprouting up. Entire villages were razed to make room for new structures, including shopping malls and a grandiose government building. In 2008, there were only a few supermarkets offering a handful of Western products. Four years later came a shiny new shopping center selling Western brands such as Nike and Adidas. Better still, Qian'an had a big modern park where residents could relax at the lake or eat at one of the many restaurants. The remaining villages around the city, most of which housed heavy industry workers, abandoned their wells and adopted running water. To improve transport into the city, in 2006, Qian'an got an exit on the newly built highway that ran from Beijing to the northern provinces of Jilin and Liaoning.

The local population's standard of living improved at a staggering speed. Working for the steel companies, former peasants earned much more than they ever had from their fields. Heavy industry caused a lot of pollution, but it was also an indispensable source of income.

That was the context in which we set up our joint venture. It was the right place at the right time. Foreign companies wanting to invest in China need to check whether they can actually realize that investment. The Chinese government has categorized the different economic areas and industries into sectors in which investment is encouraged, allowed, restricted, or outright prohibited. While foreign investment over a broad range of sectors used to be strongly encouraged, that number has decreased, as many fields reduce their dependence on Western technology. For example, the cement sector allowed foreign investments, but neither tax cuts nor other benefits. Moreover, investing in China is a cumbersome procedure, because almost all government agencies need to be involved. In the case of our Sino-Belgian joint venture with an investment of close to $10 million dollars in the cement sector, categorized as a polluting industry, we were faced with a tedious procedure. It used to be that new plants were easily approved, because they provided employment for the local population and generated new revenue streams for the local government, but in 2008, environmental factors were considered more thoroughly before approval could be granted.

The City Council as Business Partner

In the months following the joint-venture contract signing, it became apparent that we needed to involve the local city government to speed things up. Qian'an's wasn't the only approval needed; the city and its neighboring Tier IV cities all belong to the administrative region of Tangshan, a Tier III city, which in turn reports directly to Hebei Province. Since a foreign company investing in Qian'an also needed the review and approval of the competent authorities in Tangshan, this meant that the two city administrations had to negotiate with each other over the application. One of Qian'an's vice mayors was the driving force behind the local settlement, and having committed to our investment going ahead with all due speed, he threw all his weight behind the project.

But despite his strong support, it became clear that the Tangshan government had more questions and comments than did the officials in Qian'an. Their view was that the region had so many cement and steel companies already, and the city was feeling the environmental effects. Around this time, the central government had begun to exert pressure on provincial and city governments to address air pollution issues more vigorously. This meant that Tangshan granting quick approval was far from a given. And as my presence as general manager of the future joint venture would help move things faster, Qian'an's vice mayor asked me to join the daily negotiations and evening banquets with the representatives of the different government agencies.

Clearly, the whole approval process was a political issue. Tangshan's city government had to be absolutely certain that Hebei Province authorities would go along. Qian'an's city government simply wanted our investment—and soon. Eventually the joint venture was approved at all government levels, but the whole process took twice as long as planned.

That Qian'an eventually got what it wanted was by no means an exception. As a matter of fact, all Tangshan's regional Tier IV cities tried to make their own mark. In a world where everything revolved around power, money, and influence, each of the cities used every possible means to attract investors. This included business conferences organized by the Tangshan government. One of these, to which my company was invited, actually took place in Shenzhen, a southern city in Guangdong Province, almost two thousand miles away. No doubt Shenzhen's sun-kissed location, right across the water from the tax-free Hong Kong and Macao casinos, was a strong selling point for investors and officials alike.

As general manager of our newly formed joint venture, I received an invitation to this conference, where I was to sign an official letter of intent to invest $10 million in Qian'an. Officials wanted to show the outside world how international the city is and how attractive their location would be to foreign investors. I quickly realized that our relatively modest investment was actually more important to the city's image than the tens of millions of dollars that the local steel giants had invested. And it was clear that Qian'an had spared no expense or effort to make me comfortable in Shenzhen. The morning after we got there, a procession of rental cars arrived at our five-star hotel to take the delegation to the conference center. The party secretary and mayor, number one and number two in Qian'an's government apparatus, rode in the first car—a black Porsche Cayenne. I found myself with the vice mayor in a luxurious BMW. I asked him if it was customary to rent luxurious cars to transport government personnel, and added that they would not do that in Qian'an, because it wasted taxpayers' money. The vice mayor answered that these cars were part of the city's image and therefore justified the costs. And he reminded me, with a little laugh, that we were in Shenzhen—far away from Qian'an.

Shortly before we arrived at the conference center, we stopped at another five-star hotel where the vice mayor presented the letter of intent for the planned investment of $10 million—which actually said $30 million. When I pointed out this "mistake," he explained that the entire conference was a promotional event and juggling previously agreed amounts of money need not bother anyone. I was obliged to play along to avoid loss of face by Qian'an.

Elegant hostesses led us into the conference hall and seated the vice mayor and me behind the Qian'an party secretary, now glued to his cell phone, and the Qian'an mayor, who was struggling to stay awake. In the row behind us I noticed another foreigner and asked him which Qian'an company he represented. He replied that he was Australian and actually worked in a Shenzhen local school as an English teacher. He had been invited to come to the conference center that morning, however, where all he would have to do was mount the stage looking like a Western company representative and sign something.

Saving Qian'an's Self-Image

More than a year later, we opened our new factory in a ceremony that hosted a Belgian diplomat and some foreign industrialists. The city administration was thrilled to receive these guests. The Belgian diplomat had covered the 125 miles from Beijing in a small red Nissan, a great contrast to the procession of black Audis that came courtesy of the city council. When the vice mayor saw the nondescript vehicle with the Belgian flag and diplomatic service number plate, he asked me if this could really be an official Belgian delegation. I reassured him that it was. But the city government had also blundered. On the morning of the opening, the organizers realized that no Belgian flag was available for the official welcoming event, which caused panic. Eventually, to general relief at having avoided harming Qian'an's image, someone found one.

Qian'an suffered from the very excesses that China's central government was trying to eradicate, including rampant corruption, lust for profit, abuse of power, and nepotism. Since these negatively impacted the lives of Chinese citizens, Beijing was struggling to bring local officials under control. They ruled over their cities like little kings and cared little for what happened in the capital. Of course, not all officials are stupid machines or avaricious animals; many are knowledgeable, pleasant, and sensible. I had many opportunities to work constructively with this kind of official. However, the other variety did not miss any opportunity to take their share of the cake, and they often combined corruption with incompetence.

Local Government Debt

Ministry of Commerce data show that Chinese local government debt in 2016 (about $2.2 trillion) was equivalent to approximately 25 percent of the country's GDP.[3] Qian'an certainly did its part in this. Determined to claim their place in the Chinese sun, the city council commissioned grandiose designs to showcase Qian'an and took out huge loans to finance the projects.

For example, a square mile of the city's suburbs were flattened to create a sports park and associated shopping centers. A large indoor and outdoor sports stadium, it was hoped, would make Qian'an a future host city for national and perhaps even international sporting events—and that meant guests. The city council joined forces with a large steel company and built an enormous five-star hotel, financed with bank loans guaranteed by the council. Many projects have been funded this way. Shortly after the hotel's official opening, I booked a room—and was one of only four guests.

In China, there are many rapidly erected prestigious buildings designed to make lasting impressions, but that remain essentially empty—and, to keep costs down, cold dark, and dimly lit. In any case, these luxurious hotels do not meet the needs of the local population. The city administration has helped heavy industry in many ways, such as encouraging local steel companies to expand, even it meant borrowing heavily. The government often secured these loans, and if Tangshan city or Hebei Province refused to issue the necessary permits, the Qian'an City Council did so themselves. Some new production lines did not officially exist, and some excess production was never recorded. However, the central government in Beijing is taking action to end such practices.

Corruption

To me, signs of corruption were visible as soon as we moved to Qian'an. In our apartment complex, most of our neighbors were local entrepreneurs and senior local government officials. Since an apartment costs about $200,000, and an average government official's monthly salary ranges from $200 to $2000, it seemed strange that so many officials lived in the area. Then I learned how the system worked. Many neighbors had received their homes from some local big companies—along with their Mercedes, BMWs, Ferraris, or even Lamborghinis. I was surprised to see these cars covered with a thick layer of dust in the parking garage, but a friend explained that some were gifts from local companies that officials did not dare use, because they were too conspicuous. Entrepreneurs, on the other hand, had of course no problems in driving around in their fancy cars.

Lower-ranking officials, well aware that their superiors were laden with gifts, also wanted their share. Many companies receive surprise inspections from governmental agencies Inspectors found "problems" that served as pretexts for threatening high fines, and companies responded by giving regular gifts instead. Inspectors often came just before noon or in the late afternoon, so they could be invited to lunch and then a banquet or karaoke night. In fact, some local officials spent more time in restaurants than in their offices.

Other officials found varied ways to ensure that they were not forgotten by the local companies. For example, they often invited corporate executives to their sons' or daughters' weddings, basically with the sole purpose of receiving all kinds of gifts. At housewarming parties, the situation was often similar. And when one of the higher officials announced that his father had died, the fifty-meter line of mourners looked suspiciously like wedding guests in the movie *The Godfather*. They all had envelopes, or even suitcases of gifts for the grieving son. One friend was a young civil servant with a responsible position in the Ministry of Environmental Protection. Realizing that this position could make him a lot of money, he prepared an envelope for the recruitment officer in order to get the job, telling me that this was a worthwhile investment, because he would soon make it all back.

Even in the villages, politics were characterized by conflicts of interest. Most of our production staff came from small villages near Qian'an, so I heard firsthand about how villagers used direct elections to choose their co-leaders—the mayor and party secretary—and how a system of buying votes was the most common way of winning. Because I was a foreigner who spoke Chinese, I received countless invitations to banquets and other government events. The more I attended, the more they trusted me, and the more I got to understand their complex arrangements.

For example, during Chinese New Year 2011, I went to dinner at a senior official's home. I was shocked to see at least fifty bottles of alcohol in his kitchen, each more expensive than the last. There were also stacks of high-grade tea (which can run to thousands of dollars) and packs of cigarettes. He told me that these were gifts from friends, and that he was going to sell them to local liquor stores and earn himself a considerable extra income. The same official later invited me to a banquet with other top officials, where they spoke freely to me about their lives and work—investments and real estate deals, corrupt arrangements, self-enrichment, and plenty of other secret practices. which were open only to a limited group. By the end of the evening, it not only felt as though I were part of the inner circle but the whole experience felt like a scene from a mafia movie. Business was booming, and everyone always knew someone who could help.

Many officials have become instantly and enormously rich. Executives place their sisters and brothers in prominent positions, and authorities award lucrative contracts to their former classmates. One of Qian'an's vice mayors had previously taught at a local high school, so he knew everyone in the city—and the Old Boys network did him excellent service. The cross-fertilization between the business world and the government was inevitable; some were making ethically suspect investments, while others were installing their family members in powerful positions.

However, these unbridled practices and arbitrary decisions of local councils also caused dissatisfaction, even anger among local populations. This has led to social unrest, especially in the wake of forced land expropriations. Property developers had a deal with local governments to replace entire villages with new homes. In Qian'an, this created rows of half-empty apartment blocks. The original inhabitants were usually compensated financially and with new housing, but running water, better heating, and better hygiene could not compensate for what they had lost, namely, their family homes and their neighbors, who now all lived separately. Modernization came at a heavy social cost in Qian'an. And because the new apartment blocks were built so quickly, there was an oversupply. Buyers simply could not be found.

Tensions and Problems

Disgruntled citizens could take their cases to the town hall and approach the local administration directly. When their complaints went unheeded, they would try Beijing, sometimes by traveling there by train. The Qian'an City Council had to post a permanent observer at the local station and report when angry citizens were headed to the capital. Sometimes local politicians were summoned to Beijing to be reprimanded or make a verbal or written statement about a local problem. Because Qian'an lived entirely from heavy industry revenues, it quickly reallocated agricultural land to local businesses. This was not in line with central government planning, which envisaged a gradual development and provided a limited number of industrial or mining permits. But the city administration, which of course wanted to accelerate development, had almost all the large companies settled on formerly agricultural land. For their part, farmers saw no harm in leasing their land to wealthy companies—it was, after all, much more lucrative than growing crops.

Our company also leased arable land from the village, but even with a thirty-year contract, we had to renegotiate each year to take the ever-rising cost of living into account. In 2010, the lease negotiations dragged on for weeks. The villagers had completely unrealistic expectations and compromise seemed impossible. As the conflict escalated, some villagers began to block the port and access the road to the company. No trucks could get in or out. Now my colleagues and I had to consult the police. Officials tried to calm the residents and persuade them to dissolve the blockade, but emotions ran too high. It took a few hours, but a compromise was reached and the blockade was finally lifted.

This kind of tension is not uncommon, and citizens can take the law into their own hands, particularly when a lot of money is involved. Back in 2009, the development of a new mine had led to a veritable popular uprising. The Qian'an local government had promised to engage a company with whom they had good contacts, but seeing a way out of poverty, the villagers wanted to work the mine themselves. The negotiations failed, and the people retaliated by blocking the access roads to the village. When an official was sent into defuse the situation, they beat him to the point where he had to be hospitalized because of his injuries. The next day, the city council intervened. With the support of the police, they opened the road again.

Even without all these problems, companies found doing regular business already a big challenge. The deadly competition and rapid legal and administrative changes created a tough business climate. In 2008, we founded our joint venture for the production of slag powder for the cement industry, but this product was hardly known in the regional market. Slag powder is made from raw slag, itself a by-product of steel production, which is ground to powder. In the West, it has been a valuable recycling product for years, but in Qian'an it often ended up illegally in nearby mountains, which were used as dumping grounds. Our joint venture wanted to change that by producing slag powder on a large scale, but even our head start over our competition didn't help much. Steel companies quickly realized that their raw slag had some added value and started building factories many times bigger than ours. By 2011, three years after our joint venture was formed, we were already surrounded by serious competitors and were downgraded to a small player.

In fact, it boiled down to competing against companies whose production capacity could supply slag powder throughout Western Europe. Quickly and efficiently, the locals closed the gap that existed on the regional market, and the enormous speed with which new competitors gained a foothold in the slag powder market was phenomenal and unimaginable to Western eyes. In addition, our competitors were financially strong and bolstered by Chinese bank loans and local government support. The consequences were staggering. The rapid increase in production capacity resulted in a price decline that saw slag powder rapidly downgraded from a premium to a commodity product. The cutthroat competition also eroded profits. Since our competitors' profits came mainly from steel production, not slag powder, they saw little effect, but the consequences for our joint venture were dramatic. We had no choice but to close.

New Empires

This story is just one example of how hard it is to do business in China. Despite this—or maybe because of this—many companies and business leaders in Qian'an have become wealthy overnight. They are literally the nouveaux riches, people with little training and few of the sophisticated manners usually associated with their income. "Until a few years ago, these super-rich were just farmers," a Qian'an friend told me. "Now they are farmers with Jaguars or BMWs." The economic development of Qian'an seemed to make anything possible, and nobody ever missed a chance to show off their enormous wealth. There are as many luxury cars in the streets of Qian'an as there are in The Hamptons or Beverly Hills. Some furnished their houses in French Louis XVI style, complete with four-poster beds, while others bought Tibetan mastiffs, dogs that can cost hundreds of thousands of dollars (its red eyes make it a status symbol).

Parents brought their teenagers to my wife's shop, and left with clothes costing thousands of dollars. But at least clothing shopping is legal. As with everywhere, Chinese super-rich also create their own entertainment, which the police may or may not be aware of. An acquaintance of mine organized gambling events in luxury hotels and high-end teahouses. The owner of the Belgian company PIPA, the world leader in sales of racing pigeons, told me that one of his best customers is from the Qian'an region. He regularly buys pigeons at astronomical prices, then enters them in competitions. These sporting pigeons sell for hundreds of thousands of dollars.

But, as mentioned before, the super-rich are in some ways chained to Qian'an. They owe their success to local connections and cannot operate outside their network. "King in Qian'an, a nobody in Beijing," is the way many put it. The capital's residents look down on these farmers with BMWs, criticizing their unsophisticated behavior and strong accents. And while a fair wealth distribution is clearly absent, Qian'an is a microcosm of China. The central government in Beijing is thus making social stability and equal economic development a priority, and seeks to stamp out corruption and conflicts of interest, especially among local authorities, such as in Qian'an.

The New Qian'an

Since I lived there Qian'an went through many changes. In spring 2015, I returned to visit old friends and found Qian'an a shadow of what it was just a few years ago. As China's construction temporarily declined, so did its heavy industry. Most of the city's smallest, least efficient, and most polluting steel companies had gone bankrupt, unable to survive in a sector now beset with overproduction and stricter air pollution control. Where labor shortages once prevailed, unemployment was rising. Alcoholism and petty crime were predominant problems. Hebei Province reduced steel production by sixty million tons in 2017,[4] but large companies have become more environmentally efficient and have bought state-of-the-art machinery that enables them to increase their profits, compete with foreign companies, and enter new markets.

As always, the city administration is trying to change course and adapt to its new environment, focusing now on renewable energy investments. The vice mayor asked me if I knew any Western companies interested in investing in Qian'an.

Slowly but steadily Qian'an transformed itself and adapted to the New China. Steel still remains the dominant industry, but the city has cleaned up its act and has made remarkable steps toward everything a modern economy needs. Now Qian'an is a far cry from 2015. Most striking is the impact of President Xi Jinping's 2012 anti-corruption campaign, which brought many Qian'an officials to justice. Since being inconspicuous is the only way to survive, most officials consciously try to stay under the radar, selling their expensive apartments and luxurious cars. Even the local government has stopped providing fleets of shiny black Audis for official functions, and now opts for cheaper Volkswagen Santanas.

Every exaggerated luxury has disappeared. The big ultramodern offices where the officials worked have given way to much smaller units, and expensive banquets are becoming a thing of the past. When I lived in Qian'an, senior officials often had access to company credit cards and regularly invited guests to top restaurants. These cards have effectively now been abolished. Often, these officials even had their own alcohol suppliers, who were available day and night. At several banquets I saw an official phoning a supplier because he urgently needed an expensive rice wine or other alcohol. Qian'an liquor stores once did very good business, but now restaurants and beverage dealerships have to accept enormous income losses. Conspicuous nepotism has almost disappeared, as has direct bribery of officials. In the past, everyone in Qian'an knew that everything was for sale, if the price was right, and everyone was mixed up with everyone else. Companies that did not meet environmental requirements just bought the necessary permits. Family members that needed jobs got jobs. And life went on as usual.

At the beginning of the anti-corruption campaign, it looked as if Qian'an could avoid adhering to the new standards by lying low and waiting for the storm to pass. This hasn't happened. Beijing has strengthened its control over local government and sought to eradicate the old habits. Several local government officials are under suspicion of corruption. Some have fled the city and remain in hiding, afraid of social media. The central government has even launched an app that allows citizens to report corrupt behavior. The vice mayor, whom I met on my very first visit to Qian'an, has been suspected for some time of accepting bribes. He is now in prison. Some other officials were already been arrested and convicted of corruption. The owner of a local steelworks was also convicted of bribery and has been in jail for a year. It's strange to think that people I knew relatively well and saw regularly at banquets have suddenly disappeared. The same is true in other cities. Local officials complain that the strict rules and rigid controls have made it more difficult to "manage" the local population, but empowered citizens are standing up for their rights and recognizing the importance of laws' prevailing over relationships. Qian'an's experience is typical of the country's two decades of massive transformation. Modern China is yet again changing in many ways, and the old habits are no longer acceptable.

Notes

1. CEIC. 2018. China population: County level region. www.ceicdata.com/en/china/population-county-level-region?page=71. Accessed December 3, 2020.
2. Xinhuanet. 2017. Across China: Sock capital on the front foot. www.xinhuanet.com/english/2017-11/23/c_136774699.htm. Accessed April 4, 2018.
3. *The Diplomat*. 2017. Why China's local debt policies may spell slower growth. https://thediplomat.com/2017/07/why-chinas-local-debt-policies-may-spell-slower-growth. Accessed September 7, 2019.
4. The People's government of Hebei's province. 2017. www.hebei.gov.cn/english/10718769/10718845/12626607/index.html. Tangshan to reduce steel production capacity.

CHAPTER 11

China Goes Global

For several days in September 2015, my Chinese colleagues had been spending their lunch breaks checking their investments on the Shanghai Stock Exchange. Many Chinese like to gamble anyway, but now the stock market seemed to be their game of choice. Regardless of investment size, the entire country seemed transfixed by the stock market boom of those days. But when week after week, the stock prices kept tumbling, investors' moods were changing dramatically. Casual investors accepted their fate, laughingly telling me that they would travel a bit less for the holidays. Others who had invested hundreds of thousands of dollars, and even borrowed money to buy stocks, saw no way out. Short movies on various social media even showed individuals who had bet everything they had on the stock market jumping from rooftops. Others had lost all their savings. In the years after Western economists and analysts were wondering whether the Chinese economy was heading for a hard landing. Economic growth of 10 percent, considered normal until a few years before, had fallen to 6.1 percent in 2019.[1] The post-Covid-19 recovery short time might prove an exception but under normal circumstances this growth will continue to drop over the next few years. As the Chinese economy started rebalancing, the traditional drivers of investment in domestic infrastructure and exports abroad, are under pressure, and the U.S.–China trade war has done damage.

S. Agten, *Adventures in the Chinese Economy: 16 Years from the Inside*,
https://doi.org/10.1007/978-981-16-1167-4_11

Over the past few years, the Chinese economy has faced more challenges than ever before. Despite China's export continuous growth since 40 years, there have been two exceptions during the last 15 years: during the 2008–2009 financial and between 2014 and 2016, exports fell. That being said exports of goods and services in 2007 valued at $1.26 trillion, while in 2019 that number doubled to $2.6 trillion.[2] But the U.S.–China trade war led to consumers and businesses losing trust, which caused among others slumping car sales and a stumbling housing market. The coronavirus pandemic made things in the first half of 2020 even worse. Many companies were fighting for their lives or closing their doors. Workers were losing jobs and graduates couldn't find new jobs. Many in the real estate sector worried about a bubble. A construction slowdown means architects are dismissing staff. Meanwhile, over the past few years, the coal and steel industries have cut millions of jobs in a long-delayed restructuring that aims to scale back unprofitable state-owned enterprises and upgrade the country's manufacturing sector. In the steel and coal sector, the government announced a plan in 2016 to lay off 1.8 million people.[3] Cities almost entirely dependent on heavy industry, like Qian'an, are struggling to pay their debts, and this affects the entire country. As pointed out before huge loans assumed, sometimes irresponsibly, by regional governments account for half of China's national debt. Growing capital flight has also required the government to undertake draconian measures to keep money in China. In 2015–2016 the country lost $1.28 trillion when the economy faltered and China suddenly devalued the yuan.[4] These are all signs of major issues within the Chinese economy which needs to be addressed.

And what happens in China affects now the whole world. IMF data show that in 2018 China's contribution to the world GDP reached 21.74 percent, higher than other country.[5] China is the largest export destination for 33 countries, and the largest source of import for 65.[6] A fifth of Japanese exports go to China,[7] as do a third of Australia's.[8] China is the third-largest export market for the United States. In 2019, the United States exports to China were valued at $106.6 billion—which was a decline of 11 percent compared to 2018.[9] Despite the U.S.–China disputes, the growing Chinese middle class is increasingly important for the United States and a key driver of growth for the American economy. Germany, the main engine of the European economy, and China were in 2019 for the fourth consecutive year the biggest trade partners. In 2019 goods worth 206 billion euros were traded between Germany and

China.[10] Faced with a Chinese economic slowdown, German companies will lose sales, and employees might get laid off. Not too long ago, it was inconceivable that the Shanghai Stock Exchange could influence worldwide prices; today its importance is much more significant. Globally, commodity prices fall when the Chinese economy slows down. A hard landing for China could drag the whole world into crisis.

A Natural Economic Development

China sought to rebalance its economy following the global economic crisis of 2008–2009, recognizing that since foreign markets could falter, it could no longer mainly rely on exports and needed to develop more robust domestic consumption. Despite the trade war and economic slowdown, however, most Western media gloom-and-doom stories about the Chinese economy should be taken in context. One forgets that the 2019 economic growth rate of 6.1 percent is still phenomenal,[11] and that China has become a real economic superpower. Moreover, China is creating a modern economy, a process that takes time. Just like that of Taiwan, South Korea, and Japan in the past, Chinese growth in the past was mainly based on foreign direct investment, heavy industry, and exports. However, the 2008–2009 financial crisis was a clear signal to choose another course, one that did not rely so heavily on exports.

For several years now, China has been pursuing a policy to balance the economy, what President Xi Jinping referred to in 2014 as China's "new normal."[12] This would, among other things, decelerate growth slightly and shift economic focus from investment to innovation, as the government stimulates domestic consumption, grows its middle class, and strengthens the service sector. Manufacturing companies produce more value-added goods, which results in a slower, but—it may be hoped—more sustainable growth. However, this policy is often difficult to implement, because slow economic growth makes companies, investors, and trading partners nervous. China is undergoing a natural evolution similar to that of other countries that have evolved into modern economies. The biggest difference is that China's development has moved much faster and bigger, and been more robust, which creates both excesses and extremes. After all, this economic ship is gigantic, and it leaves a larger wake.

The transformation and the balanced economy however are slowly becoming a reality. Where exports in 2007 counted for 35.4 percent of

China's GDP, in 2019 this counted for 18.4 percent.[13] In other words, export has become relatively less of driver in China's GDP. China is also transitioning into a service-oriented economy. The service sector is now greater than either the industrial production sector or the construction sector and already makes up half of GDP.[14] The most important growth engines are no longer investment, but domestic consumption, a sector poised for significant growth. E-commerce and the sharing economy are gigantic in China. Already the country is the world's largest digital marketplace, and the Chinese internet companies are world leaders in their fields. Every year, Chinese citizens spend more and more on consumption. But whatever the engine, the Chinese economy is resilient. Cities like Qian'an, which have to adapt to the new reality, are ready to reinvent themselves to accommodate this new normal. For them, it's a choice between swimming or drowning.

Because the Chinese economy will become more dependent on the spending of its own citizens, and especially of the growing middle class, urbanization still plays a crucial role. After all, urban residents are much better consumers than rural ones.

Meanwhile, the government has also encouraged citizens to buy shares on the stock exchange, a strategy meant to offset declining real estate prices and overindebtedness. A healthy stock market would also fund innovative smaller companies and boost China's economic growth, not to mention providing an alternative to bank debt. That government encouragement however faced a bumpy ride. From 2014 to mid-2015 the Shanghai Composite Index soared roughly 150 percent till a crash sent prices down with more than 30 percent in 18 trading sessions. Global panic broke out also. The Chinese government however took notice, and spent $236 billion on a stock market bailout.[15] And this to good effect as five years later, the market bounced back to its 2015 levels, and reached a new milestone when in mid-2020 stock values reached $10 trillion.[16]

In the Western world there were fears that a collapse of China's stock market would seriously affect Chinese consumption and thus the global economy. But these worries are overstated. There are many differences between the Chinese and Western stock markets. The total value of every stock traded on China's exchanges is less than a third of its economic output, while in developed countries this is 100 percent. Also in China, less than 20 percent of household wealth is in the stock market. Instead, most are fully invested in real estate.[17] As such China's stock market doesn't indicate the health of the Chinese economy.

The Chinese government not only encourages domestic consumption, but over time has taken—mixed—initiatives to let the private sector play a more important role. In total, there are 155,000 state-owned enterprises, employing tens of millions of people in sectors such as banks, hotels, restaurants, oil companies, airline companies, etc.[18] Most are managed by local authorities, but about a hundred strategic companies are directly controlled by the central government. Although most SOEs are nevertheless actually fairly small companies, they dominate strategic sectors such as telecommunication, oil, and aviation, get the lion's share of the subsidies and economic opportunities, while tens of millions of other private companies must make do with the crumbs. SOEs are also highly overleveraged and structurally less efficient than their private peers.[19] Besides receiving better government contracts, SOEs can pay more and offer better employment conditions, which makes them able to attract more talent. Western companies often complain about the SOEs' competitive advantages in the Chinese market, but they forget that Chinese private companies actually face the same problem.

But these SOEs are still hugely important for China as they contribute to around 30 percent of the country's GDP.[20] Although SOEs have gone through a four decade reform period, and that their role has substantially changed, currently the predominant view is that Chinese SOEs should lead the country's economic and technology catch-up and turn them into world-class, globally competitive firms. These SOEs have also increasingly a global influence. In 2020 there were for the first time more Chinese than American corporations among the Fortune Global 500 (124 versus 121) but 85 percent of them are state-owned.[21] So it's perhaps no surprise that China's evolution toward a more open market economy is still too slow for many Western countries.

Despite the great importance of the state-owned enterprises, the Chinese government has also realized that a healthy private sector provides an extra long-term boost to economic growth, and will help China transform into a modern market economy. The country already has a lively, expanding private sector, and now allows more foreign investment in previously prohibited sectors. China's private sector is now the main driver of China's economic growth. Observers frequently use the numbers 60/70/80/90 to describe the private sector's contribution to the Chinese economy—60 percent of China's GDP, 70 percent of innovation, 80 percent of urban employment, and 90 percent of new jobs. The private sector is also responsible for 70 percent of investment and 90 percent of exports.[22] Clearly China is not a country where SOEs are most dominant.

However, as private internet companies like Alibaba and Tencent play an increasingly important economic role and exceed SOEs in value, the Chinese government is at the same exercising more control. After all, they are visible in all sectors of the economy and engaged in every aspect of daily life. So given the fact that control is still key for the Chinese government, there is an increasing trend toward some sort of government influence over China's most successful private companies. A notorious example was when at the end of 2020 Chinese regulators blocked Ant Financial's massive $35 billion IPO on the Shanghai and Hong Kong stock exchanges, allegedly after Jack Ma spoke out against the state-controlled banking system.[23] In China there is no doubt about who eventually calls the shot. But of course there is more. Just like in the rest of the world Big tech is increasingly coming under scrutiny, the same is happening in China. The country's new anti-monopoly law will hit the country's major internet companies, which were already fighting off rivals that were taking away chunks of their market share.[24]

Part of the story is also that in a more hostile and economic unstable world, China prioritizes security over efficiency, which means a conservative stance of increased centralization—in order to facilitate an immediate response to any economic threat. Privatization initiatives have further been delayed by this. SOEs are frequently utilized as a mechanism for implementing policy, providing socioeconomic stability, and building infrastructure. Therefore, privatization of SOEs at this stage seems to be more risky rather than rewarding.

Chinese Technology

As a result of Beijing's canny strategy and becoming a high-tech nation, China is since years now the world biggest exporter of high-technology products.[25] That was a gradual process. In return for opening its markets, China demanded already decades ago that foreign companies in many industries enter into joint ventures or partnerships with Chinese companies, which then learned enough to facilitate technology transfer. Cheap credit and land for strategic-sector companies were also part of this policy, as was reverse engineering to analyze design and gather knowledge. Chinese companies have now become technologically competitive and can respond pragmatically and significantly faster than Western ones to new market trends. Moreover, the Chinese legal system has been strengthened, and many illegal practices are no longer tolerated.

Especially in the telecommunication sector Chinese companies are globally expanding. A company like Huawei, with sales in 2019 of $122 billion has been establishing itself abroad for many years, overtaking foreign competitors in a number of areas.[26] Huawei has now become a well-known international brand and—before Trump blacklisted it—, the company's overseas sales were growing. Despite this, in 2019 still 100 million of the company's 240 million global smartphone shipments came from overseas markets.[27] And in 2018 a third of smartphone sales in Europe were Chinese brands like Huawei, Xiaomi, Oppo, and OnePlus.[28]

Chinese technology is also breaking through in other sectors. China has launched a significant number of manned rockets into space, and is planning a manned moon landing in 2024.[29] China is also producing the Comac C919, the first Chinese aircraft to compete with Airbus and Boeing.[30] Not only is China en route to becomes the world's biggest aviation market, this move also fits into China's strategy to create less reliance for its aviation ecosystem on buying foreign airplanes. The Chinese company Ninebot has quietly become the biggest source of electric scooters deployed in U.S. cities.[31] Ten years ago, the export of Chinese cars was virtually nonexistent; today, Chinese companies export nearly a million vehicles a year.[32]

China's High-Speed Train technology deserves focus also. When China was first establishing their high-speed railway industry, they contracted with the major players that were building high-speed rail: Alstom (France), Siemens (Germany), and several Japanese manufacturers including Hitachi. China required them to partner with a Chinese manufacturer and turn over all the intellectual property and knowledge necessary for the Chinese manufacturer to be able to build high-speed trains independently by the end of the contract. These contracts were very lucrative, and the international firms were happy to sign on.[33] The result is that there are now several Chinese manufacturers that have been completely brought up to speed with the latest technologies and are now building their own trains at better standards as the Europeans and Japanese. In December 2010 already, a Chinese high-speed train (HST) broke the speed record for commercial trains with a top speed of 302 miles per hour.[34] In 2020 the world's fastest driverless bullet train was launched in China with top speeds of up to 217 miles per hour.[35]

As Chinese companies developed state-of-the-art railway technology, China started to export also. In 2014, China exported railway equipment valued at $4.5 billion.[36] That year, too, Turkey opened its first HST railway line, built entirely using Chinese technology, linking Istanbul to Ankara.[37]

Chinese HST technology not only plays an important role in exports, it is also a crucial element of geopolitical integration. Chinese technology has become a tool of diplomacy. As part of the Silk Road Chinese political leaders intend to connect all of Central Asia with high-speed rail links. This will stimulate trade and strengthen China's own power—essentially creating a high-speed connection from Turkey in the West to Singapore in Southeast Asia.[38] The HST link worth nearly $3 billion between Hungary and Serbia which began construction in 2018—after years of delay—China, is also part of this scheme.[39] It is no exaggeration to say that China's geopolitical strategy depends to a great extent on its successful high-speed railway diplomacy.

Chinese companies are using aggressive marketing campaigns and international sports idols to improve their image. In 2013 already, Tencent spent $200 million on advertising for WeChat in India, Spain, Italy, and South Africa.[40] Lionel Messi and Lebron James were among the stars hired to support WeChat's expansion overseas.[41] Lenovo hired the now deceased U.S. NBA star Kobe Bryant.[42]

China as Global Player

In its quest to become an innovative and modern economy, Beijing has identified certain core sectors, including the maritime, aerospace, semiconductors, robotics, and clean energy space, in which it seeks to create new global champions. The "Made in China 2025" plan criticism in the West as it is been regarded as unfair competition since China heavily subsidizes certain sectors to develop new technologies.[43] Allegations that the plan is aimed to destroy Western leading companies are common. Among its various goals, the plan explicitly refers to how much of China's technology market could be controlled by Chinese companies and how many component parts in different products needed to be "Made in China." The end goal is self-sufficiency for domestic companies which then would enable Chinese companies to compete for a greater foothold in global markets.

The "Made in China 2025" plan has not been entirely successful either so far. Creating new technologies takes a great deal of brain power and R&D, and indeed under state capitalism, there is only a fine line between export subsidies and industrial policy. As for medical devices for instance, the plan explicitly seeks 50 percent usage of local products in county-level hospitals by 2020 and 70 percent by 2025.[44] New legislation ensures that companies contract only with Chinese firms for their cybersecurity needs, and updated policies on anti-terrorism and banking secrecy are following the same trend.[45]

The increasingly accepted narrative in the West, is that China acquires technology mostly through forced technology transfer. This however is not the case. As China still for a great deal relies on Western technology, Western companies for their part have benefited heavily from licensing deals to Chinese companies. Payments of licensing fees and royalties for the use of foreign technology have soared in recent years, reaching almost $30 billion in 2017.[46]

Some foreign firms enjoyed also quasi-monopolies in China. In certain sectors they can still operate like this in China, but it is clear the government wants to give domestic companies room to grow. In early 2015, the U.S. semiconductor manufacturer Qualcomm agreed to pay a $975 million fine after an investigation into its anti-competitive practices. One official admitted that Qualcomm had very good technical skills, but that its practices restricted innovation by other companies. Part of the decision required Qualcomm to lower royalty rates on patents used in China, which would likely help local competitors like Xiaomi and Huawei.[47]

Luxury cars used to be much more expensive in China than in the West, and given the size of the market, foreign car manufacturers were doing their utmost to keep it that way. Audi and Chrysler were both fined in 2014 for alleged price-fixing.[48] In the same year, the British pharmaceutical company GSK received a record fine of $489 million for bribing doctors to use its drugs.[49] And the shift away from foreign brands goes beyond government intervention. Apple, for example, is losing sales in favor of Huawei.[50]

Foreign companies see China's anti-monopoly laws as unfair, claiming that local firms are guilty of the same practices but pay no fines. That however is not completely true anymore, which was shown clearly when Chinese regulators slapped a record $2.8 billion on Alibaba in 2021 (www.bloomberg.com/news/articles/2021-04-10/china-fines-alibaba-group-2-8-billion-in-monopoly-probe). Besides trying to break the real monopoly that Alibaba has, the fine was probably also politically motivated. Regardless, Western companies are struggling to adapt to President Xi's new normal. Some cling to proven Western methods and business models and focus on their own new challenges, often failing to see that modern China's seismic changes mean that the old ways simply do not work anymore.

China also plays a much stronger role internationally. Chinese companies are looking abroad for new technologies to strengthen their market position, or trying to expand into new overseas markets. China was not a major player in global investment until the mid-2000s. However its outbound FDI (OFDI) grew from next to nothing to an average of almost $50 billion per year in the late 2000s to a record of more than $200 billion in 2016.[51] And at the end of 2019, China's cumulative overseas direct investment (ODI) reached $2.2 trillion, covering 188 countries and regions.[52] This also meant that in 2014, China became for the first time in its history a net exporter of capital.[53]

Some of the more notable deals were the acquisition of the Swiss company Syngenta—a global leader in crop protection chemicals—by ChemChina in 2016 in a deal worth $43 billion.[54] In Germany, the robot manufacturer Kuka was sold to Midea for $4.6 billion.[55] In the largest overseas acquisition by a Chinese automaker Chinese carmaker Geely acquired Volvo.[56] The Sheraton and Westin hotel chains are now under Chinese control, and Beijing's central government acquired New York's famous Waldorf Astoria from Chinese insurance company Anbang after the firm came under scrutiny for making bad investments.[57] Chinese conglomerate Wanda which took over the U.S. film chain AMC and once had a 17 percent stake in the Atlético Madrid football club.[58] In addition to its investment in Club Med, the Fosun Group also has stakes in the Greek luxury jeweler and watch retailer Folli Follie.[59]

Since 2016 however Chinese outbound investment has declined significantly, while the COVID-19 outbreak crippled deal making in 2020. The government shifts focus back to the domestic market, as it faces domestic macroeconomic headwinds. The resulting capital controls imposed by the Chinese government were responsible for most of China's outbound investment decline.[60] And despite Chinese companies paying taxes of $56 billion in the countries and regions where they operate, and employing 2.27 million foreign nationals,[61] Western countries started to have serious questions about this ambitious takeover policy. Chinese investors now also face more regulatory and political hurdles in the West. They believe that the emergence of China in combination with technological progress that has blurred the lines between civil and military use technologies, created greater vulnerabilities from foreign ownership of critical infrastructure and data. And as 80 percent of Chinese investments abroad come from state-owned enterprises,[62] it's clear that Western governments are on edge.

China's Growing International Influence

But if the West is putting up obstacles, the path to developing countries is an open road. Between 2000 and 2017, other countries' debt owed to China soared from less than $500 billion to more than $5 trillion.[63] As the world's largest creditor, China lends more money to nations in Asia, Africa, and South America than does the World Bank or IMF, and is involved in the construction of roads, railways, power plants, ports, and subways on five continents. The flood of capital from China helped prevent the global economy from plunging into depression during the 2008–2009 financial crisis.[64] But it isn't without controversy. Western critics compare this situation to 1970s economic conditions, when large American, European, and Japanese financial institutions provided billions in loans to commodity-rich Latin American and African countries, deals that international monitoring agencies failed to register. When raw materials lost monetary value, countries started defaulting on their loans, and the developing world was mired in a decades-long debt crisis.

But China's situation is different. In exchange for access to resources and market, and increased political influence, the country is creating massive infrastructure and a new market for its high-tech goods. As always China is taking the long view. Around 1.5 million Chinese are thought to be living and working in Africa, a group that includes entrepreneurs, IT experts, technicians, and merchants.[65] They have expanded infrastructure in Africa at an impressive pace, building dams, airports, train lines, and industrial parks across the continent.

It's clear that China has big ambitions, and former U.S. President Donald Trump's America First policy has accelerated this trend. Whenever the United States withdrew from international treaties or commitments, China moved in. When the United States reneged on the Iran deal, China started to increase its trade with the Islamic republic. The Trump administration has withdrawn from the Paris Climate Agreement, but China keeps investing heavily in renewables. During the Trump administration, the United States was focusing on gas and coal, while China is building the economic sectors crucial for the next thirty years.

China is also entering into closer partnerships with international organizations. Trump rejected the Trans-Pacific Partnership (TPP), while China pressed forward with international trade and globalization. The Regional Comprehensive Economic Partnership (RCEP) was signed in 2020 after eight years of negotiating and involves fifteen countries.[66] It creates a free-trade area between China, the ASEAN countries, Australia, Japan, South Korea, and New Zealand and is now the biggest trading bloc in the world. With 29 percent of global GDP and one-third of the world's population, RCEP is bigger than the European Union.[67] Clearly China is strong enough to counterbalance the United States, and has enough countries ready to join an organization that is de facto led by Beijing.

And just before the inauguration of President Biden in January 2021, China and the EU signed a—not yet ratified—new investment agreement, which in theory should provide a more level playing field for European companies in China. It took seven years to negotiate the deal, and wasn't exactly well received in the United States.[68]

And then of course, there is the New Silk Road. In 2013, Chinese President Xi Jinping announced the launch of both the Silk Road Economic Belt and the twenty-first-century Maritime Silk Road, two infrastructure development and investment initiatives that would stretch from East Asia to Europe and, to some extent, into the Americas. The project, eventually termed the Belt and Road Initiative (BRI) or One Belt One Road (OBOR), but sometimes known as the New Silk Road, is the most ambitious infrastructure investment effort in history.[69] Inspired by the original Silk Road, which connected Europe to Asia centuries ago and traders from the Atlantic to the Pacific, the project aims to create a new economic order in Eurasia. This could shift the balance of the world economy and disrupt the established world order.

Estimates vary but Morgan Stanley believes that total investment in the BRI could reach $1.3 trillion by 2027.[70] The scale of this initiative is unprecedented, and shows a broad, daring, and optimistic vision, typical of modern China. The vision is to create a vast network of railways, energy pipelines, highways, and streamlined border crossings, both westward—through the mountainous former Soviet republics—and southward, to Pakistan, India, and the rest of Southeast Asia. Beginning 2020 more than sixty countries—accounting for two-thirds of the world's population—have signed on to projects or indicated an interest in doing so.[71]

The long-term goal is to build new markets that use Chinese materials, products, and services, as well as to make more efficient use of what goods and services Europe and Asia already have. This would achieve unprecedented economic integration and geopolitical influence. Many Chinese mining, construction, and telecommunications companies are actively planning for this new reality. At the same time, China is embarking on a new Digital Silk Road, a $200 billion plan to install Chinese internet and communications technology within Belt and Road countries.[72] The goal is to create an internet network and telecom-GPS system entirely separate from the one built and operated by the United States and its allies, which some fear might lead to a new digital firewall.[73]

To shape these new geopolitical structures, China is now actively seeks to shape international norms and institutions and asserts its presence on the global stage. Nations have long accepted dealings with the International Monetary Fund and the World Bank, created after World War II, and led de facto by the United States. But in 2016, China established the multilateral Asian Infrastructure and Investment Bank (AIIB) with capital of $100 billion and the Chinese at the helm. Since the AIIB launched operations, its membership has grown from an initial 57 countries to a total of almost 100 today. When measured by the number of member countries, the AIIB is now the world's second-largest multilateral development institution, behind only the World Bank.[74] The United States and Japan opted out of membership, but Germany, France, and the United Kingdom joined right away. Expressly against U.S. will, almost all industrialized countries are participating in the reorganization of Asia. Seventy years ago, the United States, the great locomotive of the capitalist world, still accounted for 40 percent of global GDP.[75] Now the United States and China account for about 25 percent and 18 percent of global GDP, respectively.[76] As the economic gravity shifts toward the East, Western countries need to accept this reality.

With greater power also comes greater responsibility. In 2017, Beijing was mediating in nine conflicts abroad, a visible increase compared to only three in 2012.[77]

On many fronts, China has been taking the lead internationally. In 2015, China reached a new economic milestone when the International Monetary Fund added the Chinese renminbi (RMB) to the international basket of reserve currencies, where it joined the dollar, euro, yen, and pound.[78] The RMB's inclusion is crucial to China's economic integration into the global financial system and reflects the country's expanding role in global trade. A decade ago, China announced plans to transform Shanghai into an international financial center able to compete with London and New York by 2020.

China's integration into global financial markets is accelerating also. China's financial market has opened up now to many U.S. and other foreign financial institutions. Foreign ownership of onshore Chinese stocks and bonds is growing rapidly.[79] In 2019 also China set up the Science and Technology Innovation Board on the Shanghai Stock Exchange, commonly known as the "Star Market."[80] The new innovation board is designed to support companies that are working on technologies such as artificial intelligence and semiconductors, but is also aimed at enticing big-name Chinese technology firms, such as Alibaba and Tencent, to list domestically rather than on foreign exchanges.

Despite more integration, China's financial system however remains far from globalized. Despite China being the world's second-largest source of outbound foreign direct investment (FDI) and the second-largest recipient of inbound FDI from 2015 to 2017, there are still significant capital controls in place. In 2018, foreign ownership accounted for only 6 percent of China's stock market, and for 2 percent of the Chinese banking system.[81]

It's abundantly clear that through four years of Donald Trump's presidency, President Xi Jinping had a once-in-a-lifetime opportunity to significantly, and perhaps permanently, expand Chinese influence around the world at America's expense. By angering friend and foe alike and failing to tackle the coronavirus pandemic, Trump paved the way for a new leader to step into Washington's shoes. But at the same time it's important to understand that China's priorities still lay more internal than external. Whatever China undertakes, is still largely driven by internal motives.

Xi Jinping's Anti-corruption Campaign

Despite its growing international influence, the Chinese government, and especially the Chinese Communist Party, needed to do an internal clean up. The growing lack of morality, self-centered behavior, excessive wealth, and corruption had started to harm the country. To counter this problem, in 2012, President Xi Jinping launched a large-scale anti-corruption campaign within the party and Chinese society as a whole. And although whispers persist that the campaign is conveniently purging

Xi's enemies, the overarching goals are most likely to take on corruption and to revive the party apparatus by building a new political system, and gaining new legitimacy. In fact, the party's own survival might have depended on it.[82] Ideologically, the party was struggling to inspire members and nonmembers alike.

Past anti-corruption campaigns had only limited impact, but this change has been seismic. Since the launch of the high-profile campaign that targeted party, government, military, and the managements of state-owned companies, thousands have been arrested.

In a campaign which targets both high- and low-ranking officials, "tigers and flies," between 2013 and 2017 1.34 million officials have been punished.[83] Under the name "Fox Hunt" corrupt wealthy officials and other Chinese citizens who had fled abroad with large amounts of money to escape justice, were also targeted.[84] In the first six months, 556 suspects were extradited back to China.[85] The message is clear: China's old ways of doing business no longer apply, and there's nowhere in the world for corrupt Chinese officials to hide.

As I saw for myself in Qian'an, officials are now afraid to flaunt their luxurious lifestyles. The fact that European luxury brands from Burberry to LVMH reported sharply decreasing sales in 2012 and 2013 shows the incredible reach of the anti-corruption campaign—as well as the enormous scope of the problem.[86] But an unexpected side effect of the campaign was the temporary weakening of the Communist Party. A senior official told me that social unrest was rising, even as civil servants have become increasingly passive because they worry about making mistakes and being held accountable. This means decisions were delayed or sometimes avoided altogether. The population felt this and knew that government employees were more committed to following the rules. Therefore, in many places, people were betting more on their rights and putting more pressure on regional administrations, especially in the case of compulsory expropriation, meaning seizure of private property for state usage. The power of the Communist Party as the ultimate decision-maker was temporarily getting shaky. Laws became more stringent and *guanxi* was harder to cultivate. The fiefs of China's local "little kings" were in rapid decline. Despite wage increases, many lower-level officials are considering leaving their posts and looking for other jobs.

These times of instability however have passed now, and the situation has stabilized completely. Corruption will never become a thing of the past—nowhere in the world—but China is a much cleaner place now. China is changing in many ways. Domestically, the Communist Party still firmly holds control, with economic growth and stability as its main guidelines, while internationally China is a growing power. The world is shifting fast toward a new, multipolar global system that will affect every single one of us.

Notes

1. *Fortune*. 2020. The U.S. trade war slowed China's 2019 economic growth to its weakest pace in nearly 30 years. https://fortune.com/2020/01/17/china-gdp-growth-2019-weakest-30-years-trade-war. Accessed December 5, 2020.
2. Macrotrends. 2021. China exports 1960–2021. www.macrotrends.net/countries/CHN/china/exports. Accessed January 5, 2021.
3. Reuters. 2016. China expects to lay off 1.8 million workers in coal, steel sectors. www.reuters.com/article/us-china-economy-employment/china-expects-to-lay-off-1-8-million-workers-in-coal-steel-sectors-idUSKCN0W205X. Accessed March 5, 2019.
4. CNN. 2019. Money has been leaving China at a record rate. Beijing is battling to stem the tide. https://edition.cnn.com/2019/12/19/business/china-capital-flight-trade-war-us/index.html. Accessed January 4, 2021.
5. *Global Times*. 2019. 70 years: China's contributions to the world. www.globaltimes.cn/content/1165930.shtml. Accessed March 5, 2020.
6. McKinsey Global Institute. 2019. China and the world: inside the dynamics of a changing relationship. www.mckinsey.com/featured-insights/china/china-and-the-world-inside-the-dynamics-of-a-changing-relationship. Accessed March 5, 2020.
7. World's top exports. 2021. Japan's top trading partners. www.worldstopexports.com/japans-top-import-partners/. Accessed January 4, 2021.
8. World's top exports. 2021. Australia Top 10 exports. www.worldstopexports.com/australias-top-10-exports/. Accessed January 5, 2021.
9. World's top exports. 2021. America's Top trading partners. www.worldstopexports.com/americas-top-import-partners/. Accessed January 4, 2021.
10. Destatis Statisches Bundesamt. 2020. The People's Republic of China is again Germany's main trading partner. https://www.destatis.de/EN/Themes/Economy/Foreign-Trade/trading-partners.html;jsessionid=BE22C4DC20066A482B92841F6479CC5A.internet8721. Accessed November 22, 2020.

11. CNBC. 2020. China says its economy grew 6.1 percent in 2019, in line with its expectations. www.cnbc.com/amp/2020/01/17/china-gdp-for-full-year-and-q4-2019.html. Accessed March 5, 2020.
12. *Chinadaily*. 2017. New normal in economic development. www.chinadaily.com.cn/china/19thcpcnationalcongress/2017-10/05/content_32869258.htm. Accessed March 4, 2020.
13. Macrotrends. 2021. China exports 1960–2021. www.macrotrends.net/countries/CHN/china/exports. Accessed January 5, 2021.
14. Reuters. 2019. China's growth slowed by service, farm sectors, despite construction rebound. www.reuters.com/article/us-china-economy-gdp/chinas-growth-slowed-by-service-farm-sectors-despite-construction-rebound-idUSKCN1PG0A2. Accessed April 1, 2020.
15. CNN. 2015. China has spent $236 billion on its stock market bailout. https://money.cnn.com/2015/09/08/investing/china-stock-market-bailout-beijing/index.html. Accessed July 5, 2019.
16. Bloomberg. 2020. China's stock market closes in one $10 trillion milestone after its biggest crash. www.bloomberg.com/amp/news/articles/2020-07-13/china-s-stock-market-is-closing-in-on-10-trillion-milestone. Accessed December 4, 2020.
17. The balance. 2020. China's stock market, including Shanghai, Shenzhen and Hong Kong. www.thebalance.com/china-stock-market-shanghai-shenzhen-hong-kong-3305480. Accessed January 3, 2021.
18. *China Journal of Accounting Research*. 2020. Volume 13, Issue 1, Pages 31–55. State-owned enterprises in China: a review of 40 ears of research and practice. www.sciencedirect.com/science/article/pii/S1755309119300437. Accessed January 3, 2021.
19. World Economic Forum. 2019. The role of China's state-owned companies explained. www.weforum.org/agenda/2019/05/why-chinas-state-owned-companies-still-have-a-key-role-to-play. Accessed December 5, 2020.
20. China briefing. 2019. China's SOE reforms: what the latest rounds of reforms mean for the market. www.china-briefing.com/news/chinas-soe-reform-process/. Accessed July 5, 2020.
21. *Fortune*. 2020. The Fortune Global 500 is now more Chinese than American. https://fortune.com/2020/08/10/fortune-global-500-china-rise-ceo-daily. Accessed January 3, 2021.
22. World Economic Forum. 2019. The role of China's state-owned companies explained. www.weforum.org/agenda/2019/05/why-chinas-state-owned-companies-still-have-a-key-role-to-play. Accessed December 5, 2020.
23. *Fortune*. 2020. Why regulators sidelined Ant Financial's record-setting IPO. fortune.com/2020/11/03/ant-financial-ipo-record-alipay-hong-kong-shanghai-stock-exchange/amp/. Accessed January 4, 2021.

24. CNBC. 2020. Morgan Stanley names internet companies that will be hit by China's proposed anti-monopoly rules. www.cnbc.com/2020/11/12/morgan-stanley-chinas-draft-anti-monopoly-rules-impact-on-internet-firms.html. Accessed December 22, 2020.
25. The World Bank. 2020. High-technology exports (current US$)—China, United States, Germany. https://data.worldbank.org/indicator/TX.VAL.TECH.CD?end=2019&locations=CN-US-DE&start=2007&view=chart. Accessed December 5, 2020.
26. CNN. 2019. Huawei's sales grew in 2019, but it says next year will be 'difficult'. www.cnn.com/2019/12/30/tech/huawei-revenue-smartphone-sales/index.html. Accessed December 6, 2020.
27. cntechPost. 2020. Can Huawei save overseas sales? www.cntechpost.com/2020/03/03/can-hms-save-huaweis-overseas-sales/amp/. Accessed December 22, 2020.
28. Computing. 2019. Chinese brands claimed one-third of all smartphones sales in European in 2018. www.computing.co.uk/news/3071142/chinese-brands-claimed-one-third-of-all-smartphones-sales-in-european-in-2018. Accessed October 6, 2020.
29. Space. 2020. China unveils ambitious moon mission plans for 2024 and beyond. https://www.space.com/amp/china-planning-future-moon-missions-change-7. Accessed January 5, 2021.
30. CNN. 2020. Comac C919: China takes on Airbus and Boeing. https://edition.cnn.com/travel/article/comac-c919-china-airbus-boeing/index.html. Accessed January 7, 2021.
31. Bloomberg. 2018. Almost every electric scooter comes from this Chinese company. www.bloomberg.com/news/features/2018-12-05/almost-every-electric-scooter-comes-from-this-chinese-company. Accessed November 4, 2020.
32. Statista. 2020. Number of passenger cars and commercial vehicles exported from China from 2009 to 2019. www.statista.com/statistics/279055/number-of-vehicles-exported-from-china/. Accessed December 23, 2020.
33. Gov1. 2015. How did China become strong in high-speed rail? www.gov1.com/economic-development/articles/how-did-china-become-strong-in-high-speed-rail-MvZhPYgfL9d6eDX6/. Accessed December 5, 2020.
34. InventorSPOT. 2010. Chinese bullet train smashes world rail speed record. www.inventorspot.com/articles/chinese_highspeed_train_smashes_world_rail_speed_record. Accessed February 22, 2020.
35. *The Guardian*. 2020. World's fastest driverless bullet train launches in China./www.theguardian.com/travel/2020/jan/09/worlds-fastest-driverless-automated-bullet-train-launches-beijing-china-olympics. Accessed January 7, 2021.

36. *Chinadaily*. 2015. China takes 10 percent of global locomotive market. www.chinadaily.com.cn/business/2015-02/06/content_19510555.htm. Accessed May 12, 2020.
37. CRI Online. 2017. Chinese high-speed rail amazes world with "China speed". http://js.cri.cn/20171107/250d173b-fb5f-e072-e691-f8282d12ebd5.html. Accessed January 3, 2021.
38. *The Diplomat*. 2015. China's high-speed railway technology can help its foreign policy. https://thediplomat.com/2015/02/3-ways-chinas-high-speed-railway-technology-can-help-its-foreign-policy/. Accessed December 4, 2020.
39. *The Diplomat*. 2020. China and the Budapest-Belgrade railway saga https://thediplomat.com/2020/04/china-and-the-budapest-belgrade-railway-saga/. Accessed December 23, 2020.
40. Quartz. 2014. WeChat is nothing like WhatsApp-and that makes it even more valuable. https://qz.com/179007/wechat-is-nothing-like-whatsapp-and-that-makes-it-even-more-valuable/. Accessed October 2, 2019.
41. *Venture Capital Post*. 2013. China's WeChat goes global with Lebron James, Lionel Messi. www.vcpost.com/articles/12031/20130725/chinas-wechat-goes-global-lebron-james-lionel-messi.htm. Accessed May 29, 2020.
42. Business Insider. 2013. Watch Kobe Bryant play 'Moonlight Sonata' in a Chinese Lenovo ad. www.businessinsider.com/kobe-bryan-lenovo-commercial-2013-8?IR=T. Accessed May 4, 2020.
43. China Briefing. 2018. What is Made in China 2025 and why has it made the world so nervous? www.china-briefing.com/news/made-in-china-2025-explained/. Accessed September 20, 2020.
44. L.E.K. 2018. Innovation in China, "Made in China 2020" and implications for healthcare MNCs. www.lek.com/sites/default/files/insights/pdf-attachments/Chinas-Healthcare-Innovation-by-Made-in-China-2025-and-Implications-for-MNCs_JUL06.pdf. Accessed July 4, 2020.
45. *The New York Times*. 2015. New rules in China upset western tech companies. www.nytimes.com/2015/01/29/technology/in-china-new-cybersecurity-rules-perturb-western-tech-companies.html?_r=0. Accessed November 3, 2020.
46. PIIE. 2018. China: forced technology transfer and theft. www.piie.com/blogs/china-economic-watch/china-forced-technology-transfer-and-theft. Accessed March 22, 2020.
47. Reuters. 2015. Qualcomm to pay $975 million to resolve China antitrust dispute. https://www.reuters.com/article/us-china-qualcomm/qualcomm-to-pay-975-million-to-resolve-china-antitrust-dispute-idUSKBN0LD2EL20150210. Accessed June 29, 2020.

48. *USA Today*. 2014. China fines Chrysler, Audi in ongoing monopoly probe. https://eu.usatoday.com/story/money/cars/2014/09/11/china-chrysler-audi-fine-monopoly/15471999/. Accessed December 3, 2020.
49. Reuters. 2014. China hands drugmaker GSK record $489 million fine for paying bribes. www.reuters.com/article/us-gsk-china/china-hands-drugmaker-gsk-record-489-million-fine-for-paying-bribes-idUSKBN0HE0TC20140919. Accessed January 4, 2021.
50. *South China Morning Post*. 2020. Apple's iPhone loses out to Huawei in China as locals turn to the Chinese smartphone brand. www.scmp.com/abacus/tech/article/3096001/apples-iphone-loses-out-huawei-china-locals-turn-chinese-smartphone. Accessed November 4, 2020.
51. Rhodium Group. 2020. Buying the dip? China's outbound investment in 2020. https://rhg.com/research/chinas-outbound-investment-in-2020/. Accessed December 3, 2020.
52. Global Times. 2020. China's outbound investment to drop 20 percent year-on-year: expert. www.globaltimes.cn/content/1201042.shtml. Accessed October 5, 2020.
53. *Chinadaily*. 2015. China now a net capital exporter. www.chinadaily.com.cn/business/chinadata/2015-01/21/content_19367818.htm. Accessed March 3, 2020.
54. Reuters. 2018. China-owned Syngenta plots growth in challenging home market. www.reuters.com/article/us-china-syngenta/china-owned-syngenta-plots-growth-in-challenging-home-market-idUSKBN1KE1B3. Accessed November 4, 2020.
55. *Chinadaily*. 2016. Midea reaches binding investment agreement with Kuka. https://www.chinadaily.com.cn/business/2016-06/30/content_25911385.htm. Accessed January 4, 2020.
56. Forbes. 2018. Volvo & Geely: the unlikely marriage of Swedish tech and Chinese manufacturing might that earned record profits. www.forbes.com/sites/pamelaambler/2018/01/23/volvo-geely-the-unlikely-marriage-of-swedish-tech-and-chinese-manufacturing-might-that-earned-record-profits/?sh=204abf04ecc8. Accessed August 18, 2020.
57. *Architectural Digest*. 2018. The Waldorf Astoria is now owned by the Chinese government. www.architecturaldigest.com/story/waldorf-astoria-now-owned-by-chinese-government. Accessed April 4, 2020.
58. Reuters. 2018. Exclusive: China's Dalian Wanda seeks to reduce AMC stake—sources. www.reuters.com/article/us-dalianwanda-amc-exclusive/exclusive-chinas-dalian-wanda-seeks-to-reduce-amc-stake-sources-idUKKCN1LL2DZ?edition-redirect=uk. Accessed November 3, 2019.

59. *The Straits Times*. 2019. Collapse of Thomas Cook a reality check for China's Fosun. www.straitstimes.com/business/companies-markets/collapse-of-thomas-cook-a-reality-check-for-chinas-fosun. Accessed May 4, 2020.
60. Rhodium Group. Rhodium Group. 2020. Buying the dip? China's outbound investment in 2020. https://rhg.com/research/chinas-outbound-investment-in-2020/. Accessed December 7, 2020.
61. Global Times. 2020. China's outbound investment to drop 20 percent year-on-year: expert. www.globaltimes.cn/content/1201042.shtml. Accessed October 5, 2020.
62. *Journal of World Trade*. 2014. When China's national champions go global: nothing to fear but fear itself? Vol 48, No. 6, 2014. Pg 1127-1166. https://eprints.lancs.ac.uk/id/eprint/71782/1/TRAD_48_6_Ming_Du_Final.pdf. Accessed March 4, 2020.
63. CNBC. 2019. About half of China's loans to developing countries are 'hidden', study finds. www.cnbc.com/2019/07/12/chinas-lending-to-other-countries-jumps-causing-hidden-debt.html. Accessed December 4, 2020.
64. Der Spiegel. 2019. Vast Chinese loans pose risks to developing world. www.spiegel.de/international/business/chinese-loans-pose-risks-to-developing-world-a-1275643.html. Accessed October 5, 2020.
65. Der Spiegel. 2019. Vast Chinese loans pose risks to developing world. www.spiegel.de/international/business/chinese-loans-pose-risks-to-developing-world-a-1275643.html. Accessed October 5, 2020.
66. BBC. 2020. RCEP: Asia-Pacific countries form world's largest trading bloc. www.bbc.com/news/world-asia-54949260. Accessed January 5, 2021.
67. BBC. 2020. What is the regional Comprehensive Economic Partnership (RCEP)? www.bbc.com/news/business-54899254. Accessed January 4, 2021.
68. CNN. 2020. Europe strikes major investment deal with China despite US concerns. https://edition.cnn.com/2020/12/30/business/eu-china-investment/index.html. Accessed January 3, 2021.
69. Council on Foreign Relations. 2020. China's massive Belt and Road initiative. www.cfr.org/backgrounder/chinas-massive-belt-and-road-initiative. Accessed December 5, 2020.
70. Morgan Stanley. 2018. Inside China's plan to create a modern silk road. www.morganstanley.com/ideas/china-belt-and-road. Accessed December 5, 2020.
71. Council on Foreign Relations. 2020. China's massive Belt and Road initiative. www.cfr.org/backgrounder/chinas-massive-belt-and-road-initiative. Accessed December 5, 2020.

72. *Science Focus*. 2018. The digital silk road—China's $200 billion project. www.sciencefocus.com/future-technology/the-digital-silk-road-chinas-200-billion-project/. Accessed September 5, 2020.
73. Bloomberg. 2019. China's Digital Silk Road Is Looking More Like an Iron Curtain. www.bloomberg.com/news/features/2019-01-10/china-s-digital-silk-road-is-looking-more-like-an-iron-curtain. Accessed December 5, 2020.
74. Federal Ministry of Finance. 2019. Asian Infrastructure Investment Bank achieves major milestones in its first three years. www.bundesfinanzministerium.de/Content/EN/Standardartikel/Topics/Financial_markets/Articles/2019-04-03-AIIB-milestones.html. Accessed February 4, 2020. Accessed March 5, 2020.
75. Forbes. 2016. U.S. role in global economy declines nearly 50 percent. www.forbes.com/sites/mikepatton/2016/02/29/u-s-role-in-global-economy-declines-nearly-50/amp/. Attached December 1, 2020.
76. Statistics Times. 2020. Projected GDP ranking. http://statisticstimes.com/economy/projected-world-gdp-ranking.php. Accessed January 5, 2021.
77. Eyewitness News. 2018. China's role as a conflict mediator is growing fast. https://ewn.co.za/2018/10/09/china-s-role-as-a-conflict-mediator-is-growing-fast-here-s-why. Accessed February 20, 2020.
78. International Monetary Fund. 2016. IMF adds Chinese Renminbi to special drawing rights basket. www.imf.org/en/News/Articles/2016/09/29/AM16-NA093016IMF-Adds-Chinese-Renminbi-to-Special-Drawing-Rights-Basket. Accessed October 4, 2020.
79. PIIE. 2020. China's financial opening accelerates. www.piie.com/publications/policy-briefs/chinas-financial-opening-accelerates. Accessed January 4, 2021.
80. ChinaPower. 2020. How dominant are Chinese companies globally? https://chinapower.csis.org/chinese-companies-global-500/. Accessed January 3, 2021.
81. McKinsey Global Institute. 2019. China and the world: inside the dynamics of a changing relationship. www.mckinsey.com/featured-insights/china/china-and-the-world-inside-the-dynamics-of-a-changing-relationship. Accessed March 5, 2020.
82. *The Diplomat*. 2014. 4 misconceptions about China's anti-corruption campaign. https://thediplomat.com/2014/08/4-misconceptions-about-chinas-anti-corruption-campaign/. Accessed February 4, 2020.
83. Reuters. 2017. Chinese watchdog says 1.34 million officials punished for graft since 2013. www.reuters.com/article/us-china-corruption/chinese-watchdog-says-1-34-million-officials-punished-for-graft-since-2013-idUSKBN1CD04B. Accessed March 5, 2020.

84. *The Diplomat*. 2014. 'Fox Hunt 2014: China's overseas campaign against corrupt officials, https://thediplomat.com/2014/10/fox-hunt-2014-chinas-overseas-campaign-against-corrupt-officials. Accessed July 22, 2020.
85. *Chinadaily*. 2015. 556 fugitives captured in 'Fox Hunt 2015'. https://www.chinadaily.com.cn/china/2015-10/29/content_22311686.htm. Accessed February 4, 2019.
86. *Fortune*. 2015. The worst may be over for luxury goods in China. www.fortune.com/2015/12/07/luxury-goods-china-corruption-probe/amp/. Accessed December 5, 2019.

CHAPTER 12

The Great Decoupling and a New Cold War

On January 24, 2020, the last day of the Chinese lunar December, our family was as usual in my spouse's hometown, Tai'an, to celebrate the Chinese New Year or Spring Festival. For a few days, however, Chinese media had been talking about a new coronavirus—later dubbed COVID-19—that was apparently spreading rapidly in Wuhan, Hubei province, and seemed to infect people at unprecedented speed. There was no major concern yet among the general population, but the streets were less crowded than normal, and people seemed increasingly to avoid public places. Most people still remembered the SARS coronavirus, which killed 774 people and infected 8098 between November 2002 and July 2003.[1] The SARS virus had sent a shockwave through the country and hurt the Chinese economy. Many cities went into lockdown, and business came to a temporarily halt. I myself had arrived in China a year after the SARS epidemic, but my spouse, who experienced the situation then, has vivid memories of that time. She now thought it would be wise to return to our home in Shanghai at the earliest opportunity. She was concerned that whole cities and regions would be put under lockdown in order to stop the virus from spreading freely. Already there were reports of train and bus services being suspended. If Shanghai, as an international hub, were to be sealed off from the outside world, we probably would be stuck in Tai'an for months on end. Consequently, we returned home the next day in a train that was as good as empty. Virtually all passengers were already

S. Agten, *Adventures in the Chinese Economy: 16 Years from the Inside*, https://doi.org/10.1007/978-981-16-1167-4_12

wearing face masks. It was clear that everybody had started to prepare for the worst.

The damage done by COVID-19 to people's health and the world economy in general has become increasingly clear. Starting in China, the virus quickly spread all over the globe, infecting millions of people, and killing hundreds of thousands of them. But the damage in China in terms of lives lost was relatively low. Official numbers beginning 2021 indicate there were around 96,000 cases and fewer than 5000 deaths in the country.[2]

Most Chinese believe, however, that the actual numbers were much higher than this. In the beginning, no one had a clear overview of the situation, and locally in Wuhan, chaos reigned. Soon, however, the scale of the outbreak became clear to the general population. People in Wuhan were dying, and hospitals were overcrowded, and the local authorities were unable to get the situation under control. And as the virus also seemed to spread rapidly to other regions within China, the whole country was at risk. Many of my friends abroad had the distinct impression that the whole of China was under an obligatory lockdown, that people were dying on the streets, and that the situation was completely out of control. But, as usual, media reports were gravely exaggerating the situation. Actually, quite the opposite was true. Because of the widespread use of the internet and the fact that there were hourly updates about the situation, the Chinese reacted to the crisis with lightning speed. Within days of the news, basically the whole Chinese population decided to stay at home in self-imposed lockdown, so did our family. After getting back to Shanghai, we basically didn't leave our home for the next six weeks. It was truly amazing to see how a whole country stopped all activities within days and focused on one thing only: stay at home to keep safe and stop the virus spreading. China and its people understood what needed to be done.

In hindsight, it seems that the Chinese government clearly could have reacted faster. Early detection and isolation are key, and it's here where China might have dropped the ball. Reportedly, the first case of COVID-19 recognized was in November 2019 in Hubei province, and by the end of December doctors in Wuhan suspected widespread direct human-to-human transmission. Only beginning January 2020—a bit over one month after the first COVID-19 case was recognized—Chinese authorities announced publicly that a new coronavirus had emerged and measures to contain it were being taken.[3] Whistleblowing doctors and citizen journalists who tried to speak out about the mysterious virus in Wuhan in December were silenced, and the full extent of the threat to public health only became clear later. The question thus arises of whether China initially did enough to control the virus, something for which the country has been heavily criticized by the rest of the world for this. The answer might be not that straightforward. China definitely did a great job on controlling the virus, but it might be started a bit late with it.

It's however not so China acted completely on its own, sealing off the news from the rest of the world. At the end of December China informed the World Health Organization (WHO) about the outbreak. And already at the very beginning of January 2020, the U.S. Centers for Disease Control (CDC) received reports on the novel virus from Chinese colleagues. The National Security Council was being informed also.[4]

But as soon as the Chinese government was willing (or able) to face the real scale of the problem, it successfully implemented drastic and unprecedented measures to contain the virus. It was this response that eventually contained the spread of the virus, something for which the WHO already early on praised the Chinese government.[5]

In mid-January, movement in and out of Wuhan and fifteen other cities in Hubei province, home to more than 60 million people, was stopped.[6] Within weeks, some 760 million people were being told to stay home, and only venture out for absolute necessities.[7] China implemented a zero contact policy, closed all schools and cinemas, and banned large gatherings and events.[8] Daily life ground to a halt overnight, and New Year events all over the country were canceled.

At the same time, large-scale tracking, tracing, testing, and controlling became key. China deployed hundreds of thousands of neighborhood watches, workers, and volunteers to battle the virus.[9] Undergoing temperature checks became standard procedure when entering grocery stores, office buildings, or residential compounds. Everybody was wearing mouth masks. China's sophisticated surveillance network became an ally in fighting the virus. Infrared temperature detection techniques and thermal cameras were installed in all leading cities.[10] Big government and big tech worked hand in hand in response to the pandemic. The Chinese government joined hands with Alibaba and Tencent to develop a color-coded smartphone health rating system that tracked millions of people daily. Nearly everyone with a smartphone, including myself, was assigned three colors—green, yellow, and red—on the basis of their travel and medical histories. Only people with a green color code were allowed in public spaces. This meant that every time I entered places like office buildings, hotels, or metro or train stations, I needed to show my green code. In all, more than two hundred Chinese cities used this system.[11] Using a centralized database, big data, and machine learning, the government was able to track people with whom an infected person had been in close contact and order them to self-isolate themselves.

Contrary to the Western world where government measures were being questioned, almost all Chinese citizens supported the government's tough measures. Chinese are much more willing to give up personal rights for the sake of general well-being than Westerners, for whom individual rights and freedom are culturally engrained. Quarantining oneself for weeks or wearing masks was never an issue in China. This however also had some perverse effects. At the beginning of the crisis, many people in Shanghai argued that the local authorities should lock down Wuhan to protect the rest of the country. And some even believed Shanghai itself should be sealed off from the rest of the country in order to create a safe bubble. Despite support for Wuhan by many people, for months after it was declared safe again, its residents were often denied access to hotels elsewhere in China, or were obliged to undergo a fourteen-day quarantine when they visited other cities. For a whole there was some mistrust of anybody coming from Wuhan.

China's whole population was willing to make great sacrifices in order to stop the virus. The response to the pandemic actually created a sense of civil order, a feeling that everybody was in the same boat, and a sense of reassurance that the outbreak would be contained. Never during this whole period was there widespread chaos or panic. So when China managed to contain the crisis from March 2020 onwards, while at the same the virus was increasingly spreading globally, many Westerners living and working in China agreed that China was the safest place on earth.

Eventually, China managed to contain the virus relatively fast. But while China was fighting the virus with drastic measures, the Western world unfortunately reacted in a very slow fashion. Probably thinking that Covid-19 was a Chinese problem, both the United States and European countries did little to prevent it from coming to their shores. As a result, cases in the United States, Europe, Brazil, and many other places soared, with millions of Covid-19 cases and hundreds of thousands of deaths.

Many Chinese viewed the response in Europe and especially the United States with a sense of disbelief. They couldn't understand why Western governments were not taking preventive measures, seeing what was going on in China.

The Great Decoupling

Covid-19 itself was a global disaster, but it also accelerated international tensions which had been going on since the start of the Presidency of Donald Trump in 2017. Economic tensions between China and the United States are nothing new, but Trump's taking office has sent the conflict soaring to new heights. The rise of China on the global stage has increasingly caused alarm in the Western world in general, but particularly in the United States—the only surviving superpower after the U.S.–Soviet cold war. In effect, for years now the United States has tried to decouple from China politically, economically, financially, and technologically. The basis is there for a new cold war. The old Western-led world order is threatened, and there was bound to be a reaction.

Trump has long contended that China has exploited the U.S. economy for its own enrichment at the expense of the American worker. Demanding an equal playing field, in 2018 Trump initiated a tariff war that eventually applied to goods valued at around $550 billion and sought to pressure China to open up its markets faster. China reacted by setting tariffs in $185 billion worth of American goods.[12] As a result bilateral trade decreased by 15 percent in 2019, after it had surged by an annual average of 11 percent from 2001 to 2018.[13]

At the same, the Covid-19 crisis has exposed the very significant dependence of the Western world on Chinese production, especially in global supply-chain operations. The factory of the world shutting down in the beginning of 2020 sent ripple effects throughout Asia, Europe, and North America. This was for instance all too clear in the field of medical supplies. Shortages of masks, swabs, ventilators, and other necessities have taught the United States the valuable lesson that it cannot rely on deliveries from overseas that become uncertain in time of crisis.

Consequently many Western companies are rethinking their China operations. This however is nothing new as moves to reconfigure supply chains have long been underway. Increasing labor costs forced foreign companies to adopt the so-called China + 1 sourcing strategy, which led to manufacturing moving to third countries rather than back to America's industrial heartland.[14] So the idea that increased tariffs on China will move jobs back to the United States, is far from reality.

But even moving out of China is not easy either. Yes, labor costs are cheaper in other developing countries, but with everything accounted for, costs in other countries could end up 30–40 percent higher than in

China.[15] China offers world-class logistics, a highly experienced, educated workforce, a stable political environment, unparalleled supply chains for components of all kinds, and low crime rates. In other words it's a stable country where business can be done relatively smoothly, without major disruptions. Having world-class infrastructure is also a major reason why China will not lose its manufacturing dominance in the near future despite the trade war. And despite all of Trump's efforts, the U.S.–China trade deficit has remained the same. In 2016 the trade deficit was $347 billion, while in 2019 it was marginally $2 billion less.[16] Surveys from the European Chamber of Commerce and the American Chamber of Commerce in China in 2020 also show that only some 4–11 percent of Western companies in China are considering moving.[17] In other ways, breaking up is not so easy.

The so-called trade war is, however, more about technology than trade. Both the United States and Europe are unhappy with Beijing's tactics, which include coercing foreign companies to hand over trade secrets in return for access to the Chinese market, forcing foreign businesses to license technology in China on unfavorable terms, and using state funds to buy up foreign technology. For its part, China is not willing to open all its markets, fearing they will come under foreign companies' control. That technology is a big part of the China–U.S. antagonism became clear in 2018 when the U.S. government tightened its security review system and made Chinese investment in any form of U.S. tech company virtually impossible. Consequently, in 2019 Chinese investments in the U.S. firms fell to barely $3 billion, down from $27 billion in 2017.[18]

In 2019, things went even further when Huawei was added to the so-called Entity List, which restricted its access to American technology. In practice Huawei cannot use anymore Google's Android operating system, which it has relied on for years.[19] Even if there is no evidence of wrongdoing by Huawei on behalf of the Chinese state, according to the United States, as the world's biggest vendor of telecommunications equipment, Huawei is effectively an intelligence-gathering arm of the Chinese Communist Party.[20]

Most likely however the move against Huawei has much deeper reasons. Together with ZTE—another Chinese communications technology supplier on the Entity List[21]—, Huawei is one of the world's top patent developers and leaders in high-speed 5G network development. The impact of a U.S. ban on the sale of technology products—notably telecom parts and components—to Huawei and ZTE cannot be underestimated. China annually imports chips valued at some $300 billion, exceeding even the cost of its oil imports.[22] Huawei and ZTE, key players in China's telecommunications industry, are very much dependent on U.S.-made components, as are China's high-speed rail, air traffic control, and telecommuting networks. Moreover, Since Chinese companies are installing their telecommunications equipment throughout the Digital Silk Road, a ban on sales to Chinese companies has far-reaching effects. At its core, the prohibition is a clear attempt to stop the country's technological rise and global influence.[23]

The question however is whether this ban will harm Chinese companies or spur on their innovation? Huawei has been forced to develop its own operating system—HarmonyOS—which it unveiled in September 2020.[24] So it seems that here a ban spurred on innovation. In the semiconductor sector, the story still looks a bit different. Since 2014 already China has invested about $150 billion in the semiconductor industry, but till today, China has no leading-edge semiconductor manufacturing facility.[25] Despite all these investments China is still facing a big technology lag in semiconductors. At the same time however it would be a grave mistake to think that China's semiconductor catch-up efforts will fail. Instead, China is likely to continue pursuing multiple pathways to industrial catch-up in semiconductor manufacturing, leveraging a combination of indigenous development, foreign talent attraction programs, joint ventures, etc.

Also in other fields America is taking the defensive measure. Mid-2020, the United States announced plans for a so-called Clean Network initiative, aimed at isolating large parts of the Chinese internet. "The Clean Network program is the Trump Administration's comprehensive approach to guarding our citizens' privacy and our companies' most sensitive information from aggressive intrusions by malign actors, such as the Chinese Communist Party," former U.S. Secretary of State Mike Pompeo has said. The program aims to exclude untrusted Chinese apps from U.S. app stores; prevent Chinese smartphone companies from preinstalling U.S. apps; keep U.S. data of Chinese cloud services; and protect undersea cables.[26]

In 2020, a financial decoupling also started to be underway when the Trump administration started to push for the delisting of Chinese companies from American stock markets.[27] Hundreds of Chinese companies went public in the U.S. stock market over a decade ago, mostly via reverse mergers, in which mostly dormant U.S. companies were merged with Chinese companies. Not only were some of these mergers frauds, but among the listed companies, there were also a few Chinese state-owned enterprises. The key issue is that despite U.S. regulatory requirements, some Chinese companies don't provide access to their audit records.[28] With the geopolitical situation and relationship with China changing rapidly, some U.S. politicians have pushed to delist Chinese companies altogether from U.S. markets if they don't follow U.S. auditing standards and other financial regulations. This effectively cuts them off from American investors.

To top it off here are also increasingly tensions in the area of education. Already in February 2019, Christopher Wray, the head of the Federal Bureau of Investigations (FBI), said that not only the Chinese government, but the whole of Chinese society represented a threat to the United States.[29] As a result the United States is taking actions to reduce the amount of Chinese students at American schools. In May 2020, the Trump administration started planning to cancel the visas of Chinese graduate students and researchers who have direct ties to universities in China affiliated with the People's Liberation Army. According to the U.S. government, the new regulation targets students who present a significant risk of engaging in espionage or intellectual property theft. Although again there is no evidence of any wrongdoing and this decision only affected 3000 of the approximately 360,000 Chinese students studying in the United States, it opens the door for further restrictions.[30] This will, however, have negative effects for the United States also. Not only will it lose access to Chinese talent, but it also forfeits the chance to familiarize these Chinese students with American values, part of the country's soft power. As a result American universities are pushing back against the new policies. While the intellectual merits of international educational exchange are clear, there is also a financial consideration—loss of tuition payments from foreign students, especially from the large group of students from China.[31] The United States used to be an attractive place for Chinese students and families, but given its current poor handling of the Covid-19 outbreak and emergence of strong anti-Chinese sentiment, many Chinese students are now looking elsewhere.

For some within the Trump administration the China–U.S conflict is an ideological war between Good and Evil. It seems that for the more hawkish members of the Trump administration, undoing forty years of ever-closer economic relations with China and rolling back U.S. reliance on Chinese factories, firms, and investment was always the end game. In this view, the offshoring of U.S. jobs for the past forty years has been a "misguided experiment" that should be abandoned.[32]

Looking at the long list of sectors where the United States tried to decouple, President Trump was seemingly ready to go all the way. In May 2020, Trump said that the United States could do many things in relationship to China, including cut off the whole relationship, which according to him would save his country $ 500 billion.[33]

The new Biden administration might have a slightly different approach in dealing with China, but the general consensus within the Republican and Democratic Party remain very much anti-China. This means that the general strategy of containing China will not change, and thus that the U.S.–China antagonism will remain for years to come. In the United Stated anti-China feelings run high, sometimes seemingly often more ideologically than rationally driven.

An Internationally More Assertive China

America's experience with COVID-19 has hastened its decoupling from China further. Since the United States accused China of putting the world at risk because of the lack of transparency in its handling of the virus and failure to control it adequately, COVID-19 created an increasingly bad image of China in the rest of the world. President Trump from his side called COVID-19 during many occasions "the China virus."[34]

Besides Covid-19, 2020 was also in other respects devastating for the relationship between China and the Western world. Feeling bullied and threatened, China has started to take a much more aggressive stance. Traditionally, Beijing rarely reacted on criticism of its political or economic policies, often stating that these were internal affairs. At the same time it barely ever would commend on other countries' internal issues, nor engage in any other way. That changed in 2020, when President Xi Jinping started flexing China's military, economic, and technological muscle. Politically, it seems that China is envisaging a new post-COVID-19 foreign policy strategy. Examples of the heightening tensions include the new Hong Kong Security Law, which makes it easier to crack down on protestors and limits the city's autonomy[35]; the China's more assertive stance on the issue of reunification with Taiwan; conflicts with China's neighbors over disputed islands; and a Himalayan border clash that claimed the lives of more than 20 Indian soldiers.[36]

Many Western observers have pointed out that China has embarked on a more aggressive foreign policy, dubbed "Wolf Warrior" Diplomacy. China is reacting on criticism and strikes back. China and Australia clashed, for instance, when the latter demanded that the international community receive access to the labs in Wuhan to study COVID-19. The Chinese government responded by putting tariffs on key Australian imports such as beef and barley and warning Chinese students not to go to Australia to study. For Australia the stakes are high as an all-out trade war could cost hurt the Australian economy 6 percent of GDP.[37]

Just like the United States, China also rallies its allies if needed. For instance when China was condemned for the detention program of Uyghurs in Xinjiang and twenty-two nations, including Australia, urged the UN Human Rights Council to call on China to end this, Beijing swiftly signed up 37 countries, including many with majority Muslim populations, to defend its rule there. Not surprisingly it enlists the support of countries that have received Chinese development loans to win votes in global bodies.[38]

Geopolitics and the struggle for regional and global influence are, of course, central to all this. Hong Kong is a prime example of a geopolitical battleground. When Hong Kong's streets were flooded with protestors in 2019 and 2020 to demand more rights and freedom, they received support from the United States, which not only backed the protestors,[39] but even funded the protests.[40] Since the British handover in 1997, Hong Kong has been part of China, however. So this is as though China were to fund the Black Lives Matter movement in the United States. American support for the protestors obviously serves other purposes too. Clearly, destabilizing China is on the agenda. So in this context, it's not surprising that China enforces the new Security Law in Hong Kong because it needs stability in its own country.

China already had a policy of rewarding its allies economically and punishing others. Trump's administration was now about to do the same. Just like China, it was about to make the economic relationship between the two countries hostage to geopolitical competition. Demanding that a G-7 communiqué refer to COVID-19 as the "Wuhan virus" and blocking mask shipments to close allies are just some examples of the nasty turn things have taken.[41] The Trump administration also started to talk about an "Economic Prosperity Network" of like-minded countries, organizations, and businesses. The aim is in part to persuade U.S. firms to extricate themselves from China and do business with members of this so-called alliance of "trusted partners" so as to reduce U.S. economic dependence on Beijing, which is seen as a key national security vulnerability.[42] If a U.S. manufacturing company can't move jobs from China back to the United States, for example, it could at least move those jobs to another more U.S.-friendly country, such as Vietnam or India.

Not only politically, but also economically China is also embarking on a new course. Just as in the financial crisis of 2009, China is leading the way in the global economic recovery after the COVID-19 pandemic. Despite the Chinese economy retracting by 6.8 percent in the first quarter of 2020 at the height of the corona crisis in the country,[43] this was still a small hit compared to the U.S. economy, which shrank with 32.9 percent in the second quarter of the same year.[44] And as I witnessed myself, much of the Chinese economy was back on track after May 2020, when the virus was largely contained domestically and things went back to normal. When European and American airports were still empty for months to come, Chinese domestic air travel was also soon back to normal.[45] During the so-called Golden Week in October 2020, 637 million Chinese took a trip within China.[46]

In 2020 China was the only major economy with positive growth. And the Organization for Economic Cooperation and Development (OECD) is forecasting that China will lead economic growth in 2021, growing 8 percent to account for around one-third of the world's economic recovery.[47] This is not without consequences as this would mean it's the first time that an economic cycle would only have restarted in China. The big surprise comes from the transformation: China was the workshop of the world; now it gradually becomes the engine of the world. While demand has remained solid in many countries as people order from home, local factory output has been disrupted. Made in China has filled the gap.

A New Cold War

China is clearly looking to the future again. And it's not willing to bail out the world economy again, like in 2009. In 2020 China launched its dual circulation strategy which places a greater focus on the domestic market, or internal circulation, and is China's strategic approach to adapting to an increasingly unstable and hostile outside world.[48]

It also has used the COVID-19 crisis to pave the way for a wide-scale digital transformation of its domestic industrial power. Following the declines in industrial output because of the virus, and because of its relative need for foreign technology, China decided to change course and deepen its domestic technological upgrading. Investing heavily in 5G, blockchain, and artificial intelligence, China wants its tech companies to become world leaders. China has also launched a blockchain service network that aims to become a blockchain hosting platform for small and medium-sized enterprises (SME's) and individuals, creating a standardized blockchain across public networks, regions, and business sectors.[49] In other words, it wants the whole country to use blockchain. For China ensuring AI and blockchain leadership are top priorities. It will apply blockchain at scale in supply chain and quality control to dramatically reduce cost, enhance food and drug safety, accelerate the shift away from physical money, reduce risk in the financial system and direct money to places that it wants it to go, and avoid dependence on the United States for any aspect of blockchain technologies.[50] China's central bank, the People's Bank of China (PBoC) is also launching a national digital currency DCEP (Digital Currency Electronic Payment). It will be then the first major central bank to issue a digital version of its currency. Trials were already underway in a handful of cities in 2020.[51]

All these trends also show that although China is a global power in terms of scale, that has not always translated into integration. China's Fortune Global 500 companies earn less than 20 percent of their revenue overseas. China has vast amounts of capital, but only 6 percent of foreign ownership in its financial markets. China boasts 160 million outbound trips, but has less than 0.2 percent of global migrants. There are close to a billion Chinese online, but this is only equivalent to 20 percent of U.S. cross-border data flows.[52] China is huge and continues to grow, but its integration with the rest of the world is not growing at the same rate.

So it's perhaps no surprise that the United States and increasingly Europe are more and more suspicious of China. After all, the differences between these two sides of the world remain huge. Germany, China's biggest trading partner for instance, has for a long time maintained good relations with China. In the wake of the events of 2020 however, the German mood toward China started to shift. Despite the willingness to maintain good economic ties, the German Foreign Minister has called China "a partner, competitor and rival."[53] In 2019, the European Union labeled China as a "systemic rival."[54] It hasn't yet gone so far as to demonize China, as the United States is doing, but clearly the European attitude to China is shifting. So far European action has been limited mainly to rhetoric. A genuine shift would require European countries to accept the economic fallout, however, as China doesn't shy away from using its economic leverage to get what it wants.

Many Western countries thus increasingly tend to have a negative view of China. Not only is there an information war where every side spins its own narrative, but Chinese citizens for their part increasingly support their own country. Chinese people used to admire the United States, and looked up to it. That mood is shifting gradually. Most Chinese don't feel hostile to the United States, but when China is threatened, nationalistic feelings are on the rise.

The COVID-19 pandemic has actually heightened this feeling. China managed to handle the situation relatively fast and in a controlled way. Many Chinese believe that their government is doing the right thing, despite all its failures, and that the future still looks bright. After all, China has enjoyed 40 years of economic growth and stability. Many Chinese believe that Western governments are increasingly not up to the job anymore and basically undermine their own future and that of their people. It's an idea that's gained more support from the COVID-19 pandemic. At the same time, the Black Lives Matter movement and the 2020 presidential election soap opera in the United States, the Yellow Vests demonstrations in France, and Brexit show many Chinese that Western societies have many more problems to deal with than just COVID-19. They see that increasingly large sections of Western society are unhappy about the way things are being done. As a result, for many Chinese, values such as freedom and democracy, which used to be perhaps something to aspire too, are now becoming hollow words. In their eyes, the Chinese system works and benefits the general population, and the Western democratic systems increasingly don't. Simply speaking for many Chinese, these values don't seem to mean anything anymore if it doesn't ensure stability, safety and economic growth. And there is thus less and less the Western world has to offer that Chinese citizens aspire to.

China opened up economically, politically, and culturally until about 2012, and now it is becoming very selective toward foreign investment, goods, people, and ideas. It is abundantly clear that the United States, Europe, and China are entering a new phase in their relations. Economic, digital, technological, and financial barriers are going up between the United States and China, and the global consequences have yet to be determined. From all sides, the United States has China under attack. These U.S.–China tensions have presaged a worldwide recession. China and America creating two distinct, rival global systems and power structures may be inevitable. All signs point to a decades-long cold war between the United States and China, one reshaping global alliances, politics, and economies. Countries will need to choose which side they will be on. One clear example is the current COVID-19 crisis where China exported the most valuable commodity of all vaccines. Beginning of 2021 at least 70 countries and territories either approached the Chinese vaccine or struck deals to receive doses from China. As such Beijing attains a new kind of soft power internationally (Nikkei Asia. 2021. China emerges as the big winner in vaccine outreach. www.asia.nikkei.com/spotlight/datawatch/china-emerges-as-big-winner-in-vaccine-outreach).

The trade war is a skirmish in a much bigger and broader battle for global influence. As shown above, the two superpowers are competing for intellectual property and technological mastery, as well as political influence across the developing world via economic assistance. A major difference however is that U.S. power is partly based on its military apparatus, while China's rise has until now largely been focused economically. Seeing China as a threat to the world is therefore a rather misleading idea.

But in any case, the prospects for every country and every company in this new bilateral world couldn't be more challenging. A new cold war is developing rapidly. If 2009 and the financial crisis will be viewed as the year that Wall Street let the global financial system spiral out of control, and China started to lose trust in the global leadership abilities of the United States, 2020 will be remembered as the year when China stopped aspiring to the American way of life with covid uncontainment, Trumpism and presidential election issues tarnishing the brand of the United States. Both years will prove to be pivotal in the rise of China.

The only real question thus is how far the decoupling will go. Complete decoupling, while unlikely, if not practically impossible, would send historic shockwaves through the global economy. The rise of China will—literally—change the world.

Notes

1. France 24. 2020. Coronavirus death toll in China exceeds 720, set to surpass total from SARS. https://www.france24.com/en/20200208-the-death-toll-from-china-s-coronavirus-outbreak-hits-722-surpassing-the-total-from-sars. Accessed November 4, 2020.

2. Statista. 2021. Cases in China from January 20, 2020 to January 3, 2021. www.statista.com/statistics/1092918/china-wuhan-coronavirus-2019ncov-confirmed-and-deceased-number/. Accessed January 8, 2021.
3. Hudson Institute. 2021. Coronavirus timeline. www.hudson.org/features/coronavirus. Accessed January 5, 2021.
4. Hudson Institute. 2021. Coronavirus timeline. www.hudson.org/features/coronavirus. Accessed January 5, 2021. Accessed January 8, 2021.
5. Hudson Institute. 2021. Coronavirus timeline. www.hudson.org/features/coronavirus. Accessed January 5, 2021. Accessed January 8, 2021.
6. *Nature*. 2020. What China's coronavirus response can teach the rest of the world. www.nature.com/articles/d41586-020-00741-x. Accessed December 5, 2020.
7. *The New York Times*. 2020. To tame coronavirus, Mao-style social control blankets China. www.nytimes.com/2020/02/15/business/china-coronavirus-lockdown.html. Accessed December 5, 2020.
8. *US Today*. 2020. This is what China did to beat coronavirus. Experts say America couldn't handle it. https://eu.usatoday.com/story/news/world/2020/04/01/coronavirus-covid-19-china-radical-measures-lockdowns-mass-quarantines/2938374001/. Accessed December 21, 2020.
9. *The New York Times*. 2020. To tame coronavirus, Mao-style social control blankets China. www.nytimes.com/2020/02/15/business/china-coronavirus-lockdown.html. Accessed December 5, 2020.
10. Geospatial World. 2020. The China way: use of technology to combat Covid-19. www.geospatialworld.net/article/the-sino-approach-use-of-technology-to-combat-covid-19. Accessed December 12, 2020.
11. Geospatial World. 2020. The China way: use of technology to combat Covid-19. www.geospatialworld.net/article/the-sino-approach-use-of-technology-to-combat-covid-19. Accessed December 12, 2020.
12. China Briefing. 2020. The US-China trade war: a timeline. www.china-briefing.com/news/the-us-china-trade-war-a-timeline/. Accessed December 5, 2020.
13. Bloomberg. 2020. The great decoupling. What's next for U.S.-China rift? www.bloomberg.com/news/articles/2020-06-15/the-great-decoupling-what-s-next-for-u-s-china-rift-quicktake. Accessed December 5, 2020.
14. Bloomberg. 2020. The great decoupling. What's next for U.S.-China rift? www.bloomberg.com/news/articles/2020-06-15/the-great-decoupling-what-s-next-for-u-s-china-rift-quicktake. Accessed December 5, 2020.
15. Titoma. 2020. Moving out of China. US & Euro companies are not doing it. https://titoma.com/blog/manufacturing-moving-out-china. Accessed January 4, 2021.
16. *The Financial Times*. 2021. Why Trump no longer talks about the trade deficit with China. www.ft.com/content/081e6d25-8d67-4caa-918a-2765a66f0052. Accessed January 6, 2021.

17. Titoma. 2020. Moving out of China. US & Euro companies are not doing it. https://titoma.com/blog/manufacturing-moving-out-china. Accessed January 4, 2021.
18. American Enterprise Institute. 2020. Chinese investments in the United States. www.aei.org/china-tracker-home/. Accessed January 5, 2021.
19. CNBC. 2020. Huawei says its operating system can rival Google, Apple – but experts say it might be a struggle. www.cnbc.com/2020/05/21/huawei-says-its-harmonyos-operating-system-can-rival-google-apple.html. Accessed January 2, 2021.
20. *Forbes*. 2020. The FCC Just Designated China's Huawei And ZTE A Security Threatwww.forbes.com/sites/kenrapoza/2020/06/30/the-fcc-just-designated-chinas-huawei-and-zte-a-security-threat/#3697951a2348. Accessed November 12, 2020.
21. *Lightwave*. 2020. U.S. Commerce Department adds Fiberhome to Entity List. www.lightwaveonline.com/business/companies/article/14176645/us-commerce-department-adds-fiberhome-to-entity-list. Accessed January 2, 2021.
22. *The New York Times*. 2020. Huawei's U.S. restrictions expose a high-tech Achilles' heel for China. www.nytimes.com/2019/05/21/technology/huawei-china-us-trade.html. Accessed January 3, 2021.
23. *The Diplomat*. 2019. China's digital silk road: a game changer for Asian economies. https://thediplomat.com/2019/04/chinas-digital-silk-road-a-game-changer-for-asian-economies. Accessed November 14, 2020.
24. Huawei Central. 2020. HarmonyOS: (HongMeng OS): Everything you need to know. www.huaweicentral.com/harmonyos-hongmeng-os-everything-you-need-to-know/. Accessed December 22, 2020.
25. *The Diplomat*. 2020. Can China become the world leader in semiconductors? https://thediplomat.com/2020/09/can-china-become-the-world-leader-in-semiconductors/#:~:text=China%27s%20most%20modern%20foundry%20only,Corporation%20(SMIC)%20in%20Shanghai.&text=As%20a%20sign%20of%20their,the%20following%20two%20node%20generations. Accessed January 5, 2020.
26. Business Insider. 2020. The Trump administration unveiled a wild plan to wall off China from the US internet. www.businessinsider.com/us-unveils-blueprint-to-seal-off-chinese-tech-giants-2020-8?r=DE&IR=T. Accessed January 9, 2021.
27. CNBC. 2020. A 'financial war' with China could be brewing on top of the trade war. www.cnbc.com/2020/07/09/a-financial-war-with-china-could-be-brewing-on-top-of-the-trade-war.html. Accessed January 2, 2021.
28. CNBC. 2020. A 'financial war' with China could be brewing on top of the trade war. www.cnbc.com/2020/07/09/a-financial-war-with-china-could-be-brewing-on-top-of-the-trade-war.html. Accessed January 2, 2021.

29. Business Insider. 2018. The director of the FBI says the whole of Chinese society is a threat to the US—and that Americans must step up to defend themselves. www.businessinsider.com/china-threat-to-america-fbi-director-warns-2018-2?r=DE&IR=T. Accessed October 5, 2020.
30. *The New York Times*. 2020. U.S. to expel Chinese graduate students with ties to China's military schools. www.nytimes.com/2020/05/28/us/politics/china-hong-kong-trump-student-visas.html. Accessed January 10, 2021.
31. *The New York Times*. 2020. U.S. to expel Chinese graduate students with ties to China's military schools. www.nytimes.com/2020/05/28/us/politics/china-hong-kong-trump-student-visas.html. Accessed January 10, 2021.
32. *The New York Times*. 2020. The era of offshoring U.S. jobs is over. www.nytimes.com/2020/05/11/opinion/coronavirus-jobs-offshoring.html. Accessed December 29, 2020.
33. Fox Business. 2020. Trump on China: 'We could cut off the whole relationship'. www.foxbusiness.com/politics/trump-on-china-we-could-cut-off-the-whole-relationship. Accessed December 5, 2020.
34. *The Conversation*. 2020. Donald Trump's 'Chinese virus: the politics of naming'. www.theconversation.com/donald-trumps-chinese-virus-the-politics-of-naming-136796. Accessed December 4, 2020.
35. *The Wall Street Journal*. 2020. What is the Hong Kong Security Law? www.wsj.com/articles/hong-kong-security-law-11590088410. Accessed November 11, 2020.
36. *The New York Times*. 2020. Battle in the Himalayas. www.nytimes.com/interactive/2020/07/18/world/asia/china-india-border-conflict.html. Accessed December 3, 2020.
37. *Nikkei Asia*. 2020. China-Australia clash: how it started and how it's going. https://asia.nikkei.com/Politics/International-relations/China-Australia-clash-How-it-started-and-how-it-s-going. Accessed January 4, 2021.
38. *The Conversation*. 2020. Behind China's newly aggressive diplomacy: 'wolf warriors' ready to fight. back. https://theconversation.com/behind-chinas-newly-aggressive-diplomacy-wolf-warriors-ready-to-fight-back-139028. Accessed December 4, 2020.
39. CNBC. 2019. China accuses US of 'sinister intentions' after Trump signs bills supporting Hong Kong protestors. www.cnbc.com/2019/11/28/china-condemns-us-bills-supporting-hong-kong-protesters.html. Accessed March 3, 2020.
40. *South China Morning Post*. 2020. US has been exposed for funding last year's Hong Kong protests. www.scmp.com/comment/opinion/article/3091438/us-has-been-exposed-funding-last-years-hong-kong-protests. Accessed November 21, 2020.

41. *Foreign Policy*. 2020. China's post-coronavirus aggression is reshaping Asia. www.foreignpolicy.com/2020/06/18/china-india-aggression-asia-alliances. Accessed December 14, 2020.
42. Reuters. 2020. Trump administration pushing to rip global supply chains from China: officials. www.reuters.com/article/us-health-coronavirus-usa-china/trump-administration-pushing-to-rip-global-supply-chains-from-china-officials-idUSKBN22G0BZ. Accessed October 22, 2020.
43. *The Diplomat*. 2020. China's new digital industrial transformation. https://thediplomat.com/2020/06/chinas-new-digital-industrial-transformation. Accessed October 11, 2020.
44. BBC. 2020. Coronavirus: US economy sees sharpest contraction in decades. https://www.bbc.com/news/business-53574953. Accessed November 3, 2020.
45. BBC. 2020. Coronavirus: flights within China to 'fully recover' next month. www.bbc.com/news/business-53927980. Accessed November 5, 2020.
46. CNBC. 2020. More than 600 million people traveled in China during 'Golden Week'. www.cnbc.com/amp/2020/10/09/china-attractions-630-million-people-travel-during-golden-week.html. Accessed December 19, 2020.
47. CNBC. OECD lifts global economic outlook on vaccine progress, sees China driving recovery. www.cnbc.com/2020/12/01/world-economy-oecd-lifts-outlook-on-vaccine-progress-sees-china-driving-recovery.html. Accessed December 22, 2020.
48. *South China Morning Post*. What is China's dual circulation economic strategy and why is it important? www.scmp.com/economy/china-economy/article/3110184/what-chinas-dual-circulation-economic-strategy-and-why-it. Accessed December 1, 2020.
49. Ledger Insights. 2019. China's national blockchain infrastructure takes shape. www.ledgerinsights.com/chinas-national-blockchain-infrastructure-bsn/. Accessed December 1, 2020.
50. McKinsey. 2020. What can we expect in China in 2020? www.mckinsey.com/featured-insights/china/what-can-we-expect-in-china-in-2020. Accessed January 5, 2021.
51. Bloomberg. 2020. How China is closing in on its own digital currency. www.bloomberg.com/news/articles/2020-09-08/how-china-is-closing-in-on-its-own-digital-currency-quicktake. Accessed October 20, 2020.
52. McKinsey Global Institute. 2019. China and the world: inside the dynamics of a changing relationship. www.mckinsey.com/featured-insights/china/china-and-the-world-inside-the-dynamics-of-a-changing-relationship. Accessed December 3, 2020.

53. Germany Federal Foreign Office. 2020. "China is a partner, competitor and rival". www.auswaertiges-amt.de/en/newsroom/news/maas-rnd/2367552. Accessed December 6, 2020.
54. Politico. 2019. EU slams China as 'systemic rival' as trade tension rises. www.politico.eu/article/eu-slams-china-as-systemic-rival-as-trade-tension-rises. Accessed October 5, 2020.

Afterword

China is developing very fast. Accordingly, most books about it are out of date before they even appear. This one is no exception. Social and economic trends follow each other at a rapid pace in China. The economy is constantly creating new opportunities, making all sorts of new segments more interesting, while other industries are slowly disappearing. Statistics and data are often things of the past before they can be collected and analyzed.

Instead of the nearly 900 million as described in the book, there might be already one billion internet users in China by the time this book is published. The shopping centers under construction are likely to face even more serious challenges from e-commerce. Air pollution may rapidly become a thing of the past, faster than expected. Global society is and always has been moving, with younger consumers increasingly going their own way and setting new trends. But that does not change the global impact of the major social, economic, and cultural trends that continue to occur in China, and with which we are all increasingly confronted. Every day, China offers many reasons for admiration, but certainly also a shake of the head. No two days are alike, but one thing is certain: China never gets boring. Sometimes you really have to wonder how the Chinese manage to keep up with all the changes. Stability is important, but there is no country in the world that moves forward with such big leaps. In many aspects a return to Europe for a family visit or trips to North America often feel like a journey back in time.

S. Agten, *Adventures in the Chinese Economy: 16 Years from the Inside*, https://doi.org/10.1007/978-981-16-1167-4

The outbreak of Covid-19 was a global game changer, which especially sharpens the relation between the Western world and China. It's abundantly clear that the two political, economic, and social systems are clashing. A prolonged cold war looks to be the most realistic scenario. This increasingly creates a bipolar world—the United States and China. In nearly every sector decoupling seems to be the rage. This creates two internets and digital spaces, two political spheres of influence, two very different economic systems, etc. The Western world has an increasingly negative view on China, while China will no longer accept the global leading role of the United States. But divorcing is not easy, so intertwined in our world. Western companies need China for production and sales; Chinese consumers like Western products. China also needs to sell its products globally, and wants to assert itself more internationally.

But just as ten years ago nobody could predict what would happen in China, nobody knows where China will be in twenty years. Pessimists predict that the country will continue to enter into unprecedented levels of debt to boost economic growth. In this scenario, China would inevitably head for a recession. Optimists believe that China can make the transition to an innovative industrialized country with a thriving middle class, since the economy is so dynamic and can compete with the rest of the world. However, one thing is sure, the world will have to take China increasingly seriously: its growing role on the international stage, the shift from quantitative to qualitative growth and the associated accelerated production of high-tech products, its investments abroad, and the emerging Chinese middle class, which increasingly determines what products and services multinational companies produce.

The economic balance will continue to shift toward the East, which should be an eye-opener for the Western world. China won't be contained anymore. It's the logical and historical evolution of things. The United States desperately needs to align itself with Europe and clean up its domestic issues. Europe must be careful not to lose the balance between the United States on the one hand and China on the other. But eventually we will all have to face the opportunities and challenges that China offers.

Head on head collision might not be the answer, but more pragmatism and mutual understanding will. A proactive but constructive China-policy might be the answer. You have to adapt to the reality and find ways to work with instead of against China. It is essential to get to know and understand China better, to gain insight into the how and why of this country. When we better understand why it does exactly what it does, it's easier to handle. Too often the saying "unknown is unloved" also applies to China. We like to call China the best-kept secret in the world because so few people know what's really going on there. However, it is not that China acts illogically, as is often assumed. It is only a question of understanding, and an opening to the Chinese perspective on world affairs. It's not as complicated as it seems at first glance. Everything happens for a reason, especially in China. The Chinese citizen is seriously interested in the Westerner, wants to learn from us, and is ready to show China as it really is. It's also easy to make new friends as long as you're open to them.

As always, mutual respect is crucial. It does not matter if you live in China for three or twenty-three years, the lucky ones among us have been able to gain personal experience of what unconditional friendship means. Many Westerners do not know this aspect of China. Many of them come home with Chinese horror stories, but that often has more to do with them than with China. Not only because you have physically lived (or are still living) in China, you also automatically understand the country. It is therefore not surprising that there are so many companies in China that are confronted with a multitude of problems. The cultural misunderstandings that characterize everyday life in China could fill another book. China is a very dynamic country with many opportunities, which, despite its gigantic problems, is optimistic about the future and always moves forward with its own strength. It is also a country that has outpaced the rest of the world in some areas, while in other places it still has a lot of catching up to do. The economic, social, and cultural trends that are emerging in China are important, not only for the Chinese, but for all of us.

Company names and institutions

S. Agten, *Adventures in the Chinese Economy: 16 Years from the Inside*, https://doi.org/10.1007/978-981-16-1167-4

Geographical Index

S. Agten, *Adventures in the Chinese Economy: 16 Years from the Inside*, https://doi.org/10.1007/978-981-16-1167-4

Name Index

S. Agten, *Adventures in the Chinese Economy: 16 Years from the Inside*,
https://doi.org/10.1007/978-981-16-1167-4

Subject Index

S. Agten, *Adventures in the Chinese Economy: 16 Years from the Inside*,
https://doi.org/10.1007/978-981-16-1167-4

S

The manufacturer's authorised representative in the EU is Springer Nature Customer Service Centre GmbH, Europaplatz 3, 69115 Heidelberg, Germany. If you have any concerns regarding our products, please contact ProductSafety@springernature.com

Printed and bound by CPI Group (UK) Ltd, Croydon, CR0 4YY
30/09/2026
02225455-0009